ALSO BY RONALD HAVER

David O. Selznick's Hollywood
David O. Selznick's "Gone With the Wind"

A STAR IS BORN

THE MAKING OF THE 1954 MOVIE AND ITS 1983 RESTORATION

RONALD HAVER

PERENNIAL LIBRARY

Harper & Row, Publishers, New York
Grand Rapids, Philadelphia, St. Louis, San Francisco
London, Singapore, Sydney, Tokyo, Toronto

First PERENNIAL LIBRARY edition published 1990.
LIBRARY OF CONGRESS CATALOG CARD NUMBER 89-45667
ISBN 0-06-097274-2
90 91 92 93 94 FG 10 9 8 7 6 5 4 3 2 1

THIS BOOK IS FOR

Fay Kanin
Gene Allen
James and Clarissa Mason
Douglas Edwards

Contents

Illustrations follow pages 50 and 210.

Acknowledgments

The saga of *A Star Is Born* is really two stories separated by nearly thirty years. Part One concerns the actual production of the film, while the second part deals with the Academy Foundation's 1983 project to restore the film to its original form.

Part One came about because of the work involved in this restoration effort. As I tried to track down the missing sections of the film, I began talking to various people who had been involved in the production of the picture. The stories they related of the difficulties in making the film were fascinating—the technical uncertainties, the interplay of personalities, the struggle to reconcile the opposing forces of artistic endeavor and commercial movie-making. I began to wonder how and why there could be so much dissension, indecision, and conflict in the making of a movie in the heyday of the studio system. For my own satisfaction, I determined to piece together the complete story of the making of this version of *A Star Is Born*. To do this, it was necessary to start with the original source material, which meant the Warner Bros. studio files on the film. These are all carefully and meticulously maintained at the Doheny Library at the University of Southern California by Robert Knutson and his staff, who were extremely cooperative and generous in their efforts to locate anything and everything that had to do with *A Star Is Born*. Leith Adams was particularly diligent in locating contracts, inter-studio memos, correspondence, script drafts, and, most important, the daily production log of the picture—a record of everything that happened on the set on any given day. This production log was invaluable as basic original source material; armed with this and the studio memoranda I could jog the memories of the interviewees who had worked in or on the film. First of these, of course, was Sid Luft, the producer of *A Star Is Born*, who gave me two candid sessions outlining the genesis of the project, its myriad problems, and the tug-of-war over the finished film.

Earlier Mr. Luft had given extensive interviews on the subject of *A Star Is Born* to Gerold Frank for his biography *Judy;* I'm grateful to Mr. Frank and to his publishers, Harper & Row, for allowing me to use material from the book relating to this period. Both Earl Bellamy and Russ Llewellyn, the assistant directors on the film, were generous in their time and their memories of the film. Bellamy in particular deserves a major thank-you from me, as our first interview was completely ruined by a malfunctioning tape recorder; he kindly consented to do the whole thing over (all four hours of it!). Gene Allen, the production designer for the film, took time out from his busy schedule as the then president of the Academy of Motion Picture Arts and Sciences and the executive director of the Society of Motion Picture and Television Art Directors to explain the function of a production designer, the problems of this particular film, and the exhilaration of working with George Cukor. Al Harrel very kindly supplied me with an extensive interview he had taped with cinematographer Sam Leavitt that dealt extensively and frankly with the problems of photographing *A Star Is Born.* Makeup artist Del Armstrong shared his remembrances and his insights, on both the production and Judy Garland, as did actress Lucy Marlow and photographer Bob Willoughby. James Mason was extremely frank and forthright in the many conversations we had about *A Star Is Born* during our tour of the six cities that premiered the reconstructed version. His death meant the loss of a true gentleman, a gifted artist, and a warm, albeit brief, friendship. I am grateful to Hamish Hamilton, the British publishers of his autobiography, *Before I Forget,* for allowing the use of excerpts concerning *A Star Is Born,* and to David Ehrenstein for supplying me with an interview he conducted with Mr. Mason in mid-1983. S. Dell Scott and Kurt E. Wolfe, trustees of the estate of Ray Heindorf, and Tina Heindorf Morrow kindly allowed the use of excerpts from an oral history of Mr. Heindorf conducted by the late Irene Kahn Atkins. Kitty Carlisle Hart generously gave permission for the examination and use of the Moss Hart papers at the Wisconsin Center for Film and Theater Research, Madison, Wisconsin. Irving Lazar talked to me about the genesis of the film, as did Lauren Bacall, who was, as usual, forthright, frank, and astute in her observations and memories of the period 1953–54. William Hendricks, for years Jack Warner's personal assistant, was also helpful in illuminating some of the murkier aspects of the making of the film, and Lawrence D. Stewart graciously gave permission to quote from his unpublished piece "Ira Gershwin and the Man That Got Away." Selznick Properties, in the person of Jeffrey Selznick, allowed use of material from the David O. Selznick Collection at the University of Texas at Austin.

Trying to place all these events in the context of Hollywood at the time meant detailed research, and for helping in this task I am very grateful to Joan Cohen, Joseph McBride, Ned Comstock, and Ray Holland; and to the staff of the Margaret Herrick Library at the Academy of Motion Picture Arts and Sciences, particularly Linda Harris Mehr, Sam Gill, Bob Cushman, the late Carol Epstein, and Howard Prouty. A special note of appreciation is due Sandra Archer of the Margaret Herrick Library, who was never too busy to answer any query or locate any item, and who generally made this author's quest more pleasurable. Robert Osborne of *The Hollywood Reporter* shared his memories of conversations with George Cukor; the late Carlos Clarens made an enormous contribution by allowing me access to material he was gathering for a biography of George Cukor, and John Fricke supplied valuable papers on the production and distribution of the film. At Warner Bros., both Fred Talmage and Lillian Wilson were enthusiastic and helpful, while the late Evelyn Lane spent much time and effort locating the camera reports and the editor's log for *A Star Is Born,* both of which were invaluable to an understanding of how the picture took final shape. Folmar Blangsted's widow, Elsa, talked to me at length about her husband, *A Star Is Born,* and Hollywood in general. Marshall Silverman at Warners' legal department was helpful in obtaining the necessary clearances and permissions to quote from Moss Hart's screenplay and the inter-studio correspondence on *A Star Is Born,* as well as granting permission for the use of frame enlargements from the film. Of course, the person at Warner Bros. who deserves thanks most of all is Robert Daly, the chairman of the board—for without his wholehearted enthusiasm, cooperation, and financial support, there would have been no reconstruction of *A Star Is Born* and no reason for this book.

The interviews and notes and portions of the manuscript were transcribed and typed by Bill La Vallee, while Carole Logie did the final typescript (over and over and over again). For their tireless efforts, my heartfelt thanks. Writer/historian Rudy Behlmer was kind enough to read the first draft, and his sharp eye caught errors of fact and misstatement that only someone with his detailed knowledge and generous spirit would have noticed and corrected, while Robert Cushman greatly aided the quest for accuracy with his examination of the text. Copyeditor Patrick Dillon did a detailed and valuable job in ordering the syntax, catching inconsistencies, and making suggestions which added greatly to the overall quality and readability of the text. The late Bill Whitehead spent some of the last weeks of his life reading an old friend's manuscript, and his comments and suggestions were detailed, sensible, and humorous. Bill Whitehead was unique, and his untimely passing leaves a void in my life; I think everyone who knew him feels the same.

And a note of appreciation is due Alec White and Lou Hickam, both of whom provided assistance and encouragement.

I'm grateful to Earl A. Powell III, director of the Los Angeles County Museum of Art, for allowing me to take time off from my duties there to finish the manuscript.

Special thanks to Robert Cornfield, my agent, for his enthusiasm, his support, and his talent for finding the best publisher for a project. In this case that is Alfred A. Knopf, Inc., in the persons of Martha Kaplan and Bob Gottlieb. Martha is the most patient person on earth; she listened to almost two and a half years of complaints, excuses, and all the other lamentations that insecure authors can find to explain why they aren't delivering a manuscript. She did this with warmth, humor, understanding, and affection, all of which are typical of Martha. Added to that are her considerable gifts as an editor—and a chef. In the words of Ira Gershwin, "Who could ask for anything more?"

And then, of course, there is Robert Gottlieb, the man who—as he is constantly reminding me—picked me up out of the gutter and gave me several reasons to believe in life: VCRs, plastic purses, Japanese films, and a one-month trial subscription to *The New Yorker.* To Robert, I'll just say thanks—for the belief, the encouragement, the intelligence, the advice, the affection, the friendship. And his (almost) never-failing sense of humor.

Finally, my gratitude to Jack Warner, George Cukor, Moss Hart, Harold Arlen, Ira Gershwin, Judy Garland, Charles Bickford, Jack Carson, Tommy Noonan, and the 220 other people who worked on this version of *A Star Is Born.* Without their efforts, there would have been nothing to write about in the first place.

R.H.

January 1988
Hollywood, California

A STAR IS BORN

Prologue

The piercing beams of huge arc lights sweep the night sky above Holly-wood. They circle and criss-cross in a stately minuet of their own; outlining, for a brief moment in a stream of light, the Hollywood Hills, the panorama of the city gleaming in neon below the Hills and seeming, as they flash across the horizon, to endow the legendary landscape of Hollywood with the very magic it sends forth to the four corners of the world.

These words of Moss Hart's, which open his screenplay for the 1954 remake of *A Star Is Born,* distill as much as two sentences can the essence of the marvelous flummery that engulfed Hollywood on premiere nights and enthralled any tourist lucky enough to be in the vicinity.

On the day of this particular premiere, close to one hundred thousand visitors from all over the world are basking in the eighty-degree heat of Los Angeles and its environs, of which Hollywood is the most famous part. They have arrived by car, by bus, and in the new dieselized transcontinental trains offering lavish service and cut-rate fares. Some, more adventurous, have flown into the city on one of the new twice-daily low-cost flights offered by most of the major airlines. It's the second year of the Eisenhower administration, and the postwar boom is giving the United States a decade of unparalleled prosperity. The Korean "police action" ended in an uneasy cease-fire in July 1953, and the ensuing peace, while tempered by fears of atomic war with the Soviet Union, is putting money into the pockets and the bank accounts of most Americans, giving them, for the first time in a generation, security and the leisure time to enjoy themselves. And for people seeking surf and the all-pervasive glamour of the movies, Los Angeles is the Emerald City.

Most of the tourists have come from the Midwest and the South. White, middle-class, high-school-educated families, they suffered the rigors of the Great Depression, World War II, and the Korean "conflict" while simultaneously being nurtured on the myths of the movies. The same movies that fed their fantasies reinforced their values and beliefs by demonstrating that hard work, honesty, fidelity, and faith in God, government, and the guy next door inevitably made for a better life.

And a better life is what most Americans have this September 29th. Unemployment is low, unions are strong, the forty-hour work week is in force, and the average family income hovers around $4,000 yearly. You can buy a two-bedroom house in the suburbs for $16,000, furnish it completely for another $1,500 (including a seventeen-inch Magnavox TV set), feed a family of four for $15 a week, and put a brand-new Ford convertible in the garage for another $2,400—and finance it all through a bank at the prevailing interest rate of 4 percent. If you decided to drive that new car on a cross-country vacation, gasoline costs you an average of twenty cents a gallon, hotels and motels two dollars a night, and meals in a first-class restaurant can be had for a dollar fifty. For some recreational reading, you may have taken along one or two of the current best-sellers: Morton Thompson's novel about the medical profession, *Not as a Stranger,* is the number-one book in the country, followed by Daphne du Maurier's historical romance *Mary Anne;* singer Lillian Roth's candid autobiography, *I'll Cry Tomorrow;* Norman Vincent Peale's self-help treatise, *The Power of Positive Thinking;* the harrowing *Cell 2455, Death Row* by convicted murderer Caryl Chessman; Herbert Philbrick's account of his career as a counterspy, *I Led Three Lives;* and John Steinbeck's tribute to Monterey cannery workers, *Sweet Thursday.*

As you head west on your trip, you depend on your car radio for news of the world. All seems quiet on the international front. Secretary of State John Foster Dulles is heading a United States delegation to a conference in Manila that is trying to establish the Southeast Asia Treaty Organization to deal with the future of Indochina—specifically, South Vietnam. On the domestic front, you're hearing a great deal about a new subject, school desegregation: in May the Supreme Court declared unconstitutional the "separate but equal" concept that had been used in seventeen states to keep black children from officially mixing with white. The Senate is also in the news, with a subcommittee recommending that Senator Joseph McCarthy of Wisconsin be censured for "conduct unbecoming a member of the

United States Senate" and for tending "to bring the Senate into disrepute." And the World Series pits the Cleveland Indians against the New York Giants.

As you drive across the country, you can't escape the ubiquitous disc jockey with his top ten tunes of the week. Rosemary Clooney is everywhere this last week in September; she has two hits on the charts: "Hey There" ("This is the one where she talks to herself, folks!") from the Broadway musical *The Pajama Game* and "This Old House," with its novel basso-profundo male vocal. Hot on her heels is a new group called the Crew-Cuts with their nonsense song "Sh-Boom" *("yatata yatata yatata").* Eddie Fisher is belting out "I Need You Now"; Doris Day is singing "If I Give My Heart to You" (". . . will you handle it with care?"); Kitty Kallen sings "In the Chapel in the Moonlight" while the DeCastro Sisters raise many eyebrows with their suggestive "Teach Me Tonight." If you're driving through the South, you hear a new sound: a group called Bill Haley and His Comets is pounding out something called "Shake, Rattle and Roll," whose rhythms and ideas are outraging parents and delighting teenagers. Some songs are hits regionally: if you drive through parts of Mississippi and Tennessee, you may hear a raucous new voice belonging to the unlikely name of Elvis Presley singing his second record, "Good Rockin' Tonight." Then, of course, there are songs from the movies. As you near California, Hollywood is literally in the air: Don Cornell is singing the number-three song, "Hold My Hand" from *Susan Slept Here,* while LeRoy Holmes and his Orchestra have an even bigger hit with the theme from *The High and the Mighty,* the John Wayne movie about a crippled airplane. And as you finally reach the outskirts of Los Angeles, you hear a new song from one of the most anticipated pictures of the year, "The Man That Got Away" from *A Star Is Born,* sung by Judy Garland. If you're a teenager, you have vague memories of Judy Garland at kiddie matinees of *The Wizard of Oz,* but you haven't seen her in a new movie for a long time. Your parents like her, but then they like a lot of those old stars: Bing Crosby, Gary Cooper, John Wayne, James Stewart, Randolph Scott, Bob Hope. You have your own list of favorites: Elizabeth Taylor, Susan Hayward, Dean Martin and Jerry Lewis, Marilyn Monroe (though if you are a girl, you think she looks "cheap" with all that thick red lipstick), and people like Jane Powell, Robert Wagner, Terry Moore, and Pier Angeli.

If you are a teenager in 1954, you're definitely a movie fan. You have the movie habit—you've been going twice a week almost all your life. The first-run theaters downtown are the most expensive, twenty-five or fifty cents depending on your age or the picture, but they are the most fun— cavernous, imposing palaces, with rainbows of indirect colored lighting and multiple balconies, redolent with the odors of popcorn, musty air conditioning, and disinfectant. Uniformed ushers come by with flashlights to tell you to keep your feet off the seats or to stop talking. It's an exciting time to be going to the movies; to paraphrase a trade term of the time, "Movies are bigger than ever." *This Is Cinerama* opened the movies up wide; 3-D made them deeper, if not better; then CinemaScope and stereophonic sound arrived with *The Robe, How to Marry a Millionaire,* and *Knights of the Round Table:* big pictures, literally and figuratively, and with the new technology of the times they are dazzling in their impact. If you are a teenager, you are part of the first stereophonic generation; the effect of the images that engulf you and the sounds that surround you with orchestral fury in "four-track magnetic splendor" leave you reeling with the conviction that what you are experiencing is truly magnificent. You talk about these movies with your friends, discuss them in your drama or English classes, read about them in the fan magazines in the supermarket.

Westerns are still the pictures you see more than anything else—not because you like them best but because that's usually what's playing. And sometimes they are good: *High Noon* or *Shane* or even *Gun Fury*. Romantic dramas on the order of *Magnificent Obsession* and *Three Coins in the Fountain* or action adventure stories such as *The Wild One* and *Creature from the Black Lagoon* are the next two most popular categories of movies. These three categories make up the bulk of the 350 Hollywood movies that you could see in the year leading up to your September vacation. And all (or most) of them are made in Hollywood.

If you are a movie fan and you are there that day and night of September 29, you see Hollywood live up to its legend, and then some. For while it is first and foremost the home of the movies, it is also where most of the country's favorite radio and TV shows are done; if you wrote far enough in advance, you may have tickets and actually watch them make "I Love Lucy," "You Bet Your Life" (the Groucho Marx show), or "Queen for a Day," the daytime sob-and-sorrow show. NBC Studios are located at the corner of Sunset and Vine, an address that has become even more famous than Hollywood and Vine, mainly due to the thousands of radio and television broadcasts that originate there. Two blocks east on Sunset are the local stations of CBS. Most of CBS's national television programs, however, originate from the year-old multimillion-dollar complex dubbed Television City, located in the mid-Wilshire area at Third Street and Beverly Boulevard, adjacent to the famous (and expensive) Farmer's Market. This is just one of the spots that any self-respecting tourist wants to visit after checking in at one of the numerous motels that line the streets of the city, offering rooms for a dollar fifty a day, or two dollars if you want a TV set. To properly see all the sights spread throughout the Los Angeles basin, you have to get a free map from any of the hundreds of gas stations, or perhaps buy one of the maps to the stars' homes that are hawked on the streets and boulevards by sandwich-boarded preteens.

As you head east from Fairfax on Santa Monica Boulevard, you pass the Samuel Goldwyn Studios, which used to be United Artists and, before that, Pickford-Fairbanks, making Goldwyn one of the oldest studios in the city. If you start out early enough and park by the main entrance gate, you may see Marlon Brando or Frank Sinatra or Jean Simmons reporting for work on the musical *Guys and Dolls.*

Turning down LaBrea Avenue to Melrose and continuing east to Gower Street, you find the distinctive radio tower perched atop the concrete globe of the world that announces the RKO Radio Studios. Under its eccentric and reclusive owner, multimillionaire oil man and aviator Howard Hughes, the twenty-five-year-old RKO is almost a ghost town; nothing is in production, and its imminent doom is evidenced by the fact that only two films are advertised on the numerous billboards that surround the facility: *Susan Slept Here* and a B western: *Cattle Queen of Montana,* starring the eminent Barbara Stanwyck and the not-so-eminent Ronald Reagan.

A block further along Melrose are the wrought-iron gates of Paramount Pictures, the oldest movie-making company in Hollywood, whose genesis was an outfit formed in 1914 by Samuel Goldfish (later Goldwyn), Jesse Lasky, and Cecil B. De Mille. (The original studio had been at Vine and Selma; Paramount moved to Melrose in 1926.) De Mille, the only member of the original trio still with the firm, is hard at work on his newest and biggest film, a remake of his 1923 *The Ten Commandments.* Alfred Hitchcock is also working at Paramount, making an uncharacteristic little comedy called *The Trouble with Harry,* with a newcomer named Shirley Mac-Laine and a minor leading man named John Forsythe.

Your sightseeing tour includes a stop at Hollywood Memorial Cemetery on Santa Monica Boulevard, to see the elaborate mausoleums of the departed great, including Douglas Fairbanks, Sr., and the modest wall crypt of Rudolph Valentino. If you have an eye for such things, you notice that Los Angeles, and particularly Hollywood, seems to be obsessed with death: billboards, trolley cars, radio, and newspapers all extol the virtues of funeral homes and cemeteries, both human and animal. Forest Lawn in Burbank, across the river from Warner Bros. Studios, is a likely stop on any tourist's itinerary, being "world famous," as its ads repeatedly inform you.

If you drive further up Gower Street, you pass Columbia Pictures, which occupy the oldest movie-making facilities in Hollywood, established in 1911 by the Horsley Brothers on the site of an abandoned bar when Hollywood was bean fields and a few homes. At Columbia, Janet Leigh, who you know is married to Tony Curtis, is making *My Sister Eileen* with newcomer Jack Lemmon and a young dancer named Robert Fosse. Here, James Stewart is making *another* Western, this one called *The Man from Laramie,* while the new science-fiction craze is being catered to with *The Monster From Beneath the Sea.*

Still further up Gower, you're heading directly for the Hollywood Hills and the famous HOLLYWOOD sign, which seems, for no reason that you can figure out, slightly askew, with some letters higher or lower than others. To examine this landmark at closer range, you wend your way up into the topmost reaches of Griffith Park, only to find that the trail to the sign is blocked; but telescopes at the green-domed Griffith Park Observatory show that the sign was erected rather hastily on the hillside, and the eccentricity of its layout is due to the rough terrain. It was originally an advertisement for a real-estate development, "Hollywoodland," in the 1920s, and the remnants of this, the letters L-A-N-D, are lying face down on the hillside: an apt symbol, for if you turn and face south from the Griffith Park hills, you can see thousands of acres of land. The whole Los Angeles basin stretches out before you, a horizontal, decentralized, low-density area, filled with homes, business districts, and irregular, isolated patches of green— masses of trees line the street, vying for attention with billboards, neon signs, and parking lots. Looking south to Baldwin Hills and west to the Pacific Ocean, you might guess that Los Angeles is the flattest major city in the United States, possibly even in the world. An ordinance passed in 1911 prohibited any building taller than thirteen stories; legend attributes this to the fear of earthquakes, which shook the area frequently. But the truth is less dramatic and more quaint. The City Council and the Planning Department imposed the 150-foot height limit to give the city "harmonious lines" and because "people come to Los Angeles to get away from the dark, walled-in streets of Eastern cities." So for forty-three years, the city stayed predominantly flat, with only the downtown City Hall rising twenty-seven stories to dominate the surrounding landscape. One other group of buildings raised its height above its neighbors: the La Brea Towers, an apartment complex built by the Metropolitan Insurance Company in the mid-Wilshire flatlands in the early 1940s. But for those two exceptions, there is a uniformity of space and texture to the entire area that disorients and discomfits most visitors from other, older cities. But this same uniformity gives the city a strange and compelling impact, especially when viewed from the surrounding hills, or from approaching planes. It is impressive by day and spectacularly beautiful at night: the boulevards and avenues lined with amber street lamps, while the red and white lights of moving autos give movement and color to the entire metropolis. It's a city built for the automobile; its vastness and the rectangular grid that is its main design element endow it with a contemporary character, a sensibility clean and modern, befitting a city that owes no allegiance to the past.

Los Angeles has grown out instead of up, and as the settlers moved in from all over the nation in the early part of the century, the city spread along the main east-west arteries: Wilshire, Sunset, Hollywood, and Olympic; then filled in the north-south byways: Vermont, Western, Highland, La Brea, La Cienega, until the entire checkerboard of land was sketched in, laid out, and gentrified. True, there is no center to the vast sprawl, except for the older downtown Los Angeles proper, where you can find the financial center of Southern California. This downtown, which was built up around the turn of the century, most closely resembles the older, Eastern cities, with its major department stores, shops, restaurants, legitimate theaters, and motion-picture palaces. The sidewalks and thoroughfares are jammed with shoppers, workers, and hundreds of other pedestrians. Aside from this downtown area, the teeming street life that characterizes most major cities of the world is largely nonexistent in Los Angeles; and to the tourists and other noninitiates, the constant driving in search of recognizable civilization is frustrating and fruitless, as the expected scenes never materialize. Instead, you are faced with endless miles of streets, avenues, and boulevards, lined with storefront windows, interspersed with long stretches of green grass, trees, and vacant lots. Only a few isolated pockets of business and social centers in Beverly Hills, the UCLA/Westwood area, and the Miracle Mile shopping district on Wilshire Boulevard midway between downtown and Hollywood offer visible signs of thriving city life.

But then, of course, there's the Sunset Strip, that glamorous, neon-lit adjunct of nightlife, Hollywood style, with its lavish, expensive nightclubs (Ciro's, the Mocambo, the Trocadero), restaurants, and gambling spots. The area was named after its location: a winding strip of Sunset Boulevard that snakes its way through an unincorporated section of Los Angeles County and hence was not subject to the local laws. On the eastern boundary of the Strip, at Crescent Heights Boulevard, stand two of the more famous Hollywood landmarks: the Garden of Allah, the legendary apartment-hotel complex built in 1921 for actress Alla Nazimova, has long been a haven for visiting Eastern writers, actors, intellectuals, and other eccentric persons of note; it's a great spot for celebrity watching—if you have the patience. A block east is the equally famous Schwab's Drugstore, which—so everyone thinks—is where a teen-aged Lana Turner was discovered sipping a soda at the counter. Like many Hollywood legends, it isn't exactly accurate; she *was* found in a drugstore by a talent scout, but it was across the street from Hollywood High School, and it wasn't Schwab's. If you read movie fan magazines, you know that one of the original perpetrators of that legend, and of many other bits of Hollywood lore, has his unofficial offices at Schwab's: Sidney Skolsky, chronicler of the stars' careers and love lives, the man who first posed the immortal question "Do you sleep in the nude?" His byline and his column are widely syndicated, and his sign-off line, "But don't get me wrong—I love Hollywood," has become a national catch phrase. Skolsky's second-floor, glass-fronted office at Schwab's overlooks the extensive magazine rack, where you can scan the latest publications while perhaps rubbing shoulders with small-time actors and big-time agents and producers and occasionally glimpsing major stars, old and new.

Leaving Schwab's and driving east on Sunset Boulevard, you turn left at La Brea (noticing the row of English Tudor–style cottages a block south and realizing they are the studios of Charlie Chaplin, now in self-imposed exile in Switzerland because of McCarthyism and other related hate campaigns), past Tiny Naylor's Drive-In, with its cantilevered, amoebalike canopy—one of the more distinctive examples of 1950s Hollywood architecture. At Hollywood Boulevard, you turn right and look down a broad avenue filled with autos, trolley cars, and tourist buses, dotted with pepper trees, and lined with shops, restaurants, department stores, hotels, and theaters. The first building you notice to your left is, oddly enough, a church—odd because you never associated Hollywood with religion. A block east is an imposing four-story, white Italian Renaissance structure that bears the name Garden Court Apartments. Diagonally across the street from it is the even more impressive Hollywood Roosevelt Hotel, bustling with activity, its twelve stories boasting some of the most elegant rooms and housing some of the most prominent people in the city. And across the street from the Roosevelt is the famous Grauman's Chinese Theatre. As familiar as it is from photographs seen over the years, its architecture has a formidable impact: to eyes unused to Southern California eccentric, the towering pagoda entrance, the curved walls surrounding the elliptical forecourt, and the coolie-costumed employees may seem the very essence of colorful Hollywood folderol. But the theater is an icon, a shrine of sorts, the only place in the world dedicated to preserving tangible elements of Hollywood's past for the moviegoing public. Built in 1927 by legendary entrepreneur Sidney Patrick Grauman, it has become known over the years not just for its architecture (which has been referred to as "Chinese Chippendale") and its lavish premieres but primarily for its forecourt, wherein are set down for posterity the footprints and handprints of some of Hollywood's most famous inhabitants. It's the closest thing there is to a Hollywood Hall of Fame. The practice started accidentally in 1927, when the theater was under construction and a visiting Norma Talmadge (so the legend goes) stepped onto some wet cement, leaving the impression of her shoe. Showman that he was, Grauman immediately saw the beauty of the idea and began a practice of having stars leave their imprints and autographs in wet cement on the occasion of their first premieres at his theater. Over the years, the ritual has become as famous as the Academy Awards, and by 1954 there are close to one hundred of filmdom's elite immortalized in the sand and gravel of Grauman's front yard. (After Grauman's death in 1950, the theater was taken over by the Fox West Coast chain, the exhibition arm of 20th Century–Fox. It was Fox's corporate mentality that in late 1952 dictated the removal of Charlie Chaplin's hand-, foot-, and cane prints—set down at the 1928 opening of *The Circus*—because of his alleged pro-communist sympathies.)

But it was not just hand- and footprints that were set down in the forecourt. At the 1942 premiere of MGM's *Mrs. Miniver,* a complete print of the film had been encased in a time capsule in one of the concrete slabs. One of the latest additions, from September 1953, was a bronze plaque commemorating the opening of *The Robe,* the world's first CinemaScope movie. At that time, 20th Century–Fox, one of the principal owners of the theater, and Fox West Coast, the landlord of record, had defaced the open-air front of the facade by installing a flashing neon sign fifty feet wide and twenty feet high advertising both *The Robe* and CinemaScope—a sign so spectacular and gaudy that it, of course, was deemed a valuable addition to the theater's architecture and stayed in place even after *The Robe* vacated the premises. (It now heralds Darryl F. Zanuck's production of *The Egyptian,* starring newcomers Edmund Purdom and Bella Darvi, which by all accounts is proving to be the big-budget turkey of the year.) Day and night, the forecourt of the theater is jammed with tourists, performing the time-honored rituals of putting their feet into the concrete imprints to see if theirs match any of the famous and having their pictures taken in front of the stone "celestial dogs" that guard the front entrance. In the gift shop you can buy coffee mugs, posters, photographs, and other miscellaneous delights sure to arouse the envy of everyone back home.

Diagonally across the street from Grauman's, sandwiched between the Masonic Temple and the massive Barker Bros. department store, is the Hollywood Paramount, the local outlet for—what else?—Paramount Pictures. The theater is playing one of the big hits of the week, *Sabrina,* Billy Wilder's adaptation of the Samuel Taylor play *Sabrina Fair,* starring Humphrey Bogart, William Holden, and Audrey Hepburn. Directly across the street, at the corner of Hollywood and Highland, stands one of the landmarks of the town, the venerable Hollywood Hotel. Built in 1903, the four-story clapboard building was for years the social center of Hollywood life; it achieved nationwide fame during the 1930s and 1940s when Louella Parsons initiated a series of weekly broadcasts with big-name stars and musical entertainment. In 1938 Warner Bros. released a movie called *Hollywood Hotel,* featuring the song "Hooray for Hollywood," which quickly became the town's unofficial anthem. The reality of the somewhat dowdy edifice, fronted by palm trees, with wide, shaded verandas, is a far cry from the image created by the movie and the broadcasts, and the dichotomy between the real and the imagined is disappointing to most tourists.

In fact, aside from the theaters and some of the more famous restaurants, Hollywood itself has an extremely ordinary, nondescript look to it, much like a small midwestern city. As you walk about, you notice that most of the buildings seem to have been built in the 1920s and 1930s; and while they are, for the most part, well maintained, signs of decay are beginning to creep in, especially in the facades of some of the older structures, which have been converted to other uses, with a jarring juxtaposition of uninte-grated old and new. But still, the aura of the place, the cleanliness of the shops and the streets, and the very fact that it's Hollywood tend to suffuse the whole with an indefinable glamour—especially when you notice some-one like Gary Cooper stopped at a red light in his silver Rolls-Royce, or when you walk down the forecourt of another of Sid Grauman's temples of exotica, this time "the world famous Egyptian Theatre," built at the height of the 1920s craze for all things Egyptian. (It's incongruous, you think, that *The Egyptian* is playing at the Chinese while "MGM's fresh-as-a-daisy musical" *Seven Brides for Seven Brothers* is holding forth at the Egyptian.)

Thinking there might be something at the Egyptian akin to the foot-prints in the Chinese's forecourt, you search for some commemoration of Hollywood's past glories. You finally find a printed cardboard sign that lists some of the famous premieres held at the theater, beginning with Douglas Fairbanks's *Robin Hood* in 1922 and ending with the "repremiere" of *Gone With the Wind* in August 1954, just last month. One thing that is lacking in Hollywood is a place to see these famous films that are com-memorated in stone, song, and cardboard lists; most of them are as inacces-sible as entree to the studios themselves. Only one theater in the entire area specializes in showcasing "old" films, the tiny Silent Movie Theater on Fairfax Avenue—and that is largely a labor of love on the part of its owners, John and Dorothy Hampton, who show films from their own extensive collection, with no help from either the studios or any other organization supposedly devoted to the perpetuation of Hollywood's past. True, there are the occasional mass reissues of older films, such as *Gone With the Wind* and *King Kong* and the Disney films. But most of the films that you hear your parents talk about are never seen; and if you want to find out anything about them, you have to read about them in books, and there aren't too many of those, either. If you go into the Hollywood library and ask to see books on the history of the movies, you'll have a choice of approximately seventy titles—histories of the business, biographies, a few sociological studies. But hardly anywhere in town can you view anything that is dis-cussed in these books. There are film courses at UCLA and USC, and the Academy of Motion Picture Arts and Sciences occasionally holds screen-ings of older films at its theater at Melrose and Doheny; but none of these are open to the public. Ironically, the only way for most people to see an older film is on television, which is beginning to open the eyes of a new

generation to the wonders (and the trash) of Hollywood's past. The New
View Theatre on Hollywood Boulevard, next door to the Larry Edmunds
Book Shop (which specializes in "Books on Cinema and Theatre," as its
sign proclaims), has just recently begun a policy of showing reissues. But
even this is at the mercy of the major studios' practice of mistreating their
older films. You notice that the New View is running a double bill of *The
Black Swan* and *To the Shores of Tripoli*, both originally filmed in Technicolor but reissued in black and white. The week before, the theater
showed two Humphrey Bogart films, *The Treasure of the Sierra Madre* and
Key Largo, which Warner Bros. had decided to shorten by ten minutes
each to feature them on a double bill.

The Hollywood studios' and distributors' prevailing attitude toward
older films is that they don't exist, except as occasional subjects for remakes
or the infrequent reissue to fill a distribution need. Except for some independent producers and distributors, the heads of the major studios turn
down all requests for their film backlogs to be shown on television; myopi-
cally, they view the new medium as a competitor, a threat to the continued
success of theatrical exhibitions. Until 1952 most of the studios owned large
chains of theaters that supplied them with much of their income. Marcus
Loew, a pioneer exhibitor and founder of Loews Incorporated, the parent
of MGM, had said it succinctly: "We don't sell tickets to movies; we sell
tickets to theaters." This attitude continues to prevail even in 1954, five
years after the Justice Department, in a landmark antitrust suit, forced the
film companies to divorce their production-distribution arms from their
exhibition outlets. The studios obeyed the letter of the law, but just barely,
for Paramount theaters still largely play Paramount pictures and Loews
theaters still play MGM products; the same is true of the RKO theaters
and the Warner and Fox theater chains.

As a typical moviegoer, though, you are unaware of any of this, and you
continue your tour of Hollywood Boulevard. On Las Palmas Avenue, directly around the corner from the Egyptian Theatre, is a newsstand proclaiming WORLD'S LARGEST SELECTION OF OUT-OF-TOWN NEWSPAPERS! You
probably stop to look through your hometown paper to see what's been
happening there. Out of curiosity you may start leafing through the fan
magazines or the "trades": the green-bordered *Daily Variety* or the distinctive red-and-black *Hollywood Reporter.* If you look through some of the
magazines this September 29th, you'll see *Time*'s cover story asking the
question "What Is the American Character?"; *Look* featuring Arthur

Godfrey's article on underprivileged teachers and a paean to a World Series hero, "What Is So Rare As a Willie Mays?" by the unlikeliest of authors, Tallulah Bankhead; and *Newsweek* profiling hotelier Conrad Hilton. Rock Hudson, the new romantic idol, is on the cover of *Photoplay,* and the story inside, "Rock's Magnificent Obsession," is tied in to publicize his newest, biggest hit. There are stories on veteran star Bill Holden ("The Guy with the Grin"), new stars Debbie Reynolds and Tab Hunter, young marrieds Barbara Rush and Jeffrey Hunter, and superstars Marlon Brando, Jean Simmons, and Doris Day. If you look at the *Hollywood Reporter,* you learn that Merian C. Cooper, famed for his *King Kong,* has dropped his affiliation with the Cinerama Company (for whom he co-produced the innovative blockbuster *This Is Cinerama*) and is going back to his fifteen-year-old partnership with John Ford in the Argosy Corporation, whose biggest success was 1952's *The Quiet Man.* Thumbing through the trades, you also learn that Warner Bros. has five pictures in production at its Burbank studios, among them *Mister Roberts,* starring Henry Fonda in his acclaimed stage role; a John Wayne/Lana Turner vehicle called *The Sea Chase;* and *Jump into Hell,* an action melodrama about the recent French defeat at Dien Bien Phu in Indochina. You discover that at the San Fernando Valley studios of Universal-International, one mile west of Warners, World War II hero turned movie star Audie Murphy is appearing in his autobiographical *To Hell and Back,* while girl-next-door June Allyson is playing a heavily dramatic part opposite Jose Ferrer in *The Shrike,* an adaptation of another stage play; and that at the Beverly Hills studios of 20th Century–Fox, ten miles south, Billy Wilder is directing Marilyn Monroe in *The Seven Year Itch,* still another stage-hit adaptation, and Richard Todd and Jean Peters are appearing in the true-life inspirational drama *A Man Called Peter.* And you learn that MGM's Culver City stages, two miles south of Fox, are busy with a remake of the 1920s musical comedy *Hit the Deck,* with a cast of new favorites including Debbie Reynolds, Jane Powell, Russ Tamblyn, and pop singer Vic Damone and veteran dancer Ann Miller; that *Interrupted Melody,* the biography of polio-stricken opera singer Marjorie Lawrence, is being filmed with Eleanor Parker and Glenn Ford, while master director Fritz Lang is making a costume adventure film called *Moonfleet* with Stewart Granger. Reading the box-office statistics from across the country, you learn that the biggest hits of the week are *This Is Cinerama* (in its second year and still going strong); *On the Waterfront,* the gritty drama about labor-union corruption with a bravura performance by Marlon Brando; *Betrayed*, a mediocre romantic drama with Clark Gable and Lana Turner (which marks the end of Gable's twenty-three-year association with MGM); Hitchcock's *Rear Window*; and the medieval action epic *The Black Shield of Falworth*, Universal's first CinemaScope production, starring the husband-and-wife team of Janet Leigh and Tony Curtis. The corresponding top-rated television shows across the country that week are "I Love Lucy"; "The Jackie Gleason Show"; Ed Sullivan's variety show, "The Toast of the Town"; "Disneyland"; and "The Jack Benny Show." "Dragnet," the Jack Webb police program that makes a virtue of its Los Angeles locations and a national anthem of its theme song, is number six in the ratings, followed by "I Led Three Lives," about an American agent posing as a communist; "Amos 'n' Andy" and "The Life of Riley," both carryovers from radio; and "The Liberace Show," starring the dimpled darling who takes piano playing and candelabra to new depths of bourgeois delight.

If you're looking for an evening's entertainment, the trades offer ads for some unique offerings in the Los Angeles area. In a section referred to as "Theaters—Spoken Drama" you learn that Miss Helen Hayes ("The First Lady of the American Theater") is appearing at the new Huntington Hartford Theatre on Vine Street in Hollywood, in James M. Barrie's *What Every Woman Knows*. Downtown at the Philharmonic Auditorium, the Civic Light Opera Association is presenting Mary Martin in a new musical version of the same writer's *Peter Pan*. Other productions include *The Drunkard*, now in its twenty-second (!) year, and "a brilliant new musical revue called *That's Life*" at the tiny Las Palmas Theatre in Hollywood.

In both trades, however, the most interesting notice is a six-page advertising section announcing "The Most Anticipated Event in Entertainment History!"—the world premiere that very evening at the RKO Pantages Theatre in Hollywood of *A Star Is Born*, the Judy Garland movie whose hit song "The Man That Got Away" you've been hearing on the radio all across the country. The ad is in the form of thank-you notes from Garland to everyone connected with the film and the same from Jack Warner, head of Warner Bros., the company that co-produced the movie with Transcona Enterprises. The studio was publicizing not only Garland but the amount of money that the film cost and the length of time it took to produce ("$6 million and 2½ years to make it!"). In fact, if you peruse the magazine rack, you suddenly realize that Garland and *A Star Is Born* are featured in just about every major magazine: *Collier's, Redbook, Parents, Look, Cos-*

mopolitan, and—most impressive to you as a moviegoer—*Life,* whose cover shows a close-up of a freckle-faced urchin with the caption "Judy as Gamin." If you need any further proof that this is a major filmland event, the list of stars attending the premiere is a veritable Who's Who (and Who Was Who) of Hollywood. According to the ads in the trades and in the Los Angeles *Times,* the *Herald-Express,* and the *Hollywood Citizen News,* more than two hundred and fifty major personalities will be there, ranging from Anna Maria Alberghetti to Mai Zetterling. For those unfortunates in other parts of the country, the premiere will be covered live by television and relayed all across the United States, the first time anything like this has ever been done. As a tourist, however, you can have a front-row seat at a ritual that, at least according to the publicity, promises to be the most exciting, glittering, and glamorous affair of this or any other year—a throwback to the fabled premieres that you've read about in the fan magazines and caught glimpses of in the newsreels. On impulse, you buy a copy of *Life,* just in case you have the chance to get her autograph at the premiere.

As night falls, an array of searchlights near Hollywood and Vine forms a multipointed star over the Pantages Theatre, signaling to everyone for miles around that something extraordinary is about to take place. As you near the intersection, you realize with dismay that maybe you've waited too long to get to the theater. The entire two-block area around Hollywood and Vine is filled with a swaying, shoving mass of humanity—you overhear one reporter estimate the crowd at twenty thousand. Barricades have been set up all along Hollywood Boulevard for two blocks on either side of the theater, while bleachers on both sides of the theater entrance have been erected for fans smart enough to arrive early, some of them as early as nine that morning—they're the ones lucky enough to have ringside seats for the show.

And what a show it is! The limousines began arriving around eight, disgorging more celebrities than have been seen in one spot in Hollywood in years, including at the Academy Awards. There are Hedda Hopper and Louella Parsons and Sophie Tucker and Joan Crawford with Cesar Romero and the Gary Coopers and the Tony Curtises and the Dean Martins and the Clark Gables and Rock Hudson. They drive up five cars across and hundreds deep; as far as you can see down Hollywood Boulevard, limousines are lined up waiting to discharge their glamorous occupants to the light-splashed entrance. The thousands in the bleachers and on the streets raise a crescendo of sound ranging from applause to shrieks as their favorites emerge from the sleek black autos, tuxedoed, bejeweled, smiling, waving: Lauren Bacall and Humphrey Bogart, Elizabeth Taylor and Michael Wilding, Edward G. Robinson, Robert Stack, Kim Novak, even Marlene Dietrich, arriving in a vintage open-front limousine with director Elia Kazan. And there's Liberace!—and Mickey Rooney, Olivia de Havilland, Lucy and Desi, and the Alan Ladds, Frank Sinatra, Donna Reed, Fred MacMurray, television's Wild Bill Hickok (a.k.a. Guy Madison), Charlton Heston, the Jack Bennys, and Groucho Marx. As they arrive, you notice, they are greeted by four beautiful hostesses and taken through an interview circle where they are announced by Jack Carson, one of the stars of the picture, or, later, by George Jessel. From there they are shepherded over to the television cameras and introduced by emcee George Fischer to fans across the country. As you watch all this—or try to from deep inside the crowd, everyone straining for the same view—you are amazed and astounded at the hysteria, the noise, the cars, the confusion, and the glamour that is panoplied and paraded in front of you before disappearing inside the theater. If you have the chance, you may notice that James Mason, Garland's co-star, and George Cukor, the picture's director, are nowhere to be seen. But a huge roar emerges as Judy Garland, her husband, Sid Luft, and Jack Warner arrive in a frenzy of police escorts, flashbulbs, reporters, and shoving, pushing, screaming fans. Any hopes you may have had about getting Garland's autograph are drowned in the sea of surging people, held at bay by phalanxes of police on horseback and on foot. As you watch, you can see George Jessel greet both Garland and Warner warmly. Anything being said over the loudspeakers is drowned out by the continued screams of the crowd. Garland and her party are hurried into the theater, and almost immediately the crowd noise diminuendos, the lights begin to fade, and the throngs, realizing that the show is over, begin to slowly disperse . . . except for the patient hundreds who wait outside three hours for the film to unreel. They then gawk and scream all over again as Hollywood's aristocracy file out of the theater into the waiting limousines and are whisked off to a midnight postpremiere party at the Ambassador Hotel.

Lacking that kind of patience, a weary tourist, you decide to have something to eat before going back to your motel. Clutching your copy of *Life*, you walk a half-block down Vine Street to the World Famous Hollywood Brown Derby, where, surrounded by caricatures of more of Hollywood's famous, you order a Cobb salad and contemplate excitedly what you've just seen. Opening your copy of *Life*, you read the article on Garland

and the movie, devouring the behind-the-scenes gossip. You're surprised at the accounts of her temper tantrums and at the time, money, and effort that it took to make the picture. Reading all this over your dessert, you might even wonder idly just how a movie like *A Star Is Born* came to be made in the first place.

PART ONE

ONE

A

STAR

IS

BORN

Preparation

Today there is only one person who remembers how this version of *A Star Is Born* got started, and it isn't Jack Warner. He, as they say, is no longer with us; but even as far back as 1955, he couldn't, under oath (in a deposition taken in a suit against Warners by David O. Selznick over his rights to the 1937 version of *A Star Is Born*), recall how the picture had come about:

> Q: Mr. Warner, can you tell us . . . the first time you ever discussed [this movie]?
> A: Oh, it has been too long ago to remember. . . . I don't know.

At the same hearing, his older brother Harry (the president of the company), couldn't remember either:

> Q: When did you first hear that Warner Bros. . . . was to produce . . . *A Star Is Born?*
> A: After it was started . . . I only knew about it when the cost came to my attention.

No, the one person who remembers *exactly* how the film came about is its producer, Michael Sidney Luft: "We were rehearsing for Judy's Palace Theater opening [in 1951]. We had twelve dancing boys and were in a dance studio on La Cienega and Beverly Boulevard in L.A. and I picked up the paper one day and I read that Ed Alperson had the remake rights to *A Star Is Born* . . . and I just parked that in my head."

The Judy he refers to was Judy Garland, legendary ex–MGM musical star who had been fired by that studio two years earlier after almost two decades of stardom, because of her "unreliability." She and Luft had met shortly thereafter in New York City, around the time her last MGM film, *Summer Stock,* had been released. By then she had survived a suicide attempt, a subsequent nervous breakdown, and a divorce from her second husband, director Vincente Minnelli. Luft's colorful career had included stints as a test pilot, an entrepreneur, and a B-picture producer. He was a divorced (from actress Lynn Bari) man-about-town who loved horse-racing. Garland, at that point in her life, was a proven winner who'd been put out to pasture prematurely. So Luft picked up where MGM had left off and, under the sponsorship of Abe Lastfogel of the William Morris Agency, shepherded her though a series of concerts in England, beginning at the London Palladium. The success of these led to an offer for her to bring vaudeville back to New York by opening her show at the legendary RKO Palace Theatre on Broadway, which had abandoned live performances almost twenty years earlier. It was in preparation for this that rehearsals were being held in the dance studio with the twelve dancing boys. Luft remembers: "We were sort of noodling the show together over a two-week period, and after rehearsal one night I said, 'Judy, I've got a great idea, perfect for you' . . . and I told her about *A Star Is Born* and she smiled and I said, 'What's the big smile?' And she said, 'I've done it on the Lux Radio Theatre, and after I did it I went to L.B. [Mayer] and told him I wanted to do it and he thought it was a good idea, so he called Nick Schenck [the head of MGM in New York] . . . but Schenck said no, we won't take a sad and tragic story like that and do it as a musical for our precious Judy'—that's what she told me. We both decided it was a good idea . . . [but] there was nothing I could do about it then because I was concentrating on getting this whole troupe to New York and opening at the Palace."

Garland opened her show on Broadway on October 16, 1951, to tremendous critical and public acclaim. Her career seemed to be back in high gear. "After we opened," Luft recalls, "maybe a week or two after, I called Abe Lastfogel and told him what my notion was about *A Star Is Born* and for him to see if he could possibly call Alperson and see if the property was for sale. Two, three days later, I get a call back from him; he says that Alperson is not interested in selling the property at any price, nor is he interested in Judy Garland doing it . . . he has other ideas, and that was it."

Alperson's professed disinterest in Garland didn't deter Luft at all. "A couple of days later," Luft relates, "I called Johnny Beck, an agent at the

William Morris office. I said, 'John, do me a favor. See if you can set up a meeting with Eddie Alperson—I'm flying in and I want to talk to him.' He called me back in a couple of days, says, 'Eddie Alperson is coming in on such-and-such a day.' I said, 'I'll be there.' While we're in the meeting, it dawned on me what was bothering Alperson: he didn't want anything to do with the Morris office. [After the meeting] I walked out with him and I said, 'Eddie, I'm going back to New York; Judy's not feeling well. Are you coming with me?' He said, 'I'll go home and pack.' "

Edward L. Alperson was a thirty-two-year veteran of the movie business, an independent B-picture producer who by 1951 was releasing his low-budget product through 20th Century–Fox. Before that he had been president of Grand National Pictures, a 1930s purveyor of B pictures; chairman of the board of Cinecolor, a cheap two-color process; and president of the bizarrely named Pawnee Bill Productions and of Film Classics, a firm specializing in reissuing older films. It was his connection with Film Classics that had led him to buy the rights to the original 1937 *A Star Is Born* when Selznick International, the company that had produced it, disposed of its assets upon going out of business in the early 1940s.

Alperson and Luft flew to New York in mid-November 1951; and over the next few weeks, as he saw the effect Garland was having on audiences and the extent of the publicity she was generating, Alperson's intractability regarding casting her in *A Star Is Born* softened to the extent that he, Luft, and Garland formed a corporation called Transcona, after a town in Manitoba where Luft used to fly. Transcona was designed as a holding corporation, its assets being the rights to *A Star Is Born:* Alperson held 20 percent of the corporation; Garland as star and Luft as producer held 75 percent; and the remaining 5 percent went to Luft's millionaire friend and racing partner, Ted Law.

All was seemingly neat and orderly—but there was one tiny flaw that no one involved noticed: Alperson didn't own *all* the rights to *A Star Is Born*. He had the story and remake rights, true; but exhibition rights to the original film in some thirteen foreign countries had been reacquired by the picture's original producer, David O. Selznick, who fully intended to exploit them, which meant that anyone who made a new version of the story could not show it worldwide without violating Selznick's copyright. It was, at the moment, a minor legal snag which neither Luft nor Alperson noticed; their main concern was in shopping the property and Garland around.

Garland, recovered from her much-publicized suicide attempt, had filled the Palace Theatre twice daily for almost four months; she had been covered, profiled, photographed, and recorded so often that for a while in the winter and spring of 1951–52, it seemed as if Judy Garland was everywhere, except television. Her "comeback" was almost complete; all it lacked was a movie. But even with all the press attention, the men in charge of the studios were still leery of her. Singing a few songs on stage was one thing; building a big musical picture around someone with a proven record of "unreliability" was quite another, expensive matter. This was the prevailing attitude that Luft and Alperson faced—until April 21, 1952. That was the night when Garland brought her show to the Philharmonic Auditorium in downtown Los Angeles and was "welcomed home" with an extravagant celebrity turnout and a spectacular party afterwards at Romanoff's restaurant. The warmth generated by all this melted the solid wall of resistance that Transcona had encountered, and cautious feelers were extended to Luft about Garland doing a picture.

But Luft knew what he wanted: Warner Bros. "They'd just divorced themselves from their theaters and they had all this money in the bank to finance independent production. [Under the terms of the U.S. government antitrust settlement against the major studios, Warner Bros. sold its three hundred theaters to the Stanley Company for $6,000,000 in December 1952.] And just before we had opened at the Palace in New York, I saw Jack Warner at a party. I watched him pull up a chair and sit next to Judy and talk with her at length. I knew that Warner was interested in Judy. Eddie [Alperson] set up the meetings . . ."

Jack Warner, born in London, Ontario, in 1882, was the youngest and most flamboyant of the four brothers who, in 1923, had founded the company that bore their name. A self-described "lighthearted man," he had been a legendary Hollywood mogul since 1926, when he and his brothers had given the world Vitaphone and the first commercially successful talking pictures, thereby transforming their tiny company into one of the major production forces in Hollywood. Jack's older brother Harry was president of the company; his brother Albert was treasurer; and Jack was vice-president in charge of production at the firm's Burbank, California, studio. (Sam Warner had died in 1926.) A frustrated performer, he had started out in show business as a boy soprano under the stage name Leon Zuardo, singing in nickelodeons to clear the house between shows. Like many other of the film pioneers, Warner didn't have much of a formal education; he was what is now called "street smart"—shrewd, manipulative, with a collection of the worst jokes in the world, which he would tell anywhere and everywhere, usually making everyone cringe. He was a high-stakes gambler at any casino from Monte Carlo to Reno, and he ruled his suzerainty in Burbank just as loudly and as expansively as he gambled. He was a practical, thrifty (some would say cheap) man who went around the studio turning out lights to save on electric bills. (His brother Harry, with whom he maintained a strained relationship, was equally thrifty: he would walk around the studio streets picking up nails for reuse—an idiosyncrasy carried over from his early training as a cobbler.) Jack insisted on a full day's work for his money and on absolute loyalty to the company. One classic story that illustrated his attitude is the "happy gateman" episode. On one of his frequent forays around the studio to see that everyone was at work and no time being wasted, he heard a new gateman singing operatic arias in a quite respectable voice. Talking to the man, he learned that he was a serious student of voice, practicing daily. "Which would you rather be," Warner inquired, "a singer or our gateman?" "Oh, a singer, of course," the man assured Warner, thinking this was his big break. "You're fired," replied Warner and walked away.

As vice-president in charge of production, he was responsible for, in his own words, "engaging the people who produce the pictures: the writers, directors, actors, the technical branches of our studios. This is all done through department heads. Also, the buying of the stories, assigning writers, directors, producers . . . in many cases I [decide] the principal players, the stars, and occasionally the supporting players, the shooting of the pictures and things like that . . . as far as deciding what pictures should be produced. . . . I talk it over in general with producers and other executives. . . . On some pictures I have final say . . . [but] sometimes my final say is voted down . . . I think I should add that. I don't want [to give] the impression I do everything because I don't." One of his ex-executives, Hal Wallis, who started his producing career with Warner, characterized him as "a dynamo. Nervous, restless, he couldn't sit still a minute. He was like a jumping bean, endlessly interested in everything that was going on. . . . Jack was a great administrator . . . and a very skillful man in his dealings with the stars . . . he understood them, knew how to feed their egos. [He] was a showman who played his instincts. I never saw him read a script, let alone a book. Just from glancing at a title or riffling through a few pages, he could sense whether [something] would interest millions of people all

over the world. He was usually right." Playing by his instincts had kept
Warner Bros. from losing money since 1933. In the fiscal year 1951–52 the
company had a profit of $9.4 million—down from the postwar high of $22
million in 1947, but that was the year that 90 million Americans went to
the movies twice a week. In 1951, 54 million went once a week; the rest
of the time they stayed home and watched their new television sets. In
1946, there had only been 8,000 sets in the United States; by late 1952,
that number had multiplied astoundingly to 15.5 million! *Life* magazine,
in an extensive article on the movie industry in its August 13, 1951, issue,
related a young married moviegoer's explanation of how the moviegoing
decline came about: "There was a picture my wife and I wanted to see
. . . we began to add up [how much it would cost us]. Two tickets at 60¢
each—that's not so bad. But then there was the babysitter. Three hours
at 50¢ an hour plus car fare is $1.70. Parking the car—that would be
another 50¢. Figuring gas and oil would be another 50¢. Add a Coke or
something afterward, say another 25¢. That's over $4.00. So we stayed
home."

But there were still enough moviegoers to whom a night out at the
movies was worth the price; and to tempt these faithful, Jack Warner,
gambler that he was, staked nearly $28 million to make 26 features in 1952,
roughly two a month, in addition to the 88 shorts and 120 newsreels that
would carry the distinctive Warner Bros. shield insignia. Warner was proud
of that shield, and with good reason. The people he hired to make pictures,
and the pictures they made, had won eighty-five Academy Awards since
1927. Some of the best films ever made in Hollywood were actually made
in Burbank by Jack Warner and company. And that was still true on March
20, 1952, when the Academy Awards for 1951 were given out in a (not yet
televised) ceremony at the RKO Pantages Theatre on Hollywood Boulevard. Out of fourteen nominations for the company, five Oscars went to
pictures made or released by Warners.

The distinction between "made" and "released" is an important one, for
it points up a subtle change in the manner in which Warners, and indeed
many of the other studios, "made" its pictures. For thirty years, it had been
industry practice for a studio to buy a story, or have an original story written
by a staff writer, and then cast the picture from the studio's contract roster,
under a staff director, with support from the studio's technical departments. Everything would be financed by the studio, which retained ownership of the story and the film and all monies derived therefrom. But

beginning in 1937, when William Randolph Hearst took his independent Cosmopolitan Productions unit away from MGM and moved it twelve miles north to Warners' Burbank studios, Jack found a new way to obtain first-class product to carry the company's shield. And that was to finance "outside" producers who had a "property," usually a story, and sometimes a star to go along with it (in which case the "property" became a "package"), for which Warner Bros. would provide the financing, studio facilities, and the all-important distribution network. From Hearst's Cosmopolitan, the list of "outside" producers expanded to include Hal Wallis Productions in 1941, Cagney Productions in 1943, and ultimately Charles K. Feldman and his Group Productions, which made *A Streetcar Named Desire* for release by Warners. *Streetcar* grossed almost $5 million and won four of the five Oscars earned by Warner Bros. for 1951. So when, in early August 1952, Transcona, in the persons of Luft and Alperson, came to see Warner about Judy Garland in *A Star Is Born*, they found him not only receptive but ready to make a deal.

"Eddie and I had a whole list written out," Luft recalls, "of what we wanted, as opposed to what Warners was offering—we knew we wanted this, and that we'd have to trade with that. One day I met with Jack by myself. He had a scissors on his desk. I said, 'All right, Jack, you want that? Then I want this—cut this out. . . .' He'd cut out that paragraph, cut this out, put this over there. We chopped up this whole piece of paper [till] it looked like cut-up paper dolls. After [Eddie and I] concluded the trading back and forth with Warner, we made a nine-picture deal, predicated on *A Star Is Born*. Eddie brought a property called 'Snow Covered Wagons,' which was about the Donner Party, and I owned the rights to the story 'Man O' War' about the great racehorse. Those were the three properties we went in with. We made this deal in late '52 and were hopefully going to get going on one right away. We had a writer working on 'Man O' War,' which we hoped to start in early '53, then possibly get to *A Star Is Born* in the middle of '53."

On June 8, two months prior to his initial meeting with Warner, Luft had put Garland under a more personal kind of contract when he and the singer were married. On July 19, they had thrown what the papers referred to as "a huge brawl" at their new home on Mapleton Drive in Beverly Hills with a hundred and fifty guests in attendance, some of the cream of Hollywood society. Betty Comden and her writing partner Adolph Green were there, taking a break from working on MGM producer Arthur Freed's new film, *The Band Wagon,* starring Fred Astaire. Howard Dietz and Arthur Schwartz sang some of the new songs they had written for the picture, including a rouser entitled "That's Entertainment." Everybody involved seemed very high-spirited and carefree, despite the fact that that same week MGM had announced that all contract personnel, executives and stars alike, would be taking salary cuts of 25 to 50 percent, thereby effecting an annual saving of $5 million for the beleaguered studio. It was a harsh acknowledgment that an era of munificence and extravagance had ended. Also in the trade papers that week were two small, seemingly unrelated items. A New York outfit called Cinerama, Inc., had leased the Broadway Theater from the Shuberts to exhibit what was referred to as "a new three-dimensional process," beginning in September. And in Hollywood, a promoter named Sid Pink was taking the unusual step of screening "rushes" (daily footage) for potential investors in a new independent movie called *Bwana Devil,* directed by Arch Oboler and photographed in something called "Natural Vision 3 Dimension." These two items were buried in the back pages of the trades; the headline news that week, after the MGM economy measures, was the story of the disastrous fire that had swept the Warners lot, raging for almost three hours in the mid-afternoon and causing $5 million in damages. While these events swirled and eddied around them, the Lufts were celebrating not only their marriage but also the news of her pregnancy, an impending recording contract with Capitol Records, and what looked to be a very important picture deal with Warners.

On September 8, 1952, Jack Warner made it official: Warner Bros. would finance and distribute three films from Transcona, the first to be a musical remake of *A Star Is Born* with Judy Garland.

Transcona's nine-picture deal was altered slightly so that the six pictures to follow the initial three were to be taken as options on the part of Warners every six months, with Garland having the lead in two after *A Star Is Born.* Once agreement had been reached among Luft, Alperson, and Warner, the actual working-out of the contract was turned over to the Warners legal department, which promptly began negotiating with Transcona's attorneys. While the lawyers met, Luft recalls, "we were kicking around names [of people to work on] the picture. We knew we wanted Harold Arlen to write the music because of his association with Judy on "Over the Rainbow," and we kicked around [the names of] guys to write the screenplay. Judy loved Moss Hart, she knew him personally, so we went to Jack and said we wanted Moss for the script if we could get him. Jack went along with us, thought we couldn't do any better."

Moss Hart and Harold Arlen had one thing in common—they were both represented by Irving Paul Lazar. Pint-sized, dynamic, and shrewd, Lazar was one of the fastest-rising literary agents in Hollywood. He had not yet been nicknamed "Swifty" by an admiring Humphrey Bogart—that would come in 1955, when in the course of one afternoon he made six separate picture deals for Bogart—but in 1952 he already was known for the speed, dexterity, and imagination that characterized his business deals. He maintained an enviable circle of friends which included the Bogarts, Luft and Garland, Billy Wilder, Frank Sinatra, and George Cukor. A prominent bachelor-about-town, Lazar was in noticeable attendance at just about every major social function, public or private, held in Hollywood or New York, several of which he hosted himself. He was at the July 19 party that Garland and Luft gave, and undoubtedly at that time he had conversations about Moss Hart.

Lazar had met Hart when the two were in the service in World War II. Lazar, a former MCA agent, was a second lieutenant, and Hart was already a famous, well-established playwright. Lazar persuaded Hart and General "Hap" Arnold that the Air Force needed a fund raiser; the result was *Winged Victory,* which netted $5 million for the Air Corps relief fund and marked the beginning of a long and close friendship between Hart and Lazar. "Moss anointed me," said Lazar. "He said, 'You are a literary agent now.'" Lazar not only took Hart at his word but took him on as his first client, obtaining an unprecedented $150,000 for Hart's screenplay for Laura Z. Hobson's novel *Gentleman's Agreement* in 1947.

Five years later, in October 1952, Lazar broached the subject of *A Star Is Born* to Hart, who was in Philadelphia with out-of-town tryouts for his play *The Climate of Eden,* which he had adapted from a novel and was directing. According to an Ed Sullivan column of the time, Hart

> was dining in the Ritz Hotel when his West Coast agent Irving Lazar arrived from the airport. Hart said, "I've read that Warners is planning to re-make *A Star Is Born* with Judy Garland. Is that on the level?" Lazar told him that the oft-discussed idea was a reality. "I'd very much like to write it for Judy," said Hart. "I've known her a long time and I'd enjoy it." Lazar asked the waiter to connect a phone at the table and put through a call to Sid Luft in Hollywood. "Sid wants me to fly right back and sign the deal," Lazar said.

"But you haven't even had dinner," objected Hart. "When it comes," grinned Lazar, "you eat it for me. I'm rushing to the airport."

Apocryphal though the story may be, it certainly enhanced Lazar's reputation as a whiz at deal making—as did the actual deal he made with Luft for Hart's services: $100,000 and a house in Palm Springs in which to work. It was a felicitous arrangement and worth every penny, for Hart was one of the pre-eminent figures of the Broadway theater. Since his first success in 1930 as the co-author, with George S. Kaufman, of the Hollywood satire *Once in a Lifetime,* Hart's name, as author or co-author, had been on some of the most famous plays in the American theater, including *You Can't Take It With You,* for which he shared a Pulitzer Prize with Kaufman in 1937. He wrote some of the best dialogue Broadway ever heard, and his direction of plays and musicals was equally skilled. In collaboration with Kaufman, Richard Rodgers, and Lorenz Hart in the 1937 Franklin D. Roosevelt spoof *I'd Rather Be Right,* and then with Kurt Weill in *Lady in the Dark* in 1941, Hart managed to change the style and direction of the Broadway musical theater. He had created one of the first truly integrated original musicals, in which song and dance arose from character and story instead of being dragged in as divertissements. *(Oklahoma!,* which many point to as having pioneered this approach, was an adaptation of the play *Green Grow the Lilacs.)* Hart's choice of subject matter for *Lady in the Dark*—psychoanalysis—had been derived from his own experiences and had brought drama and a new maturity to the rather innocent and carefree musical theater libretto. As a screenwriter, Hart had earned an Academy Award nomination in 1948 for *Gentleman's Agreement,* his adaptation of Laura Z. Hobson's novel about anti-Semitism in America; and just as Lazar was making the deal for Hart to work on *A Star Is Born,* Samuel Goldwyn's new film, *Hans Christian Andersen,* for which Hart had written the screenplay, was opening around the country to excellent reviews and even better business. One of Hart's recurring superstitions held that "every success is a combination of luck and a modicum of skill, and that with each new play the luck is bound to run out." So it was with his *The Climate of Eden,* which opened on Broadway on November 6, 1952, and closed after twenty performances, after which a philosophical Hart remarked: "Only two things matter in a man's life: Love and Work. It is possible to live without one, but not without the other. My secret dream is to get together enough money to some day give up work." With that, he and his actress/wife, Kitty Carlisle, and their two children left for Palm Springs, where Hart promised to "do magic" with the script of *A Star Is Born.*

Meanwhile, on November 21, in Los Angeles, Judy Garland gave birth to her second child, whom she and Luft named Lorna. Four days later, according to Gerold Frank's biography *Judy,* the singer once again tried to commit suicide by slashing her throat; it was only through the timely intervention of Luft that she hadn't bled to death. This fit of self-destruction evidently had been brought on by a combination of postpartum depression and Garland's long-standing and continuing dependence on barbiturates and amphetamines. Her addiction had begun innocently enough in the early 1940s, when an MGM doctor had prescribed use of the new drug Dexedrine to help her get through her rigorous daily filming schedule. Over the years, she had made valiant but unsuccessful efforts to stop using these pills. It was a truly vicious cycle: sleeping pills at night, then during the day another stimulant to neutralize the sleeping pills. Luft realized that she was happiest and felt most vital when she was working, but he also realized that if word of her latest escapade leaked out, the deal with Warners would probably be called off. To quiet any rumors of problems, he and Garland decided to give a small dinner party in early December. Garland's recuperative powers were evidently tremendous, for not only was she a charming hostess but she also sang at length after dinner, the scars on her neck concealed by a high-collared dress. Luft marveled at her seeming indestructibility and almost immediately continued with preparations for *A Star Is Born,* as if nothing out of the ordinary were besetting his wife and the star of his film.

Preoccupied with their problems, the Lufts paid scant attention to the two events that were causing the rest of the film industry to sit up and take notice. On September 30, the motion picture *This Is Cinerama* opened at the Broadway Theatre in New York and quite literally created a sensation. It was something distinctly new, using three separate cameras and projectors to throw a gigantic picture on a huge, deeply curved screen which almost engulfed the audience. Coupled with this was a six-channel stereophonic sound system, utilizing, for the first time in film exhibition, magnetic tape and offering sound of astounding richness, realism, and directionality from numerous speakers placed around the theater. The process was a refinement of a World War II gunnery training device invented by Fred Waller, an ex–Paramount cameraman-director; the technique had caught the eye of pioneer broadcaster and newsman Lowell Thomas, who had interested Broadway producer Michael Todd and filmmaker Merian C. Cooper. What evolved was a travelogue of sorts, which showed the potential of the technique while literally taking audiences for a ride all over the world. That particular opening-night audience was filled with the social, political, and theatrical elite, all friends and/or acquaintances of the three impresarios; the word of mouth they generated and the resulting press attention made Cinerama an overnight sensation, with front-page stories in the major newspapers and block-long lines at the box office. Anything on film that generated that kind of money and publicity was bound to arouse the interest of the heads of the film companies; but after a careful review of the process, most of the studio executives decided that Cinerama was too complex to be practical. And there seemed to be no way to achieve the same effect in any simpler manner. Still, Cinerama did create a new excitement about moviegoing, even if it was an excitement that couldn't be exploited immediately.

Across the continent at the Paramount Theatre on Hollywood Boulevard, two months after Cinerama's New York splash, another movie opened. It was *Bwana Devil,* the low-budget potboiler that Sid Pink had been selling to investors on the strength of the dailies. The reviews of the film were merciless in their contempt, calling it "inept," "amateurish," "boring," and "ludicrous." But there were lines around the block from the moment the picture opened, so much so that a second theater booked it within the week. What was pulling people in was the "Natural Vision" gimmick, which used two cameras and two projectors in synchronization to give the illusion of depth. True, audiences had to wear special glasses to view this "third dimension," but that did not seem to deter them one bit, as they queued up to have natives' spears and leaping lions seemingly come whizzing out of the screen into their laps. Natural Vision was another sensation, but a much more economical and practical one than Cinerama, for it required no extensive theater renovations.

In the weeks after *Bwana Devil* opened around the country, the money it continued to generate attracted the notice of everybody in Hollywood, and for a while Milton Gunzberg, developer and owner of Natural Vision, was the most sought-after man in town, as most of the studios tried to sign up his process for their own use. But it was Jack Warner, who knew a good gimmick when he saw it, who got Gunzberg first. On December 19, barely two weeks after *Bwana Devil* opened, Warner gleefully announced that the Natural Vision Corporation had made a five-picture deal with Warner Bros. and that the company was planning a "full program of pictures utilizing the process." Remembering the sensation (and the huge profits) caused by the introduction of sound and color in the late twenties, Warner told *Variety* that "the three-dimensional film opens up a new avenue of expression for the film creator; an avenue, I might say on the basis of some actual experience, which offers tremendously exciting opportunities for stirring the emotions of the audience. And what is the sum total of all our effort if not to stir the emotions?" The problem of the necessary glasses he dismissed with the prediction that "audiences will wear such viewers as effortlessly as they wear wrist watches or carry fountain pens." And with that said, he donned a pair of Polaroid spectacles and posed for a *Life* magazine spread.

That same week, on December 17, Warners' legal department had sent the Transcona contract to Jack Warner for final approval. It had taken three months for all the parties to agree to the fine points, details, subdivisions, and thousand-and-one other complications that were spelled out in the eighteen-page, single-spaced document. Warners was to finance, through a series of loans, the direct production cost of each of the group of three films Transcona intended to make. The budgets were set at $500,000 for *Snow Covered Wagons*, $650,000 for *Man O' War*, and $1,500,000 for *A Star Is Born*, which were the average costs for Warners' own Westerns and musicals. Garland was to be paid $100,000 for performing in *A Star Is Born;* but, interestingly enough, there is a sentence in the same paragraph that states, "Transcona is not entitled to include in the budget of any photoplay produced hereunder any of Transcona's overhead or corporate operating expense. The contract continued:

> [If Transcona is] required to expend more than the budgeted cost of a photoplay to complete it, then Warners will advance the additional financing. If Transcona spends more than 10% in excess of the budgeted cost, then Warner Bros. forthwith has the option to elect whether it shall assume control of production of the photoplay involved. . . . Transcona will endeavor not to have the final screenplay [for *A Star Is Born*] exceed 125 pages in

length . . . and the principal photography including all montages, etc. of any photoplay (in which Miss Judy Garland) appears shall not require more than 54 production days. . . . When any photoplay has been previewed, "sneak," press, or public, on two (2) different occasions, Warner Bros. has the right, in its sole discretion, to re-cut or re-edit with a view to giving it the highest box-office appeal to the general public. Transcona grants Warners the right to retain and use all so-called cut-outs, negative trims, key shots, and deleted portions of the photoplays for its film library [or] Warner Bros. may dispose of the balance of said footage, if any remaining from said photoplays, as junk.

Under this contract, Warners received the right to distribute the film for twelve years and would split the profits fifty-fifty with Transcona after agreed-upon expenses. Warner Bros. also agreed that the "cost of advertising, publicizing, and exploitation [of *A Star Is Born*] shall not exceed . . . $175,000." For its part, Transcona agreed that it "would secure and immediately assign to Warners . . . all rights in and to the screenplay [*A Star Is Born*] . . . based on the literary property used as a basis of a photoplay . . . Transcona has the right to grant [these rights] to Warner Bros. There are not and will not be any claims, etc. against any of said photoplays which can interfere with Warners' rights." Specifically, this last referred to the chain of ownership that gave Alperson/Transcona all the rights to remake the picture and to be able to distribute it anywhere in the world. This minor sentence and the legal stumbling block it would be was just one of the unseen perils that would beset Warner, Luft, et al. before the picture was completed.

Also attached to the contract was a list of acceptable directors and players. Laurence Olivier topped the list for Garland's leading man and had already been cabled by Jack Warner to inquire about his interest: he had none. Number two was Richard Burton, a relative newcomer, under exclusive contract to 20th Century–Fox; inquiries found him unavailable, as he had been cast in Fox's biblical epic *The Robe*, which was expected to go into production shortly. Following him was Tyrone Power, also under contract to Fox—his price put him out of the running. Then, in order of preference, came Cary Grant, James Stewart, Glenn Ford, Stewart Granger, Robert Taylor, Gregory Peck, and Ray Milland. Of all these, the only name that seemed to delight everyone was Cary Grant; so it was decided that Luft, as he recalls, "would romance Cary Grant to see if he would do it."

The list of acceptable directors was short, only six names, all tops in their field: George Cukor, Daniel Mann, Charles Vidor, Michael Curtiz, Henry Koster, and John Ford. There was an early rumor that Vidor would do it, but Luft states emphatically that "Judy wanted George [Cukor] to direct. He was under contract to Metro, so we started negotiating to get him." Garland reiterated this herself in an interview in 1953: "I wanted George . . . the picture had to be the greatest . . . it couldn't be merely very good. I had too much at stake . . . I had to prove things."

George Cukor had been helping performers "prove things" since his arrival in Hollywood in 1929, under contract to Paramount Pictures as a "dialogue director" to assist silent film directors in coping with the new demands of sound. The twenty-nine-year-old had brought with him nearly two decades of intense fascination and devotion to the theater, first as a spectator, then as a stage manager/director in stock companies in and around New York. He and his sister, the only children of a well-to-do Hungarian family, were raised in an atmosphere of culture and refinement. Breeding, good manners, and civilized behavior were instilled in him by his family; but on his own he acquired an acerbic forthrightness, an irreverent attitude toward most things, and a salty vocabulary to express it. Added to this was a training in theatrical conventions and traditions brought on by attending shows two or three times a week. "I saw everything," he recalled. "New York theatre [was] at a marvelous period and I was right at the hub of it." He shocked his conservative parents by announcing that he wanted to go into the theater—"it was as if I'd said I wanted to be a pusher"—and spent the next several years happily learning, staging little-theater productions with such not-yet-luminaries as Louis Calhern, Miriam Hopkins, and Bette Davis ("I fired Bette Davis . . . because we had nothing for her, and to this day she still talks about it!"). Eventually, he landed an important job as assistant to Gilbert Miller, a leading Broadway impresario. Cukor began directing plays on Broadway at this period, working with Ethel Barrymore, Laurette Taylor, and Jeanne Eagels, all superb actresses—a breed that Cukor immediately took to: "Actresses are tougher and more realistic than men . . . you can always talk turkey to them."

Cukor had been snooty about movies; but sound changed his mind, and when he arrived in Hollywood, he "just took to the movies . . . I fell in love with the movies. . . . Then I met David Selznick and we became great friends and he recommended me to Lewis Milestone who was about to make *All Quiet on the Western Front.* I started from scratch. I watched and I learned." Quickly, evidently, for he soon received widespread praise for his direction of Tallulah Bankhead in *Tarnished Lady* (1931) for Paramount. Cukor then followed Selznick to RKO, where his years of training and his talent finally were recognized in his work on *A Bill of Divorcement*, which started Katharine Hepburn's long film career, and *Little Women*, also with Hepburn. He had been with MGM since 1933 and *Dinner at Eight*, directing some of that studio's biggest female stars in some of the most outstanding pictures of the thirties and forties. "Very few of the great stars of the thirties had theater training," recalls Cukor. "They had something . . . quite different, 'personality,' that mysterious thing which touches an audience's imagination."

It was at MGM that Cukor's path first crossed that of Judy Garland; they arrived within a year of each other. Though only thirteen, she had had years of experience in vaudeville as one of the Gumm Sisters; by the time MGM put her under contract in 1935, the sister act had vanished and in its place, alone, stood Judy Garland. (The name was a combination of Hoagy Carmichael's song "Judy" and the "Garland" from George Jessel's compliment to her, "You're pretty as a garland of flowers.") Her tremendous power and versatility as a singer, her sensitive phrasing and uncanny ability to get at the meaning of a lyric, her enthusiastic and infectious personality, marked her as a major star from almost the very start of her MGM career.

Cukor had almost directed her twice at MGM, first in her childhood classic *The Wizard of Oz* and later in 1944 in *Meet Me in St. Louis*. He had bowed out of both projects, the first because it was a fantasy, the second to join the army. But to anyone who delighted in talent the way Cukor did, Judy Garland was inescapable. He followed her career and her vicissitudes and, along with everyone else who appreciated her, was alternately amazed by her gifts, gratified by her success, and saddened by her inability to fully control her personal demons. "Judy Garland was a most vivid personality," he recalls. "She had an innate intelligence to her; she was extremely witty and one of the best raconteurs I've ever known. But she wasn't one to confide her problems in others, the great publicity about the precarious state of her emotions to the contrary. If she did, it was always in a humorous way, with Judy the butt of the situation. She could talk about the most devastating experiences of her childhood—this overweight little girl with the enormous talent—and have you screaming with laughter. She had an absolutely devastating eye, and while making fun of herself, she could also zero in on the other person being talked about with great humor and style. She was the most marvelous company." Cukor also vividly recalled something she had done for him in 1949, just before she was fired by MGM: "I gave a birthday party for Ethel Barrymore—it was her seventieth—and Judy came and sang 'Happy Birthday' to her. She did it with such feeling and emotion that I thought Ethel would dissolve in tears. Anyone who could sing like that, I thought, had the emotional ability to be a great dramatic actress. That was the first time I got the idea I wanted to direct Judy." When the offer came, in mid-December 1952, to do just that with *A Star Is Born*, Cukor jumped at the chance. He was then working on a loan-out to Columbia directing Judy Holliday in a script by his friends Ruth Gordon and Garson Kanin called *It Should Happen to You*. The previous year Holliday, under Cukor's guidance, had won the Academy Award for Best Actress in *Born Yesterday*, edging out Bette Davis for *All About Eve* and Gloria Swanson for *Sunset Boulevard*. After *It Should Happen to You* finished production in January 1953, Cukor was to take a two-month European vacation, returning to the United States in early spring of 1953, at which time he would begin working with Garland and Luft on *A Star Is Born*.

By the end of December, Luft recalls: "We had Moss working on the script, we had an agreement with George, and I'm taking Cary Grant to the races virtually every day, trying to get him to do the picture. . . . Judy and I used to go out with Cary and Betsy [Drake, then his wife] once a week—we'd go to Chasen's, to Romanoff's, their house, our house, we were so close I was beginning to talk like him. . . . We were gonna do this picture together."

At about the same time, Irving Lazar stepped in and solved a very thorny problem: Who would write the lyrics to Harold Arlen's music? Arlen had collaborated with several lyricists throughout his twenty-year career, most notably Ted Koehler, with whom he had written "Stormy Weather"; E. Y. ("Yip") Harburg, who had lyricized *The Wizard of Oz* and the hit show *Bloomer Girl*; and Johnny Mercer, who had written "Blues in the Night," "Star Spangled Rhythm," and "St. Louis Woman." Arlen's last film work had been with lyricist Dorothy Fields at 20th Century–Fox in 1952: another musical remake, *The Farmer Takes a Wife*, starring Betty Grable.

Born Hyman Arluck in 1905, Arlen was raised in Buffalo, New York; the son of a Jewish cantor, he sang in the choir of his father's synagogue as a child. His love and talent for music were shaped by his heritage, with its strong religious roots, and his environment, which was as varied as his melodies. At his mother's insistence, he began studying piano with a neighborhood teacher at the age of nine; later, he studied the classics with a downtown instructor. As his musical knowledge grew, so did his restlessness: in 1921, when he was seventeen, he dropped out of high school to pursue a career in music. He had a passion for jazz, and he refined it by arranging, singing, and playing for a group called the Snappy Trio, which found ready employment in the cabarets of Buffalo's red-light district. The trio became a quintet, the Southbound Shufflers—a prophetic name, because to anyone who loved music and show business as Hyman Arluck did, there was only one place to go.

He arrived in New York late in 1925, when the city was at the height of its influence as the center of American popular music and theater. He came armed with one published song, a piano piece called "Blues Fantasy," and a new name, Harold Arlen. His original hope was to be a singer, but in 1930 he had his first hit as a songwriter—"Get Happy," written with Ted Koehler, which ended up in a show called *The 9:15 Revue.* After that, his singing career was put to rest. He composed some of the Cotton Club's legendary shows and added work in radio, films, and particularly the Broadway musical theater. It was while composing for a 1934 revue called *Life Begins at 8:40* that he met the man who would eventually write the lyrics for *A Star Is Born:* Ira Gershwin.

In collaboration with his celebrated brother, George, Gershwin had become a gifted practitioner of the art of lyric writing. Born and raised in New York City, he was a child of the popular culture of the time, especially vaudeville and Broadway. Quieter and more introspective than his brother, Ira was a peace-loving, easygoing man with an ever-present cigar and an impish twinkle in his eyes that belied his placidity. His first published song, in 1917, gives some indication of his irreverence with its cautionary title, "You May Throw All the Rice You Desire (But Please, Friends, Throw No Shoes)." Gershwin was an erudite and learned man who spent much time studying the relationship between music and verse. He had a particular knack for utilizing slang, which he alternated with some of the most clever, literate, and graceful combinations of words ever put to music. With his brother he had co-written the songs for eighteen shows; for one of them, 1932's *Of Thee I Sing,* he became the first lyricist ever to be awarded a Pulitzer Prize. In the course of working together on *Life Begins at 8:40* (the

title was a Gershwin variation on the best-seller *Life Begins at Forty*),
Gershwin and Arlen formed a close and lasting friendship.

After George's death in 1937, Ira was coaxed out of temporary retire-
ment by Moss Hart, who prevailed on him to supply the lyrics to *Lady in
the Dark* in 1941. Following his work with Weill, he had collaborated with
the cream of American composers, including Jerome Kern, Aaron Copland,
Arthur Schwartz, and Harry Warren, on a number of shows and films.
When the offer came for *A Star Is Born*, Gershwin had just finished work
with Burton Lane on MGM's *Give a Girl a Break*, a "little" picture about
kids trying to break into show business. After seeing a rough cut, his wife,
Lenore, asked him if he owned any stock in the company. When he told
her he did, her advice was succinct: "Sell it!"

After signing Arlen and Gershwin, Sid Luft continued wooing Cary Grant.
"I'm taking Cary to the races virtually every day. I'd pick him up, we'd go
to Hollywood Park. Just because you go to the races with a guy, you don't
necessarily talk business to him. First of all, his maximum bet was ten
dollars and he'd only bet on [jockey Willie] Shoemaker." But Luft did
manage to find out what Grant's price was, and it was stiff: "His deal was
one thing and one thing only—three hundred thousand dollars against 10
percent of the gross. I told that to Jack, who said, 'Offer him a flat four
fifty'—he would not give him 10 percent of the gross at all." Warner's
willingness to go as high as he did indicates that he was already thinking
beyond the fairly modest original budget of $1,500,000. Added to the
money already committed in salaries, his offer to Grant boosted the preproduction cost of *A Star Is Born* to $1 million, which meant that the picture
could conceivably end up with a $3 million budget—a considerable sum for
what was planned as an intimate musical drama with few characters and
no lavish production numbers.

Two of MGM's most recent spectacular musicals, *An American in Paris*
and *Show Boat*, had both cost about that much, but they had been made
with people under contract to the studio, while for *A Star Is Born*, all talent
had to be contracted individually at considerably higher costs. At $3 mil-
lion, *A Star Is Born* would have to gross nearly double that just to break
even, and the highest gross on any Garland film had been the $7 million
from 1948's *Easter Parade*, in which she had co-starred with Fred Astaire.
Warner, gambler that he was, was obviously playing against the odds and

betting heavily on Garland's resurgent popularity—which, judging from the amount of coverage and audience response she continued to generate, was bigger and more broadly based than ever before.

While Luft wooed Grant and the budget escalated, Moss Hart, happily ensconced in Palm Springs, was beginning his work on the screenplay. Since no scripts of the original were available, Hart prepared himself by watching the 1937 film several times, outlining the structure, the main characters, and situations that could be retained in his musical treatment.

In the Academy Award–winning story by director William Wellman and writer Robert Carson, the heroine, Esther Blodgett, is a movie-struck kid who lives on a North Dakota farm with her uncle and her aunt, who discourages notions of "Hollywood foolishness" in her niece. Only her grandmother encourages her dreams of getting into the movies; she gives Esther her life savings to finance a trip to Hollywood.

In Hollywood, Esther is befriended by Danny McGuire, a young assistant director, who gets her a one-night stint as a cocktail waitress at the home of producer Oliver Niles. There she meets a drunken but charming Norman Maine, the biggest star in Hollywood. He is smitten by her youth, beauty, and innocence and convinces Niles to screen-test her. Niles gives her a contract because she is wholesome and natural, and he thinks public taste is swinging back that way.

As Vicki Lester, Esther gets her big break when she is given a lead opposite Maine. She becomes a star, and they are married; but his career flounders because of his drinking and his contract is not renewed by the studio. He shows up drunk at the Academy Awards ceremony, where Vicki wins the Best Actress Oscar; he interrupts her speech to tell off the assembled group and in so doing accidentally slaps Vicki across the face. Confined to a sanitarium to cope with his alcoholism, Maine is visited by Niles, who offers him a small part in a new film. A proud man, Maine refuses.

After his release from the sanitarium, Maine is publicly humiliated at the bar of the Santa Anita race track by his arch-nemesis, Matt Libby, Niles's press chief. Going off on a three-day bender, Maine is bailed out of the drunk tank by Vicki, who thereupon tells Niles that she is giving up her career to care for Norman. Maine overhears Niles tell Vicki that she is making an empty gesture, that there's nothing left of Norman to save; unable to change her mind, he wishes her good luck. Maine, unable to stand the thought that he will be responsible for the end of his wife's career, swims out to sea and drowns.

Vicki decides to give up Hollywood and go home to North Dakota, but her grandmother suddenly arrives and convinces her that she must stay, because Norman would have wanted her to. Vicki, her grandmother, Danny McGuire, and Oliver Niles go to the opening of her newest picture at Grauman's Chinese Theatre. Vicki almost breaks down when she sees Norman's footprints in the forecourt, but she pulls herself together. Invited to say something to her millions of fans listening on the radio, she introduces herself by saying, "Hello everybody. This is Mrs. Norman Maine."

Working with Dorothy Parker and her husband, Alan Campbell, Carson turned his and Wellman's story (originally called "It Happened in Hollywood") into a screenplay, with uncredited assistance from producer David O. Selznick and writers Ring Lardner, Jr., and John Lee Mahin. It was Mahin who came up with the famous curtain line, but it was John Hay Whitney, millionaire, sportsman, publisher, and chairman of the board of Selznick's company, who gave the story its new title. When queried by Selznick for an opinion on the proposed title, "The Stars Below," Whitney replied in a telegram, "Don't think it [good] . . . If poetic title [is wanted,] what about earlier suggestion of mine '*A Star Is Born*'?"

Wellman, who directed the original, always maintained that the story was made up "from things that just happened." Much of the tale is based on Hollywood legends; there was a long history of careers ruined by alcoholism and marriages destroyed by the seesaw of Hollywood success and failure. There is a popular misconception that the suicide of Norman Maine was inspired by the death of actor John Bowers, who, despondent over his inability to find work, told friends that he was going to "sail into the sunset and never come back" and did just that; his body was washed ashore at Huntington Beach on November 21, 1936. But the suicide scene of *A Star Is Born* was filmed three days earlier, on November 18.

The plot of *A Star Is Born* had a direct antecedent in a film on which Selznick and Cukor had collaborated at RKO in 1932. *What Price Hollywood?*, written by Adela Rogers St. John, Jane Murfin, Rowland Brown, and Gene Fowler, starred Constance Bennett as a movie-struck waitress at the Brown Derby who is befriended by a drunken director, who gives her a chance to act in films. She becomes a star and marries a millionaire polo player, while the director hits the skids. Grateful to him for his early generosity, she bails him out of night court and takes him to her home, where he kills himself, precipitating a scandal that ruins her career and her marriage. She retires to the south of France, where she is finally reconciled with her husband.

Aside from the basic situation, the only thing the two films have in common is a line which Selznick had liked in the 1932 film. As the actress takes leave of the director just before his suicide, he calls to her and she turns, questioningly. "I just wanted to hear you speak again," he says. Changed to "I just wanted to take another look at you," this was used twice in A Star Is Born, once at the end of Esther and Maine's first meeting and then again just before his fateful swim.

It took Wellman fifty-two scenes, two montages and 110 minutes to tell this quintessential tale of Hollywood tragedy. The enlightened attitude with which it treated movie-making and movie stars, the lavish Technicolor production, the wit and style of the script and direction, the bittersweet flavor of the romance, and the unusual tragic ending all coalesced into a classic heartbreak drama. The film had served (ironically, in viewing the remake) as a comeback vehicle for Janet Gaynor, whose career had waned in the early 1930s. One of the biggest stars of the late silent period, Gaynor was lovely, sweet, wholesome, and an actress of depth and sensitivity. She had won an Oscar* for her performances in Seventh Heaven (the first Academy Award ever given to an actress); Street Angel, in which she co-starred with Charles Farrell; and the F. W. Murnau masterpiece Sunrise. Gaynor had successfully made the transition to sound, but the type of films she made and the parts in which she was cast did not keep up with public taste, and by 1935 she was seriously considering retiring from films. Selznick, however, knew her personally and felt that her true personality had never been revealed to moviegoers. She was charming, funny, and sophisticated—qualities germane to the success of the character of Esther Blodgett; combined with Gaynor's air of innocence and vulnerability, they made her performance in the film one of her most memorable and beloved. She was nominated for an Academy Award but lost to Luise Rainer in The Good Earth. (The other nominees were Irene Dunne for The Awful Truth, Greta Garbo for Camille, and Barbara Stanwyck for Stella Dallas.) Still, A Star Is Born had accomplished one of Selznick's objectives: it revitalized Gaynor's career and made her a star all over again.

*Her award was given for three performances.

Because of the picture's constant theatrical circulation all during the forties, two presentations on the Lux Radio Theatre, and finally as a staple of early television, the tale was familiar to almost two generations of moviegoers. Hart's task was to preserve the potent appeal of this Hollywood myth while making it viable for a modern-day audience. The problem was complicated by the necessity of rewriting the part of Esther/Vicki to suit Judy Garland. The original film had walked a delicate dramatic path in interweaving the lives and careers of Vicki and Norman Maine. In emphasizing the "star power" of Lester/Garland, more screen time would have to be devoted to her, thus altering the careful balance of the original. Hart later recalled: "It was a difficult story to do because the original was so famous and when you tamper with the original, you're inviting all sorts of unfavorable criticism. It had to be changed because I had to say new things about Hollywood—which is quite a feat in itself as the subject has been worn pretty thin. The attitude of the original was more naive because it was made in the days when there was a more wide-eyed feeling about the movies . . . (and) the emphasis had to be shifted to the woman, rather than the original emphasis on the Fredric March character. Add to that the necessity of making this a musical drama, and you'll understand the immediate problems."

To make sure that his retelling accurately reflected the Garland persona, Hart had a series of informal conversations with her and Luft regarding experiences of hers that he might be able to incorporate into the script. Luft recalls: "We were having dinner with Moss and Kitty [Carlisle], and Judy was throwing ideas at Moss, cautiously, and so was I. I remember Judy telling the story of when she was a kid, she was on tour with a band and they were in Kansas City at the Mulebach Hotel—all the singers and performers stayed there. And I think her mother ran into a big producer who was traveling through and she invited him to come and see the act, and supposedly afterward he was very interested in Judy's career. Nothing happened, though. Judy thought it would be a kind of a cute idea to lay onto Moss—that maybe it might be something he could use in his writing."

Several days after this dinner conference, on Christmas Day, 1952, Luft, Garland, and one-month-old Lorna boarded a cross-country train for New York, where Garland, as a personal favor to Jack Warner, would sing at a coming-out party for Warner's daughter Barbara at the St. Regis Roof on January 3. It was to be a spectacular affair, arranged by ace party giver Elsa Maxwell, with the cream of New York society in attendance. The Lufts would stay in a suite at the Waldorf, courtesy of Warner; in return for the favor, Warner would give Garland any gift she wanted. (Hedda Hopper, in her book *The Whole Truth . . . and Nothing But,* was responsible for the legend that it was this party and Warner's request that Garland sing at it that led to the deal for *A Star Is Born.* Hopper was a good storyteller, but as a reporter she was inaccurate: the request by Warner was made several weeks *after* the contract with Transcona had been signed. Yet the rumor persists to this day and is soberly reported as fact by otherwise responsible writers.)

The couple spent a busy holiday hobnobbing with some of their more intimate chums, including the Duke and Duchess of Windsor, and enjoying a round of parties, capped by Garland's singing at the Warner party. She was by all accounts a sensation, and in the din surrounding her appearance, Elsa Maxwell extracted a promise to appear on the fifth at another party she would be giving. On that day, however, in Santa Monica, California, Judy Garland's mother, Ethel, was found dead in the parking lot at Douglas Aircraft, where she had been a clerical worker. She evidently had died of a heart attack on her way to work, and her body, wedged between two cars, had not been found for several hours.

Mother and daughter had been estranged for several years. Mrs. Gumm seems to have been a classic stage mother, pushing, scolding, and obsessively living her life through Judy. Garland's attitude toward her mother had undergone a perceptible change in 1939 when, on the anniversary of her adored father's death, her mother had married a stern autocrat named Gilmore, whom Garland detested. When the nineteen-year-old Garland married composer David Rose in 1941, it was as much an escape from her mother and stepfather's iron rule as it was a teenage infatuation with an older man.

Early in the 1940s, Mrs. Gilmore had halted the teenage Garland's much-needed sessions with an analyst, convinced that he would turn her daughter against her. Later on, in a reversal of her earlier fears of psychiatry, she sought to have Garland committed to the Menninger Clinic, for which Garland never forgave her. The final break between mother and daughter came in late 1949, after a particularly bitter argument during Garland's separation from her second husband, Vincente Minnelli. Since then Garland had refused to see or speak to her mother and had given orders that she was not to be allowed near her grandchildren.

A call from Mrs. Gilmore's doctor informed Luft, paged in the Waldorf lobby, of his mother-in-law's death. The first person he encountered after hearing the news was Elsa Maxwell; when he told her the news, she implored him to keep it from Garland until after she had sung at Maxwell's party that night. Appalled at this request, Luft told Garland the tragic news and the family flew back to Los Angeles for the funeral, while the newspapers made much of Garland's mother working in a menial job while her celebrity daughter made millions. Afterward, Garland went into a lengthy seclusion behind the closed doors of her new nineteen-room mansion in Holmby Hills.

20th Century-Fox's
Revolution

On January 8, the Hollywood film community was startled by a headline in the *Hollywood Reporter:* FOX GETS BIG SCREEN PROCESS. Apparently, 20th Century–Fox had found a way to make Cinerama practical, for the article went on to reveal that in December Spyros Skouras, Greek immigrant, former World War I flier, theater owner, and now president of Fox, had seen a demonstration in France of a photo device called the "anamorphoscope," a name derived from the Greek "anamorphose"—to transform, to form anew. Invented in the late 1920s by Henri Chrétien, it was a cylindrical lens that compressed a picture horizontally by 50 percent; used on cameras and projectors, it provided a picture twice as wide as the normal motion picture image, while keeping the same height. After seeing test footage, Skouras, as he later recalled for *Life* magazine in his charmingly imperfect English, "in bed that night . . . I am dreamin' of Egyp, of Bens Hur and the Quin of Seba, of Betsy Grabble in colors, everything on a big screen. Oh, I had *wonderful* dreams." He immediately took an option on the lens, beating out a representative from Jack Warner, who had also heard about it and wanted it for Warner Bros., evidently sharing Skouras's instinct that it could be marketed as an acceptable alternative to Cinerama.

Tests with the lens were made by Fox in both New York and Hollywood, and after a week of conferences between Skouras and Darryl Zanuck, head of production at the studio, it was announced that henceforth *all* of 20th Century–Fox's films would be photographed and released using this new process, which Charles Einfeld, head of Fox publicity, christened "CinemaScope." Lifting another idea from Cinerama, the system was equipped with four-channel stereophonic sound, tied to the action on the new wide (65 to 90 feet, depending on the size of the theater stage), slightly curved screen, which put an image roughly two-and-a-half times as wide as normal in front of the audience. CinemaScope was a gamble of unprecedented proportions for a major studio: staking $30 million worth of unproduced films on a process that could not be shown in any theater in the world. Skouras and Zanuck realized that before exhibitors would invest the necessary $25,000 to equip a theater to show CinemaScope, they would need assurances that there would be a sufficient supply of films to make this investment worthwhile. On January 28, at a pandemonium-filled press conference in his office at the Fox Studios in West Los Angeles, Zanuck announced that the first film to be produced and released in the new process would be *The Robe*, the long-pending version of the Lloyd C. Douglas best-seller. The picture had actually started filming the previous week, but production would now be shut down and revamped to show off the new technique in a spectacular fashion. This production would be followed with a comedy called *How To Marry a Millionaire*, yet another adaptation of the Zoe Akins play *The Greeks Had a Word for Them*, which would star Lauren Bacall, Betty Grable, and Marilyn Monroe, thereby proving that the use of CinemaScope need not be confined to spectacles but could be equally effective with "intimate" stories. All CinemaScope films would be photographed in color, and all would have stereophonic soundtracks. To make certain that this "revolution" would be accepted throughout the industry, Zanuck announced that Fox would license to all other producers the use of the Fox anamorphic lenses and the trade name CinemaScope for a fee of $25,000 per picture. All this was predicated, of course, on the virtues of the process, which no one in the world except a privileged few had yet seen. But Skouras's brother, Charles, president of the huge Fox West Coast theater chain, didn't need any additional urging; he signed up his entire three-hundred-theater circuit to show CinemaScope films. To convince the rest of the country's fifteen thousand theaters to follow this lead, Zanuck announced that mass demonstrations of the process would be held at Fox's Western Avenue studios in Hollywood in mid-March. By then, it was hoped, there would be enough rough footage from the first two films to demonstrate the amazing impact of the system to the dubious and the recalcitrant.

One of the latter was Jack Warner; still chagrined that the Chrétien device had eluded the Warner shield, he was given a private showing of the test footage by Zanuck, to whom Warner had given his first film job thirty years earlier. It was at Warner Bros. that Zanuck had made his fame,

ABOVE: Janet Gaynor, as Vicki Lester, filming the final scene at Grauman's Chinese Theatre for the 1937 version of *A Star Is Born*. RIGHT: Sid Luft, Judy Garland, Jack Warner, and George Cukor on October 12, 1953—the first day of filming.

Judy Garland with Moss Hart and George Cukor.

Composer Harold Arlen.

Ira Gershwin working on the lyrics.

LEFT: Mason, Garland, Sid Luft, Cukor, and Gene Allen on location. OPPOSITE: Garland, costume designer Irene Sharaff, and assistant dance director Jack Harmon on the set of "Born in a Trunk."

Cukor directing Garland and Jack Carson.

Garland with choreographer
Richard Barstow.

Garland and musical director Ray Heindorf.

Cowboy star Guy Madison pays a visit.

Garland, Louella Parsons, and Sid Luft.

Doris Day, working on *Lucky Me*,
visits Garland and Mason.

RIGHT: Garland, Leslie Caron (center),
and Elizabeth Taylor on the set of
"Born in a Trunk," on the last day
of filming, July 28, 1954.

The set for the Downbeat Club.

Esther Blodgett/Vicki Lester's apartment at the Oleander Arms.

A hotel lobby.

Norman Maine's palatial home.

WARNER BROS. STUDIOS
WARDROBE TEST
FOR
"A STAR IS BORN" 386
OF
JUDY GARLAND
-AS-
EXT-INT PUBLICITY OFFICE
WARDROBE CHANGE# 12
WORN IN { SET
          SCENE 53-54-B
CUKOR   10-6-53   HOCH
W-B   SCENE 1 A 1   W-B

RIGHT: Garland having her costume ironed between takes of "Someone at Last." BELOW: Filming the Academy Awards scene, Sam Leavitt (with hat) is behind the real camera.

ABOVE: The first (Technicolor and standard screen) version of "The Man That Got Away." BELOW AND RIGHT: The second (CinemaScope and Eastmancolor) version. Note the changes in Garland's costume and makeup. The final film used still a third version, with yet another costume and makeup change (see color insert following page 210).

Norman Maine returns to the Shrine Auditorium to find the name of the orchestra that "the little dark girl" was singing with.

Esther washing her hair in the rooming house.

Norman Maine and Vicki Lester plan their dream house at the Malibu beach.

Norman Maine as a swashbuckling pirate.

From "Born in a Trunk": father and daughter (Jack Baker and Garland) sing "When My Sugar Walks Down the Street," after the death of the mother.

Esther says goodbye to the piano player
(Tom Noonan).

Norman being pulled from the ocean.

Norman leaving for location.

The "Trinidad Coconut Oil Shampoo" commercial.

Esther as a carhop (Chick
Chandler in car).

Norman at home with the "lovely
Lola Lavery" (Lucy Marlow).

The proposal scene on the
sound stage.

ABOVE AND BELOW: Norman finds Esther
in a cheap rooming house.

The "Lose That Long Face" sequence.

first as a writer, eventually ending up as vice-president in charge of production. When he and the Warners had a falling-out in 1933, Zanuck had gone on to form 20th Century Pictures, eventually merging his firm with Fox Films to form 20th Century–Fox. But he and Jack Warner had stayed friendly, and they maintained their friendship throughout a series of disputes, recriminations, lawsuits, and rivalries. At the private screening on February 2, the irony of the moment could not have been lost on the two men, for it was Zanuck who had been Jack's executive assistant when Warners had introduced Vitaphone sound in 1926. After the screening, Warner was complimentary over the process but noncommittal regarding its use by his studio. The $25,000 fee rankled, as did his resentment at having been beaten to the CinemaScope punch. Warner decided to wait and see what developed with his Natural Vision gamble before he committed himself to any other outlays of money.

While Zanuck, Skouras, Warner, et al. tugged and pulled at the shape and depth of the screen, down in Palm Springs Moss Hart was finishing the outline of his rewrite of the picture.

He had altered the beginning of the story considerably. The United States had changed complexion greatly in the fifteen years since the original was written and was now largely urban rather than rural, so the North Dakota farm sequences were jettisoned, as was the character of the grandmother. Hart now introduced the two leads almost simultaneously in his new opening sequence, which took place at a gigantic benefit for the Motion Picture Relief Fund in Hollywood. Norman is the big attraction that night, and Esther Blodgett is just a singer with the Glenn Williams Orchestra. When he staggers into her act, thinking it's his turn to go on, she earns his gratitude by saving him from making a drunken fool of himself. Later he hears her singing in an after-hours musicians' hangout and is impressed enough to offer to have her screen-tested. On the strength of his promise she quits the band, waits, but never hears from him. He's off on a distant location and can't remember where she was staying. She takes odd jobs to survive, including singing a jingle for a shampoo commercial with puppets. Norman hears this on his return and tracks her down in a cheap rooming house; he makes good on his promise and she is signed by his studio. From that point on, Hart's screenplay follows the structure of the original very closely.

In mid-January, Hart journeyed up to Los Angeles with his rough outline for discussions with Harold Arlen and Ira Gershwin at the latter's home in Beverly Hills. Hart explained the approach he was taking and the whys and wherefores of placing the songs and the type of song each spot required. Hart's outline had places for seven songs:

1. Benefit show—Esther and orchestra
2. "Dive" song—Esther and small group
3. Movie rehearsal song (happy type), partial; reprised complete at preview
4. Song on recording stage (marriage proposal with interruptions)
5. Honeymoon song in motel; to be reprised later
6. Malibu beach house song (funny song; she tries to cheer Norman up)
7. Reprise of 5, probably sung over suicide or at end.

After the meeting with Hart, Arlen and Gershwin started right in, working on the first song in the story, which would be sung by Esther at the benefit show. It needed to be a catchy, up-tempo piece—"the kind of song you can never hear the lyrics to," as Hart put it, much to Gershwin's amusement. It took almost two weeks to complete this first song, "Gotta Have Me Go With You." Once they had it, Arlen and Gershwin began work on the important "dive" song, so called because Esther sings it in an after-hours joint, a "dive." Hart felt it was crucial to the rest of the story that Norman (and the audience) realize at once that Esther is an extraordinary singer with a definite dramatic flair. "When inspiration or something else worthwhile hits Arlen," recalls Gershwin, "it is the beginning of something at some time worth mulling over, and onto an envelope or into a notebook it goes. These snatches or possible themes he calls 'jots.' " In Edward Jablonski's biography of Arlen, *Happy With the Blues*, this practice of his is elaborated on in the writing of the second song for *A Star Is Born*.

Arlen had an idea, in his usual jot form, which he played for Gershwin. "I know how Ira's ear works, [said Arlen] and was sure he would like the theme, one that I'd had for some time—an eight-bar phrase." Gershwin did like it, particularly the insistent movement of the rhythm; he listened a while and [then] suggested as a possible title "The Man That Got Away." It was Arlen's turn to be impressed. "I like" was his simple indication of approval and work began.

Jablonski points out that "interestingly, none of the music Arlen played for Gershwin is the accompaniment for the words of the title. What Gershwin heard was merely the introduction, the first four bars of mood-setting music and the melody, for which he devised:

> *The night is bitter,*
> *The stars have lost their glitter,*
> *The winds grow colder*
> *And suddenly you're older . . .**

According to Lawrence Stewart, a UCLA professor who visited Arlen and Gershwin several times while they were working on the film and who wrote an unpublished piece on Gershwin and Arlen's work on the film, the original lyric was to have been:

> *The song is played out*
> *The moon is in a fade-out.*
> *The stars won't glimmer,*
> *The autumn wind is grimmer—*
> *And all because of*
>   *The man that got away.*†

That, in turn, had supplanted:

> *There's just no sleeping.*
> *Your eyes are red with weeping.*
> *Though you know better,*
> *You're waiting for that letter.*
> *And all because of . . .*†

Equally interesting are Gershwin's rejected phrases for the end of the song:

> *Oh tell me if you can*
> *What song is sadder than*
> *The one-man woman looking for the man that got away.*†

and:

> *You always will be his.*
> *Oh what a sucker is*
> *The one woman . . .**

For a time, the two men even toyed with a structurally different ending:

> *Oh since this world began*
> *What's black and bluer than [or: What future's bluer than]*
> *The gal that hopes to find the man that got away*
> *[or: The gal who's hoping to find the man that got away].**

According to Stewart:

> Gershwin's manuscripts reveal how difficult it is to write a song such as this, where the language is the colloquial diction of the dive singer and the rhymes, rhythms and the allusions must be consistent with her character. Arlen's music for the song can be described only in Gershwin's own term, "sweet and low-down." The mournful theme, repeated and repeated in its rising climax . . . and the elongated last line brings the song to its emotional height, while the repetition of the title at the conclusion (done at Gershwin's suggestion for a sort of coda) created the effect of a resigned amen.

About his inspiration for the title, Gershwin remarked: "[Some people] called it 'The Man Who Got Away,' a whodunit title I wouldn't have considered a lyric possibility . . . but this had to be 'The Man *That* Got Away' because, actually, the title hit me as a paraphrase of the angler's 'You should have seen the one that got away.' "

When they had finished the two songs, Arlen recalled:

> We had been working about two weeks. . . . We'd been at it every afternoon and I wanted to go away for the weekend. "Ira, I want to go to Palm Springs." "Don't." "Why not?" "Well, Moss is there, and Judy [and Sid are going down] there, and you'll be playing the songs for them and it's much too early." And he was as vehement as Ira can get. He said: "You'll spoil things." I said, "Ira, I promise you. I'm not going there to see Moss and Judy; I just want a break." I went up to that golf course where Ben Hogan was the pro—the Tamarisk—and I went out that Saturday morning. Because I

wasn't feeling too well, I wasn't supposed to play. But I saw Judy and Sid, large as life, just teeing off. I said: "I'll walk around with you." Nobody said anything about the picture. Then about the middle of the round . . . I started to whistle, very softly. I don't know what tempted me. She was about twenty yards away—it was kind of a tease and I couldn't stand it. I love Ira and I love Judy, and well, I just whistled the main phrase of "The Man That Got Away." Suddenly, on the third or fourth whistle, Judy turned around. "Harold, what are you whistling?" "Nothing. I don't know." This continued. "Harold, what *are* you whistling? Don't tell me it's something from the picture." I said "No." "Harold, I've got an idea it *must* be from the picture—don't hold out on me." Finally, on the eighteenth hole, Sid hit the ball 320 yards into the sand trap, and while he dug it out, Judy insisted: "Harold, there's a piano in the clubhouse, and you've *got* to play it." I kept playing it down: "It's just something we've been working on. I don't know how well you'll like it." So I played both songs, and—well—they were the first songs, the script wasn't finished, it was their first picture—and they went wild with joy. "Ira, Shmira, he'll be happy about it," I thought. So I went to see Moss and Kitty. Same thing. They wanted to call Ira. I said, "Oh, don't! I've promised him not to play them." But they insisted and phoned Ira and said how wonderful it was, and he was delighted. And when I came back he was beaming and never said a word about my broken promise.

Hearing "The Man That Got Away" must have galvanized Moss Hart into returning to his work on the rewrite with a renewed zeal. Having completed his restructuring of the original, he now began to flesh it out with more realistic dialogue and to replace the somewhat caricatured comedy of the original with a wryly observant attitude that provoked the laughter of recognition rather than the laughter of derision. This was carried through in his approach to the subsidiary characters. The grandmother was eliminated, but the function she served at the end, the "you must go on" speech, was necessary, so Hart retained the character of Danny McGuire from the original, making him a pianist with the band, a nebbish, evidently in love with Esther and loyal to her throughout.

The character of Oliver Niles, the "famous producer," Hart left relatively intact. In both the original and the Hart rewrite, Niles is a paragon of Hollywood virtues; Hart describes him: "late forties, robust, an excellent example of the latter-day successful Hollywood executive. He is cultivated, intelligent, industrious, warm, dignified. He is the antithesis of the old-time Hollywood producer so widely parodied. He is a sophisticated and able man." Niles seems to have no life outside his studio. He sleeps alone in a small bed in a spartan room discreetly stacked with scripts. There is no overt humor either in the character or in Hart's approach to it.

The "demon publicity man" Matt Libby had been written by Dorothy Parker et al., and portrayed by Lionel Stander, as a brash, wisecracking hyperbolist of the old school: "There go a couple of rats I raised from mice," he mutters after Norman and Esther double-cross him by marrying quietly. He is forever searching for a "big angle" ("We'll have a thousand school kiddies spelling out 'LOVE' on the Santa Monica beach") and distorting facts ("Are you *sure* there's no Russian in your background? It'd make great copy!"). He is cynical, sour, and nasty, for no apparent reason. In rewriting the character, Hart recast him in the mold of a modern-day public-relations man. Hart's outline describes him as "in his early forties. He is a big man, fast with his tongue, sure of himself, expert at his work. But he is a machine. There isn't much heart or warmth here. He is not a parody of a 'Hollywood Press Agent'—he is merely more intense and less aware of some of the niceties of life." He is also, in this rendering, a much more understandable human being; the cynicism is still there, but it's leavened with an understanding of the frustrations of his job, the humiliations, the condescensions. He is coarse and brutal ("I don't like you, I never *did* like you. And nothing made me happier than to see all those cute little pranks of yours catch up with you and land you on your celebrated face"), philosophical ("This is how the world ends—not with a bang, with a whimper. T. S. Eliot, my friend"). And he is still funny, cynically so, in the execution of his duties (giving instructions for the upcoming wedding of Norman and Esther: "Have the traffic routed out of Beverly Hills for three miles on either side of the church. . . . Which church? The big one, dummy!").

But it was in the characters of the two leads that Hart made his subtlest and most illuminating changes. Hart's Esther Blodgett has little in common with the idealized Selznick original. The 1937 Esther/Vicki, though an orphan, still has a family. She is spunky, goal-oriented, movie-struck— and she desperately wants to make something of herself. Her grandmother sends her off to Hollywood with a speech that gives Esther's background and states the moral of the film: "If you're my granddaughter, you'll go to your Hollywood. . . . You've got the blood of pioneers in your veins. . . . Your grandfather and I came across the prairies in wagons because we wanted to make something out of our lives. . . . You go to your Hollywood

. . . but remember, Esther, for every dream of yours that comes true, you pay the price in heartbreak." You knew exactly where this Esther came from and what she wanted. And as sweet and tearful as she occasionally was, there was an air of invulnerability and indestructibility about her. Because her grandmother doesn't want her to be "a quitter," she gives up her own identity and becomes "Mrs. Norman Maine"—and a star is born.

Hart's description of his Esther/Vicki is deceptively similar (except for the age) to the original: "Middle twenties, petite, not really wide-eyed, but bordering on the naive. Sincere. Easily roused if her principles are questioned. The sort of person of whom people always say, when the occasion warrants, they knew she'd make it." But the similarities end there. His Esther/Vicki is a dreamer, but without goals, imagination, or ambition. She has a vague hope that "someday a big record agent will let me make a record, and it'll become a hit and I'll be made." But even that she laughingly shrugs off with a "but that'll never happen." She is shocked that Maine would think she was wasting her time singing with the band: "I'm doing fine, Mr. Maine, just fine. . . . Do you know how long it takes singers like me to get a job like this?" She has no parents, no family. She sketches her life thus: "I remember my first job singing with a band . . . then one-night stands clear across the country by bus . . . putting on nail polish in the ladies' room of a gas station . . . waiting on tables. That was a low point—I'll never forget it, and I'll never, ever do that again." She is a creature of urban rootlessness; she lives for only one thing: "I had to sing . . . somehow I feel most alive when I'm singing"—a sentiment that could easily have come from Garland herself. The song titles and the lyrics were all carefully fashioned by Gershwin to work with Hart's dialogue in explaining and illuminating Esther/Vicki's psychology: "Gotta Have Me Go with You," "The Man That Got Away," "Someone at Last," "It's a New World." They chart the emotional development of the character as surely as the speeches and the action advance the surface manifestations of the story.

This Esther is completely vulnerable, lacking in self-confidence, uncertain of her own talent, convinced that without Maine she is nothing. At the end she overcomes her insecurities, her need for Norman as the mainspring of her life; in freeing herself of him, even as she becomes "Mrs. Norman Maine," and in finally recognizing her own talent and her worth as a human being, a star is born.

As for Norman Maine, with his sturdy, rock-bound name, he is one of the more complex and completely tragic heroes of the American cinema: an amalgam of Sydney Carton, William Wellman, and silent-film director Marshall ("Mickey") Neilan. The Sydney Carton came from David O. Selznick, who had been under his spell since reading *A Tale of Two Cities* as a preteen. Wellman, of course, included elements of himself as well as incidents that had happened to him: the night court sequence, wherein Maine is verbally assaulted by a judge, happened to Wellman almost word for word. Marshall Neilan, one of the biggest and the best directors of the late teens and the twenties; an alcoholic, he had been brought down by his arrogance, outspokenness, pugnacity, and undependability. Neilan was the inspiration for the character of Max Carey, the director in Cukor's 1932 *What Price Hollywood?*

When Carey metamorphosed into Norman Maine, it was with overtones and shadings from the John Gilbert/John Barrymore sagas. Gilbert's career as a major star had ended almost overnight with the advent of talkies, not because of his voice, which is the legend, but because of poor choices in stories and roles. Sound rendered his character, the flashing-eyed impassioned lover, ridiculous, and his consequent inability to make himself popular in any other role led to his abrupt decline. Gilbert later married the young actress Virginia Bruce, and her career forged ahead while his ended in a paranoid, alcoholic daze. Gilbert's death of heart failure at age thirty-eight came in January 1936, just as work began on the screenplay of *A Star Is Born.*

There was more of John Barrymore in Max Carey than there was in Norman Maine, but the story of a romantic idol who dissipated his gifts and his career through drink had a ready parallel in the continuing tragedy of John Barrymore, who had been reduced to reading his lines from cue cards. The sanitorium sequence, where Niles calls on Maine to offer him a small part in a film, came from a similar visit George Cukor made to Barrymore, who had had himself committed in an effort to "dry out" and go back to work. Cukor related the details of his trip to Wellman and Selznick, who were working on the screenplay, and they wrote the scene into the final version.

This original Maine, while a charmer, has an element of coarseness about him. He nearly disrupts a concert at the Hollywood Bowl; he has very little regard for other people and is prone to fisticuffs and boorish behavior; he proposes to Esther at a boxing match while chewing gum and egging on the fighters. When he drunkenly interrupts Vicki's speech at the Academy

Awards to make one of his own, it is to tell off the assembled multitude
("Fellow suckers . . .") and to denigrate the award his wife has just received:
"I got one of those things once; they don't mean a thing." His saving graces
are his sense of humor, his charm, and the fact that, as he explains to
Esther, "no matter what else . . . I appreciate lovely things"—a line which
took on poignant believability when Fredric March quietly spoke it. In
March's hands and under Wellman's direction, Maine never reveals any
self-doubt or introspection. We know nothing at all of Norman, even where
he came from—not a hint of the inner turmoil that causes his alcoholic
binges. The closest we get to any evidence of self-awareness in Maine is
in the token he hands to Oliver Niles: "Good for Amusement Only." His
sole function, dramatically at least, is to be the deus ex machina—the fairy
godmother who makes everything possible for Cinderella. When she is
"born," so to speak, there is no longer any reason for his existence; and so
he does what all good gods do: he walks into the ocean and disappears,
thereby assuring his immortality.

Moss Hart's version describes Maine as "a 'movie star' personified.
Superlative good looks which bear more than just the mark of a photogenic
face. . . . There is evidence of a deep inner turmoil." The 1950s Norman
is an intelligent, semicultured man, with no visible roots or background.
Perceptive and proud, he feels a deep loathing and contempt for the
manner in which he makes his living and for the hypocrisies of so much
of "our industry," as he mockingly refers to it. He is constantly starring in
vapid romantic dramas and empty action films with titles like *The En-
chanted Hour, The Black Legion,* and *Another Dawn.* The correlative
Hollywood career was that of Errol Flynn, who had reigned supreme at
Warners for almost twenty years; his relationship with Warner was very
similar to Maine's with Niles. Flynn had been released by Warners because
of the very situation that faced Maine: drinking, undependability, and
slipshod performances in lackluster, unimaginative variations on the same
old stories. But Flynn was acutely self-aware, and so is Hart's Maine. "I
know myself very well," he says in the script, "and I'm right near the
fighting stage. . . . Unless I get my way, I begin to break up people and
things." Later, he warns Esther that she must not be in love with him: "You
come too late . . . I'm a bad lot, I destroy everything I touch."

"I never grew up," Flynn stated in his autobiography, and a childlike
quality is another thing that separates the new Maine from the 1937
original; it's emphasized by his manservant's remark "He'll smile in his

sleep in a minute . . . like a child" ("Like a child with a blowtorch," observes Matt Libby) and reiterated near the end by Vicki, who tells Niles: "He looks so helpless lying there . . . like a child." Maine's childlike vulnerability is most evident in Hart's rewrite of the proposal sequence, which he places on a recording stage, where Vicki is singing "Here's What I'm Here For" while Norman watches on the sidelines. During a choral break, she joins him and they have an extended conversation, inaudible to the camera but, unbeknownst to them, recorded by an overhead microphone. During the playback of the song, their dialogue is revealed to everyone—Norman's proposal, Vicki's refusal, her reasons ("You're irresponsible . . . you drink too much")—much to the couple's embarrassment, particularly Norman's. His humiliation is assuaged only by Vicki's change of heart: "That's much too public a proposal. I accept."

Hart carries this new dimension of Maine further in the Academy Award sequence, where instead of displaying anger and hostility, Norman humbles himself by begging the assembled moguls for a job ("I made a lot of money for you gentlemen once . . . Now I need a job"). But it is earlier in the story that Hart makes his strongest contribution to an audience's sympathy for and understanding of Maine. When he hears Esther sing at the Downbeat Club, he is struck by her talent, and tells her, "You're a great singer. . . . You've got that little something extra that Ellen Terry talked about. . . . She said that's what star quality was—'that little something extra.' Well, you've got it." Later, in trying to convince her to quit the band, he says, "A career is a curious thing. Talent isn't always enough. You need a sense of timing—an eye for seeing the turning point, of recognizing the big chance when it comes along and grabbing it. A career can rest on a trifle—like us sitting here tonight. Or it can turn on somebody seeing something in you that nobody else ever saw, and saying, 'You're better than that—you're better than you know. Don't settle for the little dream—go on to the big one.'" He instills in Esther a belief in herself and gives her the confidence and courage necessary to pursue the "big dream"—stardom. He may have started out on the make, but his speech to her and his offer to "see what I can do for you at the studio" make his intentions understandably honorable. Even while Esther is suffering greatly after not hearing from him, his frantic efforts to locate her from his location at sea and upon his return make him much more sympathetic than the 1937 Maine, for we can see that he is truly anguished at his inability to make good on his promise.

When he does find her, he carefully shepherds Esther through the perils of the Hollywood jungle, taking an active hand in getting her cast in her first major role, watching carefully in the shadows of a sound stage while she rehearses, nervously offering comfort and advice on the way to the preview of the film, and finally taking quiet pleasure at the vindication of his belief in her after the triumph of this initial public screening. He is protective and concerned but wary of becoming involved, and only does so because of the intensity of Esther's love for him: "I've done all I can for you. You've come along the road with me as far as you should. . . . Forget about me." When she protests "Don't you know that . . . nothing could make me stop loving you?," he warns her: "You've come too late." But she rejects this: "I don't believe that. . . . It's not too late—not for you, and not for me." "Don't say that, Esther—I might begin to believe it." To which she responds passionately, "Oh, believe it! Please believe it!" She finally convinces him to take the chance, much as he had convinced her to believe in herself.

All of these refinements and additions by Hart to the character of Maine make his suicide ultimately more poignant, for we know how deeply he cares for her, and how proud he is of her talent and her success.

Hart finished his rewrite of the screenplay in early March 1953 and immediately dispatched a copy to Luft and Garland. Luft recalls: "In my heart I wasn't so sure this was the right thing to do, to take this wonderful picture and see if you can make it into a musical. Mixing music with drama—I didn't know if it would work or not." But according to Gerold Frank, Luft's fears were quickly allayed:

> . . . The night a delivery boy brought the . . . script . . . to them . . . it was well after midnight and the entire house was asleep save for Judy and Sid. . . . They settled themselves in the downstairs den, reading it together. When they finished, they looked at each other and simply lost control . . . hugging each other, crying, laughing. . . . When Sid had first thought of *Star,* it had passed fleetingly through his mind, "What a twist: the rise and fall of a great male star, yet with such overtones of Judy's own story . . ." He looked at her and said, "We're going to have a great picture, Judy."

• • •

While Hart had been laboring in Palm Springs, production of new films had come to a virtual standstill in Hollywood as confusion over the three-dimensional and CinemaScope formats paralyzed the decision makers.

The start of filming on *The Robe* at 20th Century–Fox on February 23 had been carefully and nervously noted by the other studios, which adopted a cautious watch-and-see attitude. Warners, meanwhile, had gone full speed ahead on its first film using the Natural Vision 3-D system, a remake of the 1933 thriller *Mystery of the Wax Museum,* retitled *House of Wax.* It had begun filming on January 19 on carefully guarded sound stages, under the direction of one-eyed André de Toth, the only director on the lot who could not truly perceive depth, another of Jack Warner's little jokes. The picture was finished on February 21, at which time Warner ordered a studio-wide production shutdown until after the picture's April 10 premiere, when the financial impact of 3-D could be more accurately determined.

By March 18, enough footage from *The Robe* and *How to Marry a Millionaire* was available for Zanuck and Skouras to hold the first public demonstration of CinemaScope for exhibitors at the old Fox studio on Western Avenue in Hollywood. The screenings were a huge success, with theater owners from all over the country clamoring for the necessary equipment and the exclusive rights to premiere *The Robe* in their cities. And not only exhibitors: two days after the demonstrations, Fox announced that MGM, Columbia, Universal-International, and Walt Disney had joined "the CinemaScope revolution." The lone holdouts were Warner Bros., because of Jack Warner's intractability, and Paramount, which startled Zanuck and everyone else by both denouncing Cinema-Scope as impractical and, surprisingly, contesting Fox's claim to exclusive rights to the process by dusting off its own anamorphic lens. Paramount had made a similar deal with Professor Chrétien in 1932 but had never used the lens.

At the heart of the matter, however, was Paramount's fear that if CinemaScope did catch on with the public and exhibitors, the same situation that had happened with the introduction of sound would reoccur: the studios would be stuck with a backlog of outdated, unmarketable product. As of March 18, when Fox held its public demonstrations of CinemaScope, the major studios had a total of $350,000,000 tied up in unreleased two-dimensional films, which would take up to two years to play off successfully in the nation's theaters. Many veteran industry executives shared Jack Warner's privately expressed sentiment that 3-D was a good short-term gimmick, a quick fix that would hype box-office receipts but never gain lasting public favor. CinemaScope, however, was being introduced and marketed by a major studio with a long-term investment and a single-minded approach to making certain that the process's dramatic and technical standards were on a level consistent with audience expectations and comfort (i.e., no glasses). Cinerama's panoramic screen mystique seemed to be exciting audiences and press alike, whereas 3-D was meeting with critical and audience resentment: by March, *Bwana Devil* and a series of old American and British short subjects were all that the public had seen of 3-D, and while the sensation was novel, so was the eye strain and the inconvenience of the cardboard viewers necessary for obtaining the primitive depth effect. Warners was rushing *House of Wax* to completion to meet the April 10 New York premiere deadline; and Columbia had hastily added 3-D to a little B picture called, aptly enough, *Man in the Dark,* with which it hoped to make a lie of Warners' claim that *House of Wax* would be the first feature-length 3-D film from a major studio.

But even as he raced with Columbia's Harry Cohn to be first in the stereoscopic sweepstakes, Jack Warner, worried about the backlog of unreleased pictures, was hedging his bets. Still smarting from being aced out of the Chrétien process, he tried to come up with a viable alternative to both Cinerama and CinemaScope—preferably something that could be used on the studio's unreleased films. Early in January rumors began to be heard of a new projection system that Warners had developed, and suddenly the same rumor began to circulate about Paramount and Universal-International. On January 26 a secret demonstration at the Warner Wiltern Theatre on Wilshire Boulevard in Los Angeles revealed to a select few what Jack, in a fit of pique and semiplagiarism, would soon dub "WarnerScope." What it was was nothing more than the studio's 1946 musical blockbuster *Night and Day* projected through a rectangular mask and a wide-angle lens on the projector, resulting in a picture almost twice as wide as normal, giving a good imitation of "the panoramic screen" that so many had heard about but so few had actually seen. It turned out that both Paramount and Universal had already come up with the same concept, although neither had gone to the extremes of width that Warners had. To get the necessary proportion, Warners' process cropped the original image almost in half horizontally, masking the top and bottom of the picture so that when it was projected through the necessary lens, it had a long, narrow look. Paramount opted for a proportion slightly less wide, roughly one and a half times wider than normal, while Universal decided that it could stretch its picture out to one and three-quarters times wider than normal size, enhancing the width by projecting the picture onto a curved screen reminiscent of Cinerama and throwing in a multi-channel sound system as an added tonic. When Warner heard about this latter gimmick, he grabbed it gleefully, christened his version "WarnerPhonic sound," and ordered that *House of Wax* should be advertised as the first "all 3-D picture: 3-D Action, 3-D Sound, and 3-D Color"—the latter being, of course, WarnerColor (what else?).

Strangely enough, when *House of Wax* finally opened in New York, it had all the above-named Warner gimmicks except WarnerScope, which Jack evidently decided to save for a rainier day. *House of Wax* proved to be the sensation he had hoped for: on an investment of a little over $1 million, the picture grossed the staggering figure of $5.5 million, more than any other Warners release since 1947's *Life with Father*. It seemed that 3-D, if not the panacea for all the industry's ills, was certainly a potent shot in the arm; even Columbia's little 3-D potboiler *Man in The Dark* (which beat *House of Wax* into New York by one day) grossed a respectable $2.5 million.

But Paramount became the first to introduce the wide screen to most moviegoers, when George Stevens's *Shane* opened at the Radio City Music Hall on April 24, on a screen measuring 30 by 50, as opposed to the normal size of 25 by 34. The picture took in a hefty $9 million in its first year, which it probably would have done without the added width; but the lesson, such as it was, seemed to be that the public would flock in even greater numbers to see pictures that were, to paraphrase an advertising slogan of the time, "bigger and better than ever."

It was around this time that George Cukor returned from his European vacation to find a Hollywood considerably different from the one he had left in January. Hardly anybody was working. Many of the studios were at a standstill—RKO, Warners, and Universal had been closed down for weeks, while at Columbia only one film was in production; at MGM, two. But Cukor sensed a feeling of optimism and excitement in the town, and after surveying the disarray and confusion he remarked to the press that it seemed to him to be "the end of an era in Hollywood; but I think it's healthy. There is a great turnover just like the period when talkies were introduced. It's stimulating . . . it gives you a chance to keep yourself fresh . . . it takes you out of a groove and gives you the chance to work with new ideas and new people." Having said that, he reported to the Warner Bros. studio to begin the preproduction work on his thirty-seventh film, his first in color and his first musical.

Preproduction

One of the first problems confronting Cukor was what to do about the Cary Grant situation. Luft was continuing to assure everyone involved that Grant would do the part, and in fact the actor did do a reading of the entire script with Cukor. As Cukor told author/critic Robert Osborne, "Everybody wanted Cary to play Norman Maine in *A Star Is Born* with Judy, and he came here [to my home] one day to read the script aloud for me, and with me. He was absolutely magnificent, dramatic and vulnerable beyond anything I'd ever seen him do." It was under Cukor's direction in *Sylvia Scarlett* in 1935 that Grant had first stretched his talents beyond mere personality and delved into a character, feeling, according to Cukor, "that he had substantial talents as an actor. The part gave him confidence in his abilities, and I think was the real start of his career as an actor." Cukor thereafter directed Grant in *Holiday* and *The Philadelphia Story*, two films that established the actor as a major romantic leading man and box-office attraction. Now, thirteen years after their last work together, Cukor was astonished at Grant's depth and range in reading the part of Norman. "But when he finished," continued Cukor, "I was filled with a great, great sadness. Because I knew Cary would never do the role. He would never expose himself like that in public."

Cukor evidently kept his suspicions to himself, for according to Sid Luft: "George Chasin [Grant's agent] warned me that I'd never get Cary unless we made the deal he wanted. But Jack Warner was stubborn about it. Cary wanted to do it, but Jack would not give him 10 percent of the gross. Then one night a few months before we were scheduled to start, Betsy [Grant] came down to our house at midnight in her tennis outfit and said that Cary was just heartbroken, but he just couldn't do the movie. After all that romancing and racetrack and dinners he just couldn't do it—he couldn't get on the phone either, so Betsy had to come down. She was crying, Judy was crying. . . .

"So a couple of days later we all have a meeting—Jack, George, Moss, Eddie, Judy, and myself. I brought up the name Bogart. He was our neighbor, a close friend of ours, and he and I had talked about him doing it, but Jack just brushed him off quickly. His thinking was that the contrast facially between this young pretty girl and this older, withered-up man was just too much. In the original movie Freddie March was a very handsome fellow, he didn't look like any drunk, and she was very young and innocent looking, so Jack was probably right.

"So then I brought up Frank Sinatra. I'd had a meeting with Frank, long before he did *From Here to Eternity*. He was a great friend of ours, an old and close friend of Judy's. He wanted to do it. I thought he and Judy would be great together. Judy wanted him too, so I brought up his name at the meeting. But at the time he was considered poison; his records weren't selling. As a matter of fact, I went down to see him when he was at the Cocoanut Grove—must have been about thirty people in the crowd, that's all. And he was having problems with [his wife] Ava [Gardner]; she was running around with a bullfighter and making a movie in Africa. So Frank was going over to Africa to settle up with her; when he came back he wanted to do *A Star Is Born*. But the name Sinatra was taboo. Moss listened, but George wasn't too thrilled, and Jack didn't like it at all— nobody liked it except Judy and myself. So it seemed we were stuck, and we were all going to think about it. I got on the phone next day with [agent] Charlie Feldman and he brought up the name James Mason."

In 1953, James Neville Mason was forty-four years old and, at this stage of his career, in his own words, "a madly competitive actor. I was competitive because I was not getting anywhere very fast." An uncharacteristic statement, for Mason was also, in George Cukor's view, "rather reserved by nature . . . a mysterious creature with the greatest discretion. He is a complete actor." Ambition is one of the necessary components for the "complete actor," and Mason had the kind of ambition that had taken him from his early upbringing as the third son of a successful Yorkshire business family through an education at Marlborough and Cambridge, where he studied architecture in the midst of which he stage-managed a production of Purcell's *The Fairy Queen* and simultaneously played the part of Oberon. The taste of performing whetted his appetite for more, and he was soon immersed in productions of the Marlowe Society, devoting himself to plays of the Elizabethan era and drifting further and further from architecture. But it was Tyrone Guthrie and his company of actors at the Festival Theatre in Cambridge who opened Mason's eyes and mind to the infinite possibilities of the theater.

After graduation and a move to London, he discovered that the Depression had destroyed any possibility of architectural pursuits. In 1931 he began his professional theatrical career by playing the part of a thinly disguised Prince Yousoupoff in an even more thinly disguised version of the Rasputin saga called *The Rascal,* which toured the provinces; at one performance Mason, who was supposed to shoot the mad monk, discovered to his dismay that his prop gun had no bullets and administered the requisite coup de grâce by aiming his pistol and yelling "bang bang." An inauspicious beginning for a "madly competitive" actor, but hard work, perseverance, and luck worked in his favor. Luck came in the person of Guthrie, who saw Mason in his West End debut as one of John Brown's sons in a play called *Gallows Glorious,* a dramatization of the raid on Harpers Ferry. Guthrie, impressed with Mason's intensity, offered the young actor a spot in a new troupe he was assembling for the Old Vic. The company included Charles Laughton, Elsa Lanchester, Ursula Jeans, Roger Livesey, and Marius Goring, all of whom soon went on to greater fame in theater and film.

Mason's own beginning in film was shaky: the lead in a 1935 "quota quickie," *Late Extra.* Eight years later, he finally reached stardom in Britain playing a sexy nineteenth-century villain in *The Man in Grey,* one of those Regency melodramas so dear to the hearts of the war-weary British masses. A succession of such roles followed, capped by his classic "Gainsborough Gothics," *Fanny by Gaslight* and *The Wicked Lady.* But it was his bravura performance in 1945's *The Seventh Veil* that turned him into an international sex symbol, as the crippled, possessive guardian of concert pianist Ann Todd. As a saturnine Svengali figure, he was called upon to thwack her fingers with his cane as she rehearses the "Moonlight" Sonata, thereby ensuring her undying love—after a certain amount of plot development, of course.

The film was as big a success in the United States as it was in England, leading to the traditional offers from Hollywood. Being ambitious, Mason took the plunge. As he put it, "I had a clear sense of my own status in the English entertainment world. . . . I knew the pecking order: Laurence Olivier, Rex Harrison, David Niven, Michael Redgrave, Richard Greene,

Trevor Howard. . . . I also knew that the number per year of good British films could be counted on the fingers of little more than one hand. Flukes like *The Seventh Veil* were rare. I thought it more than likely that I might have to go on knocking myself out in an unbroken line of banalities, whereas the Hollywood people were liable to be much more impressed by my highly touted popularity; I would extend my range, have a wider choice." Ironically, it was fellow countryman Carol Reed who gave Mason the opportunity to extend his range in the last film Mason made before leaving for Hollywood in 1947: *Odd Man Out.* Mason's portrayal of an Irish rebel leader hunted by the police, subtle and intensely affecting, overnight gave him international credibility as a performer of power and sophistication. He was no longer considered just a smooth, sexy villain but respected as an actor of enormous range and sensitivity.

In Hollywood in 1953, he was, as he mentioned, "not getting anywhere very fast." He had appeared in a number of high-budget films in showy roles, notably as the real-life spy Cicero in *Five Fingers* and as German General Erwin Rommel in *The Desert Fox* in a much-praised portrayal. Of this early period he recalled: "On the one hand I shrank from being typecast or of becoming the long-term thrall of a major studio; on the other I wished to involve myself in filmmaking of every variety and ultimately to become my own producer and my own director or writer . . . obviously this would not happen overnight. First I must rise to a position of some power, and this could only be done by appearing in one successful picture after another. Though it may be hard to believe, this was my aim throughout my career in Hollywood; unfortunately my taste guided me unerringly to projects which were artistically unadventurous and financially hazardous, so my American career started with a run of five failures."

Carol Reed once again came to his rescue, with the meaty role of a German who lives by his wits between the East and West Berlin sectors; hence the title *The Man Between.* This role and Mason's Brutus in MGM's *Julius Caesar* (the two films were released within weeks of each other in mid-1953) brought forth glowing notices from the critics, and suddenly Mason found himself very "hot," sought after for roles in several major films.

"During these years," he related, "I practically ran the gamut of the Hollywood agencies . . . but I was best served by Charlie Feldman's agency. Charlie himself was a man of whom it was easy to become very fond. He was a generous, warm-hearted person. I had absolute faith in his judgment, so when he called to tell me about *A Star Is Born*, I thought that it would be exactly my cup of tea. The first version with Janet Gaynor and Fredric March was a superb little film, an unpretentious and credible Hollywood story; I had known for some time that Judy Garland and her husband Sid Luft were planning a remake, and now here they were with a healthy-looking contract with Warner Bros. and a new scenario by one of the top playwrights of the time, Moss Hart. When you read a good script, and this was a really beautiful, witty script of those times, you can't help thinking that this could make a wonderful film. . . .

"I was very fond of Judy . . . as a moviegoer I had admired her so much from a distance for such a long time. I got to know her very well when I first arrived in Hollywood, because one of the first films I appeared in at MGM was *Madame Bovary*, which was directed by her husband at that time, Vincente Minnelli, and I developed a fond relationship with her. . . . I loved and responded to her sense of humor. . . . She was a sharp, witty woman who as a child star at MGM had gotten into the unfortunate habit of taking things like Dexedrine to sharpen her up in the morning and sedatives to help her sleep at night. She was a party-goer, almost too eager, some may have thought, to join whoever was at the piano and sing along, while her hostess made sure that her medicine cabinet was safely locked. It was on account of this that Judy had made a bad name for herself in a commercial town like Hollywood where reliability is the big thing.

"She and Sid were kindred spirits, both mavericks, and the feeling in Hollywood at the time about *A Star Is Born* was very negative. Judy told me later that Arthur Freed, who had produced a number of her films at MGM, had said of her and Luft in the presence of one of her friends, 'Those two alley cats can't make a picture.' In Hollywood, no one would expect *A Star Is Born* with Judy Garland to be a smooth or easy ride. I was by no means the front runner for the part of Norman Maine; I know that the part was offered to Humphrey Bogart . . . and to Cary Grant . . . and there were probably others, but in the end it came to me and I grabbed it smartly before it slipped away."

Mason's "grabbing it before it slipped away" was a blessing for the film, for few performers of his caliber would have had the maturity to allow themselves to be subordinate to Judy Garland, to sit and react while she sang to them, and generally be upstaged by her. This prospect is probably what kept Cary Grant from accepting the role, even more than the impasse over salary. Actors' egos are fragile things, and it is to Mason's credit that he was able to sublimate his own for what he saw to be an outstanding role, even if it did mean playing second fiddle to Garland. His romantic appeal and his innate sensitivity would also add another dimension to the part of Maine, which, as written, offered no explanation for his alcoholic decline. Mason's gifts were such that he could communicate Maine's inner turmoil without an excessive amount of expository, soul-searching dialogue; and his considerable personal charm and magnetism would add greatly to the character's appeal.

Mason agreed to do the film in early May, just about the time that Jack Warner, luxuriating in the blockbuster that *House of Wax* was turning out to be, announced that his studio was taking up the Natural Vision option and would use the process for twenty-two more films, among them the Cukor-Garland-Mason *A Star Is Born.* At the same time he formally announced the introduction of WarnerScope (described as "a newly perfected process for the projection of all motion pictures, which has been under development by our studio for some years now"), adding one more name to the confusing welter of Scopes, Visions, and Ramas that bedeviled producers and exhibitors alike.

Meanwhile, the preproduction work on *A Star Is Born* began to move into high gear. Harold Arlen and Ira Gershwin had finished their work on the score in late April. They had written twelve songs instead of the seven requested by Hart. In addition to "Gotta Have Me Go With You" and "The Man That Got Away," there was a short jingle, "Trinidad Coconut Oil Shampoo," to be used in the sequence where Esther does a voice-over for a television commercial. Three additional songs, "Green Light Ahead," "I'm Off the Downbeat," and "Dancing Partner," were all written as alternatives for the "big number" that Hart had indicated to show the transformation of Esther the singer into Vicki the star. The "song on recording stage" for the marriage proposal sequence had become "Here's What I'm Here For," while the "honeymoon song in motel" was called "It's a New World." The Malibu beach house number, in which Esther tries to cheer her despondent husband, emerged as "Someone at Last," a parody of all movie production numbers. For the finale of the picture, Esther/Vicki's appearance at the Shrine Auditorium, there would be a reprise of "It's a New World." Additionally, Hart had added a new scene which necessitated an actual film-within-a-film production number: "Lose That Long Face" was designed to frame the dramatic scene between Esther and Oliver Niles in which, after singing the number on camera, she breaks down in her dressing room and confides her doubts about being able to save Norman from himself. When Niles promises to put Norman back to work, she goes out and finishes the song.

Seven songs was not many; the average musical of the time contained at least ten. The previous year, 20th Century–Fox's *With a Song in My Heart* had an all-time high of twenty-five, while MGM's *Singin' in the Rain* had thirteen and Warners' own *Lullaby of Broadway* offered twelve. That this seeming paucity of music was of some concern to Jack Warner was evidenced in a memo from his executive assistant Walter McEwan, who commented in his notes on the first draft of *A Star Is Born:* "As per your instructions regarding the possibility of adding one or two more songs, I looked, perhaps overzealously, for places where the screenplay might be shortened in order to make room for more music."

From McEwan, the script was sent to the timer, whose job it was to estimate the approximate running time of the finished film. Timing a script is an exacting task, requiring the ability to visualize the scenes of a script, working them out as to camera movement, staging, and dialogue delivery, all calculations based on a knowledge of cinema mechanics and the style of the particular director. The timer goes over each scene with these factors in mind and stopwatch in hand; an expert with years of experience can usually time a script to within a minute of the eventual running time. But Jack Warner didn't believe in having more people than necessary on the payroll, so script timing was left in the hands of the film editors. In the case of *A Star Is Born,* the script was given to William Holmes to estimate; he came up with an approximate running time of ninety-five minutes, exclusive of musical numbers. There was one fallacy in his estimate, however: George Cukor had never worked at the studio before, and Holmes was unfamiliar with his style. And Cukor's style was leisurely—long takes, complex staging and blocking, with the emphasis on the actors and their reactions to the script and to each other. A scene that might take two and a half minutes to play under Raoul Walsh or William Wellman might take three and a half to four minutes under Cukor. Holmes was not aware of this, so his estimate of ninety-five minutes was off the mark by a wide margin. The original version of *A Star Is Born,* directed by Wellman, ran 110 minutes, and Hart's new screenplay didn't shorten the story at all—in fact, his revision in the first half lengthened it. And the seven musical numbers, each running four to five minutes, would add approximately another thirty minutes to the picture's length. Add to this Cukor's typical meticulous attention to detail, nuance, and mood and *A Star Is Born* could conceivably end up running two hours and forty-five minutes. An experienced producer, one familiar with Cukor's style, would have detected this immediately. Luft, however, was not an expert in these matters, so it evidently never occurred to him. Warner should have known, but he seems not to have mentioned it. The evidence at hand—the memo from McEwan—indicates that Warner wanted to shorten the script, to tighten and condense it to make room for more musical numbers.

Cukor's concern was to make the script work in terms of character, to flesh out the relationships and to fill in more detail in the staging of individual scenes. One of his early suggestions to Hart concerned revamping the scene of Esther's first day of work on a sound stage. Hart had Esther doing a "hand insert," a close-up of her arm standing in for a star's and throwing a glass of champagne, evidently into an actor's face. Cukor wrote a long letter to Hart outlining his idea for the expansion of this scene:

The other day when I talked to you on ze telephone, I volunteered to write the description of a new scene which we are substituting for scene 57, the hand insert scene. But what the hell! *You* got [all those thousands] for writing the screenplay, didn't you? In my poor, halting words I will attempt to describe the action which we propose to do in scene 57. . . . We show a movie set going full blast, with the usual array of personnel. We should give the impression that an important scene is going to be shot.

It is a hot California (Burbank) day and the crew are in various states of undress, T shirts, etc. The set is a huge train shed (just a wee bit smaller than the New York Central station). It has three long tracks, on two of which are six-car trains. Through the open doors of the shed a long, picturesque tenement street can be seen. Since this (the tenement street) is not the set that is to be shot, there is the usual paraphernalia parked around—portable dressing rooms, lights, etc.

It is Esther's first day of work under her new contract, her first opportunity. Naturally she is very much on the qui vive. The assistant director takes her to the director. This action is far enough away so that we don't hear the instructions that the director is giving her, but he is pointing to the train coach. Esther drinks in his instructions and nods her head, all eagerness and tension. She gets into the "mock-up" of a railroad coach. (I will explain: This is a regular railroad car, the end of which is cut off so the camera can give the impression of being *inside* the car.) A wardrobe woman helps Esther into a large and very heavy fur coat, and she seats herself next to an open window.

We cut to the outside of the same coach where we see Esther, having taken her place at the window. . . . We also now see the reason for the fur coat. About a quarter of the outside of the railroad car in which Esther sits is all fixed up for a big snow scene. The glass is cloudy, the roof of the car is covered with snow, and there is snow on the ground as well. Icicles hang on the window. . . . The technicians are hard at work, the lights have been adjusted, and there is a sound effect that indicates that the train is about to start. We see the special effects man with a pipe, feeding the steam up into the scene as though it were coming from under the car. The director says "Camera!" Our camera now slowly trucks up past the prop camera, and we photograph the scene that the prop camera is presumably getting. Out of a beclouded, ice-frosted window of a snow-covered train, a fur-coated arm is thrust through the window. In its hand is a lace handkerchief which it begins to wave. The steam is coming up most convincingly . . . the sound effects of the train chugging away, etc. . . . Suddenly the director's voice yells "Cut!"

We cut to another shot where we see the director, who is obviously annoyed. "We saw her face!" (to Esther) "We saw your face! Keep back! Keep back!" Esther is very embarrassed. The director says, "Let's do it again. Now mind you, be careful—*I don't want to see your face!*"

The next scene should be shot from the inside of the "mock-up" coach. The prop camera still remains on the outside, photographing the scene. We hear the director say, "All right—camera!" This time Esther becomes a contortionist. She stretches her arm way out, does the waving business, but keeps her head and body safely averted.

I hope my description . . . [is] neither too garbled nor too long-winded and that you can make some sense out of [it]. Also, I trust that you're not sore at me for this continued harassing, but "ARS GRATIA ARTIS"—no, that's the wrong slogan. I have none to substitute for it, however, because I've not yet learned the Warner Bros. motto . . . but I will! If you're a good boy and do this homework well, I'll dream up some more things for you to do.

My love to you and Kitty.

Always,

Gregory Ratoff (your director)

Hart replied:

Your fascinating letter to hand—and I see no reason why all this shouldn't blossom into a kind of Shaw-Terry correspondence. . . . I'm delighted with [the scene] as outlined in your letter—[it's] excellent and infinitely better visually than what we had originally—I'm enclosing the letter back to you in case you didn't keep a copy—I see no point in just transcribing your

deathless prose and sending it back to you—it's fine as it is—just insert it—as
the girl said to the sailor. I don't know why people say you're not as good
as Lucky Humberstone.* I think you're wonderful!

Cukor's suggestions and revisions added considerable comedy and accurate behind-the-scenes views of movie-making—and they also added another four minutes to the overall running time of the picture. So even at
this early stage, the length of A Star Is Born was a problem that no one
seemed to be aware of. Sid Luft remarked: "Suddenly everybody was
getting excited about this picture . . . Moss Hart, George Cukor, Ira
Gershwin, Harold Arlen. The place was getting steamed up about this. The
word was out that this was going to be a blockbuster."

The word was out, as Luft stated, and one person who got it was the
producer and uncredited co-writer of the 1937 original, David O. Selznick.
Inactive as a producer since 1948, he had turned instead to the international marketing of his extensive backlog of films. A Star Is Born was his
baby, even if it had been adopted by others; his pride in it and the
knowledge that it was still unreleased in several European and Asian markets led him to make a concerted effort to reacquire some rights to the film,
even if these were only releasing rights in certain overseas territories. He
did this by buying up the subdistribution rights that Alperson and his
associates had sold to small independent franchises in the late 1940s, so that
by the time the remake was announced in 1952, Selznick was in possession
of rights for some thirteen countries, including Germany and Japan. As he
pointed out in a letter to his attorneys:

> This is a unique situation . . . in which apparently Warners are perfectly
> willing to have the competition of another version of the market abroad, or
> it may be that they don't even know about it. Certainly it may come as a
> rude shock to them that there is nothing they can do to interfere with the
> distribution of our version; [regardless of] whether there is anything we can
> do to interfere with the distribution of theirs. . . . I think it behooves us to
> get on the market before them, certainly at least in those countries where
> the picture has never been released before.

*H. Bruce Humberstone was a notorious "one take" director of low-budget action films and B musicals.

In order to do this, however, he needed to make color prints of the film, and this he could not do without the negative, which was in Alperson's possession. It was standard industry practice for the original distributor to supply all legal subdistributors with prints to fulfill their contractual obligations; but in this case Alperson, embarrassed by the oversight of selling the remake rights to Luft and Warners without owning *all* foreign distribution rights, flatly refused to cooperate with Selznick. This led Selznick to fume in a memo to his attorneys:

> Have seldom been so outraged as by Alperson's attitude . . . imperative he immediately be served with . . . notice [that] he will be held strictly accountable for all damages growing out of any delays in fulfilling our privileges. . . . Would not be at all surprised to learn that Warners does not know of our rights. . . . It [is] imperative that Warners know of the situation. . . . Also I think I ought to *immediately* send a letter to Judy Garland, a good friend of mine, and her husband, concerning this matter, so that they understand the situation, and perhaps will put some pressure on Alperson and Warners. If and when all else fails, then let's see what legal steps we might take, if not against Warners, then against Alperson, to *force* them to give us the negative. Certainly, the whole thing can be approached legally . . . or as a matter of fairness, or probably a combination of the two—with the Warner lawyers, *but on a friendly basis.*

Selznick's reluctance to take on Warners in this matter was due to his desire to once again produce a picture. The property he wanted to make was owned by Warners: Ernest Hemingway's *A Farewell to Arms.* On the one hand, he needed the prints of *A Star Is Born* from Alperson and Warners; but he could not risk rushing into a lawsuit without jeopardizing the possibility of getting the remake rights to the Hemingway novel.

While Selznick grappled with this dilemma, George Cukor was immersed in the thousands of daily details that go into the preproduction phase of a picture. Despite its small cast and straightforward plot line, *A Star Is Born* was a musical, and musicals by their very nature are more complex than straight dramatic films. This would also be Cukor's first official color film, although back in 1939 he had directed two weeks of Selznick's *Gone With the Wind* in Technicolor, before disagreements with the strong-minded producer had caused him to be replaced by Victor Fleming. Cukor had switched over to MGM's *The Women*, which included a Technicolor fashion show. Cukor had not directed this sequence and had thought its costumes and color design were particularly garish. Cukor was a cultured, civilized man, of whom Irving Lazar later said, "George proved that you could be in the movie business and not necessarily be a hoodlum." Cukor's home in the hills above Sunset Boulevard was elegantly designed not only for gracious living but also to be a showcase for his extensive collection of paintings and sculptures. His ideas of color and design were shaped by his love of art, and *A Star Is Born* would be his first opportunity to infuse one of his films with the same sense of understated elegance that was so characteristic of his own private surroundings. In his book *On Cukor*, Gavin Lambert quotes him as saying that "anyone who looks at something special in a very original way, makes you see it that way forever." To Cukor, Hollywood and its inhabitants were something special. From the time of his arrival in Hollywood in 1929, he had "just taken to it immediately. . . . I quickly fell in love with . . . Hollywood . . . the place and the people." It was an affection he shared with David Selznick, although not to the degree of Selznick's wide-eyed idealism: "David didn't like cheap jibes about Hollywood or its people, he had a romantic idea that the whole world loved Hollywood . . . so when we made *What Price Hollywood?* he didn't want to make anything bitchy or sour . . . he wouldn't let it become cynical. It was exuberant and a little larger than life." Cukor's down-to-earth attitude about Hollywood complemented Selznick's more romantic view of the subject. Cukor viewed the place and its people with neither a jaundiced nor a cynical eye but rather with a realistic, nonillusory view, which in the case of *What Price Hollywood?* was tempered with his own irreverent humor toward the subject. Interestingly, Selznick had wanted Cukor to direct the original *A Star Is Born;* but Cukor had not wanted to do another Hollywood story, so close in time and spirit to the 1932 film, so Wellman took on the project. In the intervening sixteen years, however, Cukor had watched from the inside the changes in the town and in the industry; he had seen the rise and fall of careers, the deaths of friends through old age, neglect, and suicide—all of which tempered his irreverence into a bemused, appreciative tolerance and understanding of the foibles and failings of the residents of the movie colony. His attitude toward all of them was that Hollywood, far from being the crazy, corrosive kind of place so dear to novelists and other detractors, was made up of a forthright mixture of the good and the bad, the strong and the weak, the talented and the not-so-talented, motivated by ambition, envy, greed, and the love of movies and movie-making. And all of this Cukor wanted to reflect in *A Star Is Born*—directly, through Hart's screenplay and the actors, and indirectly, through the interplay of mood, design, color, and the sprawling, diverse Southern California landscape.

A motion picture depends for its effectiveness on the interaction of numerous components: script, performance, setting, lighting, design, photography, music, color. All of these diverse elements are orchestrated and given emphasis and meaning by the director. And in the studio system, a director was only as good as his collaborators—a fact of film life that Cukor had learned early on. He realized the value of having fresh outlooks and new talent surrounding him; as he had put it in his press conference in March: "The chance to work with new ideas and new people . . . is stimulating. . . . It gives you a chance to keep yourself fresh."

For *A Star Is Born,* Luft, probably at Garland's urging, had turned to the Broadway theater for some of the "new" talent that Cukor found so refreshing to work with. For the settings and costumes for the film, Luft had brought in the distinguished (and expensive) Lemuel Ayers, whose reputation had been made with his designs for *Oklahoma!* in 1943. Subsequent to that he designed the settings or the costumes (in some cases both) for *Song of Norway, Bloomer Girl,* and *St. Louis Woman* and was co-producer as well as designer for *Kiss Me Kate* and *Out of This World,* all colorful, stylish, and trend-setting musicals.

In mid-June, Ayers joined the production meetings at Warners, where the picture initially began to take shape. Here, each department head, in consultations and discussions with the producer and the director, began to get a sense of how the story should be treated. Ideas were tossed out, approaches tested and accepted or rejected; costs were estimated, compromises made, and ways devised to save money while still getting the necessary images onto the screen. An example is Hart's opening line: "The piercing beams of huge arc lights sweep the night sky above Hollywood." This would be almost impossible to do realistically, so it was decided that a second-unit camera crew would photograph various panoramic vistas of

Hollywood at night, and that the searchlight beams would be added by the special effects department. Hart's description of the Night of the Stars benefit, which opens the story, takes only one paragraph in the screenplay: "The lights are being manipulated for a special event . . . Hollywood's Own is on display at its most splendid. Those stars not appearing in the show are in the audience—the men in white tie, the women beautifully gowned and jeweled—all watching the act in progress on the stage with that fine air of benevolence reserved by hard-shelled audiences for benefits in a worthy cause. The camera sweeps quickly across the auditorium; then to the row of dancing girls on the stage . . ." But in visualizing this, Cukor expanded and refined the idea so that the opening sequence became an evocation of the glamour, the hysteria, and the fatuousness that was, to his knowing eye, so much a part of these ritual events.

In addition to the audience in the theater, Cukor wanted to sketch in the pushing, shouting, shoving, screaming crowds of fans for whom the ritual is performed; and in so doing, he—perhaps inadvertently—added an important element missing from Hart's screenplay: a villain. In Cukor's *A Star Is Born*, the public is the real heavy of the tale: fawning and hysterical one moment, angry and destructive the next; demanding, fickle, righteous, and vicious in its treatment and mistreatment of its favorites. "Fan" is short for "fanatic"; and to Cukor, that's exactly what the mass public was, at least as he had seen it behave at just about every major social function in the town for the past twenty years, be it a party, a premiere, or a funeral. This idea was touched on briefly and memorably in one scene in the 1937 original, where Vicki's fans snatch off her mourning veil at Maine's funeral. Hart's treatment had indicated this kind of behavior on the part of the movie public, but it was Cukor who decided to visualize it, to depict it in all its mindless, infantile, drooling tawdriness. To do this in the opening sequence of the film would add greatly to the physical necessities of the production—an exterior of a theater, several hundred extras, dozens of cars and limousines, all the other paraphernalia of the typical premiere night—and add at least another $100,000 to the budget; but everyone involved evidently agreed that this would add excitement, spectacle, and glamour to the opening of the story.

It was at these production meetings that Cukor realized that Ayers, with all his talent and experience in the theater, had no understanding of how to design for film, at least not in the way Cukor wanted the film to look. He wanted every camera setup to be carefully drawn beforehand for composition, lighting, color, and costuming, including angles and cuts. When he tried to explain this, it was obvious that Ayers was stumped. "He was a New York stage designer and . . . didn't know anything about the movie business," Cukor later recalled. "I suggested he find someone in the art department who would understand what I was talking about and bring him to the meetings." Ayers did exactly that, locating a thirty-four-year-old sketch artist named Gene Allen who had just rejoined the Warners art department. A native of Los Angeles, Allen had grown up surrounded by the movies. He recalls: "After I finished school I went to work at Warners . . . as a blueprint boy in the art department. . . . Warners had a great art department, as good as if not better than MGM's. We had men like Anton Grot and Carl Weyl, John Hughes, and Jack Okey. I really learned how to draw, watching the sketch artists at Warner Brothers; then I went to night school at Chouinard Art Institute and studied art. At Warners in those days they had maybe twelve sketch artists working in the art department, because each art director had one of his own people that he liked to have do his sketches. A sketch artist would take the plans for the sets and turn them into three-dimensional drawings so the producer and the director would have an idea of what they would look like. They were called 'set sketches' . . . and then you worked on continuity, in which, to a certain degree, you illustrated the script—at least, the art director's interpretation of what the script should look like, so that he could talk to the director, showing the various angles, pre-editing, that sort of thing. . . .

"After the war I just got pulled back into the film business and started all over as a sketch artist, first at Fox, then at Warners, which is where I met Lem Ayers. He looked at some sketches I was doing and asked me to come and work for him doing some drawings of people backstage, and I guess he liked them, because he said, 'I'd like you to come up to a meeting with me.' So I went up with him and there were the art director, the costume designers, and the cameraman, and there was George Cukor, whom I'd heard about for years and saw his movies, and they're all sitting around talking about *A Star Is Born*. They were working on the design for the Malibu house, where [Norman and Vicki] would live after they were married. I knew that Lem Ayers was very involved with that, the design of it and all—he was interested in the kind of furniture and was working with the decorators on all that. And it was all very fascinating to me, because I'd never been in any production meetings before. . . .

"I had read the script and loved it. Then along comes a new draft and there was a scene missing that I thought was really good—the wedding scene, where they get married in a funny little jail in some small town. So at the end of one of the meetings I stuck my hand up and said I thought it was a marvelous scene and perhaps they should think about putting it back. Cukor just sort of looked up at me and never said anything, but the very next day along come the famous blue pages for that section, which means that the scene's been put back. I guess it impressed him . . . maybe he thought, 'Here's a guy who not only sketches but thinks about story' or whatever, because after that I got a lot more attention and was asked a lot more questions by George Cukor."

From the recollection of everyone involved, it is evident that the look of the film was of much concern to Cukor, especially the use of color. He did not want it to be bright and colorful as was the custom with musicals. This was, after all, basically a tragedy, a dark, poignant story. The color was to be carefully controlled to enhance the mood and define the emotional impact. He wanted it lush but subdued, realistic with a touch of stylization. The year before, he had been much impressed with John Huston's *Moulin Rouge,* which had used Technicolor in a new and innovative method to evoke the era and works of Toulouse-Lautrec. Huston had brought in the eminent still photographer Eliot Elisofon to supervise the color design of the picture, and the results had caused much excited comment in and out of the industry.

While Cukor was pleased with the ideas of his art director and set decorator, he still felt the need for an imaginative color advisor who would use the spectrum as a design element. One of his close friends was the noted fashion photographer George Hoyningen-Huene. Born in 1900 in St. Petersburg, his father was a Baltic nobleman in the service of Czar Nicholas II; his mother was the daughter of the United States minister to Russia. Living in Paris after the Revolution, he became a fashion illustrator, then a photographer, eventually rising to the top of his profession as the pre-eminent photographer for Paris *Vogue* from 1930 through 1945. His work brought life and realism to hitherto stereotyped, unnatural poses and was distinguished by the use of a dominant color, in order that, as he said, "the eyes do not get distracted." He carefully coordinated the art direction and the wardrobe people so that "it all jelled. You have to know how the camera records things." Hoyningen-Huene had moved to Los Angeles in the late 1940s. He worked when the fancy struck him. He had an inordinate wanderlust, traveling ceaselessly and extensively. In mid-1953, he was off on one of his extended wanderings, when Cukor decided that he was just the person to work on *A Star Is Born* and immediately began trying to track him down.

While production meetings on the film were getting under way, two more events took place which muddied the technological waters even more. On May 21, Universal International opened a James Stewart film called *Thunder Bay* at Loew's State theater in Manhattan. The picture did astounding business—200 percent better than normal for a Stewart western—and the reason seemed to be the heavily advertised emphasis on "our gigantic wide-vision screen and stereophonic sound." The theater had boosted its image size from 17 by 21 to 24 by 43 and curved its screen deeply in an imitation of Cinerama: the ensuing long lines of eager patrons turned the film into one of the smashes of the spring season. At almost the same time, Paramount had startled the industry by announcing that it would no longer make 3-D movies,* nor would it take up CinemaScope; instead, it introduced its own wide-screen system, called VistaVision ("Motion Picture High Fidelity"), which allowed a picture to be photographed and exhibited in any ratio from 1:33 to 1, to 2 to 1. This industry disarray and lack of agreement as to what format would be the standard played havoc with the production plans of most films of the time, especially *A Star Is Born.* Cukor had been unenthusiastic about Warners' announced intention to make the picture in 3-D, feeling that the story would best be served without annoying glasses and other gimmicks. He evidently pressed home his distaste to Warner, for in the subsequent announcements on the film there was no mention of 3-D. And Hart shared Cukor's concern about the new screen shapes; having seen the CinemaScope demonstration and taken a look at both *Shane* and *Thunder Bay* in their big-screen incarnations, he wrote Cukor, "I do hope that you can talk them into doing it with a regular size screen, and not WarnerScope or CinemaScope. It may be vital, that choice. I have a horrid suspicion that [those] might drain the emotion out of so personal a story as this." As long as the decision as to what technique to use on *A Star Is Born* was postponed, it was extremely difficult to do the physical planning of the film—a fact that was becoming obvious to everyone connected with the production meetings now going on almost daily.

By early June, the script was ready to be submitted to the Production

---

*The studio eventually made four: *Sangaree, Those Redheads from Seattle, Cease Fire,* and *Money from Home.*

Code Administration, which reviewed it for any possible infractions of the prevailing morality. Joseph Breen, the chief censor, warned against danger spots:

> At the outset, we direct your particular attention for the need for the greatest possible care in the selection and photographing of the dresses and the costumes of your women. The Production Code makes it mandatory that the intimate parts of the body, specifically the breasts of women, be fully covered at all times . . . We would like to suggest that you eliminate the jail portion of the wedding ceremony, in order to treat the ceremony in a more digni-fied and respectful manner . . . Please eliminate the expression "And Lord knows . . ." in Danny's denunciation of Esther for her conduct after Nor-man's death. . . . Also Danny's eulogizing of Norman's suicide is unaccept-able. There is, in this dialogue, a glorification and justification of suicide, which is specifically in violation of the Production Code. Particularly, we call your attention to the lines ". . . It took guts to do what he did when he found he couldn't lick it. But he did it. And the one thing he was proudest of, the only thing he ever did in his life that paid off, you, you're tossing it right back into the ocean after him. Who gives you that right? Because it hurts?" This flavor of approval to the act of suicide should be eliminated.

The PCA had just faced the first serious challenge to its authority from independent producer-director Otto Preminger, whose filming of the in-nocuous F. Hugh Herbert stage comedy *The Moon Is Blue* had used dialogue and situations strictly forbidden by the thirty-year-old Code— words like "seduce," "virgin," and "pregnant." Preminger refused to delete the dialogue, so Joseph Breen denied the film a seal of approval, the first time any film from a major releasing organization had been so penalized. The regulatory system had originally been set up in the early 1930s, when the studios controlled their own theaters, and all signatories to the Code agreed not to exhibit pictures without a Code seal. But when the govern-ment insisted that the studios divest themselves of their theaters, the exhibitors who took over the houses were not bound by this agreement. United Artists, the company that had financed and would release *The Moon Is Blue,* resigned in protest from the Motion Picture Association of America, the parent organization of the PCA, and went ahead with plans to release the picture without a seal. This created a nationwide sensation and any number of censorship problems in cities and towns whose guard-ians of morality were outraged by the words in question. It was the first successful defiance of the Code's stranglehold on filmmakers, and its impact was not lost on Cukor, who carefully noted the objections to the script of *A Star Is Born* and remarked: "The Code [is] a kind of straight-jacket. You have to find ways around all these ridiculous objections. It's not so much a question of morality, but one of taste." Emboldened by Preminger's example, he rejected outright the suggestion of dropping the jail portion of the wedding—but he did reluctantly go along with Warner's request that the speech in question be rewritten, which Hart did by simply eliminating the lines "It took guts to do what he did . . . But he did it" and "Who gives you that right? Because it hurts?" Even with these concessions, the PCA would keep a watchful eye on the film, carefully noting each change in the script and warning that "final Code approval will be based on the finished film."

In mid-July, Jack Warner announced that the studio, which had been dormant since March, would resume production the following week. The first films to go before the cameras, both filmed in 3-D, would be *Hondo*, a John Wayne Western, produced by the star for his independent Batjac Company, and Alfred Hitchcock's version of the stage success *Dial M for Murder*. In announcing the studio's return to production, Warner also dropped another technological bombshell: the introduction of his own anamorphic process, given the rather unwieldy name of "WarnerSuper-Scope," which, as he pointed out, was "not to be confused with our wide-screen WarnerScope process."* While the idea of the anamorphic lens could not be patented, the design itself could be, and Professor Chrétien had done just that; and when Fox bought his process, it also acquired the United States patents, so no one could use the lens without infringing on Fox's rights. But in late March Warner had contacted an independent producer named Carl Dudley, who earlier had joined forces with the Simpson Optical Company in Chicago to devise a lens that would be anamorphic without copying the Chrétien configuration. Dudley called his process Vistarama and had offered it in the industry marketplace as an alternative to CinemaScope. Warner immediately began negotiations with him for rights to the process, this despite the fact that his lenses were markedly inferior to Chrétien's. And even those, good as they were, had an unfortunate tendency to distort in both directions, so

---

*Two weeks after this press conference a press release announced that "WarnerSuperScope" would be shortened to "WarnerScope" and the old "WarnerScope" would henceforth be called "Wide Screen."

that horizontal lines were curved, vertical lines on the edges of the frame bowed outward; performers' faces were widened and their bodies broadened unflatteringly. Worse, the light-gathering ability of these early lenses was very slow, resulting in an image that fairly bubbled with grain. To rectify these drawbacks, 20th Century–Fox was paying nearly $3 million to the American optical firm of Bausch and Lomb to redesign and manufacture two hundred and fifty CinemaScope photography and three thousand CinemaScope projection lenses. The Vistarama lens also had these problems, along with a soft image and color-distorting factors. None of this deterred Warner, however, and he pursued Dudley, finally making a deal for the nonexclusive rights to Vistarama for $75,000—the same amount he would have had to pay Fox for three pictures in Cinema-Scope. Warner was evidently confident that whatever technical bugs his new lenses possessed could be eradicated, for he immediately signed a contract with the German firm of Zeiss-Opton for the redesign and manufacture of both photographing and projection lenses. Warner cannily announced to worried exhibitors that the lenses would not have to be purchased, as Fox was insisting on with CinemaScope, but would instead be supplied for a small rental fee along with the WarnerSuperScope feature, "just the way we used to supply the Vitaphone discs with the first talkies." When questioned by a reporter whether it wouldn't be better to standardize and join with others in a single big-screen medium, Warner replied, "Does GM go to Chrysler for its automotive developments—or vice versa? Our company has always believed in individual creation. We . . . feel that we have the process we want and have decided on a merchandising plan for its use by theaters that will ease their burden of a big layout." He then announced that the first two pictures to use Warner-SuperScope would be *Rear Guard,* starring Guy Madison, another 3-D Western, which would begin filming the next week; and *A Star Is Born,* which would go before the cameras on September 1.

This announcement of Warner's startled everyone connected with the film. Luft recalls: "It was just vanity on Jack's part, that whole Warner-SuperScope business. Zanuck went for CinemaScope, and Jack, being the kind of guy he was, was determined to have his own system. We shot some tests with these lenses and we looked at them and there was too much distortion—the whole goddamn thing was a mess. Judy, Eddie, and I kept begging him to let us do it regular flat in Technicolor, but Jack says, 'Give us a chance with WarnerSuperScope and the new lenses'

". . . I mean, what can you say to the man? So we had to wait until they got these new lenses from Germany, and there was no way we could start shooting in September, because they didn't even know when the lenses would be ready."

Cukor too was taken aback at Warner's announcement, since he had not been consulted about the scheduled starting date or using WarnerSuper-Scope. At Warners he had made some tests with the Vistarama lens and wrote to Moss Hart: "The Warner process is a very hit-and-miss business . . . they've not had time to take the kinks out of it. . . . We made some photographic tests of Judy and Mason and I thought the results were distinctly unpleasing. On Mason, the distortion was just distracting, on Judy I thought disastrous." Part of the problem with photographing Garland was that she was about ten pounds overweight, a fact that put Warner's announced start date into question. She would have to go on a rigid diet and exercise routine, and it would take her a month or more to safely shed her excess pounds.

Warner's seemingly arbitrary setting of the starting date for September 1 was actually a shrewd move on his part to galvanize everyone into action. He knew just how much preproduction work had been done, and it was not progressing at the pace he liked. Cukor was still fussing with the script; sets and costumes were being argued over; the songs had not yet been orchestrated; there was considerable confusion over who would be the cameraman and who would do the choreography. Much of this Warner must have attributed to Luft's inexperience as a producer, so he decided to take matters in his own hands and give everybody a push. In a memo to Luft dated August 9, Warner made his feelings in the matter clear:

Dear Sid:
After our talk yesterday, I am pretty sure all of us understand each other. Now that we have set a definite starting date of the first, everyone should really start things rolling. Above all it is imperative we get tests underway to get the feel of WarnerScope. With the starting date decided on, we should move everything in our power to that point. Otherwise we will find things going along with indecision, which is always costly and non-productive. It is up to you, Sid, to see that we do not waste money or go overboard. Also, that everything we do spend is photographed. I have great confidence

in you and all connected with the picture, and I know that confidence will pay off.

With the picture due to start in less than six weeks, the production meetings became more intense as everyone involved tried to come to grips with the myriad problems that needed solving and the decisions that needed to be made. Hoyningen-Huene, who had finally been located in Mexico, agreed to work on the picture at $500 weekly; he arrived in mid-August, staying at Cukor's home while he began working with the art-direction staff. Lemuel Ayers had become ill and left the picture in early August; he was replaced by Malcolm Burt, who, as Gene Allen recalls, "had been the draftsman working for Lem; he became the art director and I was made assistant art director. Mal would do all the basics; he'd hear the ideas everyone had—Mr. Cukor, Sid Luft, Judy—about the kind of settings, interiors and exteriors, and see that it was done . . . a very, very professional gentleman.

"Now, when Hoyningen-Huene came on the scene, this was the first movie he'd ever worked on—he'd made some documentaries, I think, but this was the first time he had done anything with a big production. He had very good taste, a background of art second to none—we neither of us had any real jobs, we interchanged and just talked and thought of things. He was terribly creative and helpful, and so we formed a sort of partnership. We were known as Cukor's art boys—he had a great extensive collection of art books, so he would bring in these fine art books and show the cameraman what we had in mind for color or lighting or something and they loved it."

The cameraman who was finally picked was British-born Harry Stradling, in films since 1937, who had previously photographed Garland in *The Pirate*, a lush Technicolor fantasy directed by her then husband Vincente Minnelli, and in *Easter Parade*. His work was characterized by a rich chiaroscuro look, which molded and shaped the mood of a scene. He last had worked at Warners on *A Streetcar Named Desire*, then went to Goldwyn to do *Hans Christian Andersen*, then joined the staff of *A Star Is Born* in early July.

Assistant director Earl Bellamy, who began his duties on the film at about the same time, remembers exactly when he first heard of *A Star Is Born:* "I was working with Mr. Cukor on *It Should Happen to You* in New York. I was organizing a shot in Columbus Circle at rush hour, which was very complicated and nerve-wracking, and I was having a bit of trouble with the police because they thought I'd lost my mind trying to get this shot the way he wanted it, which was in one continuous take as the car drove around. It was a bad moment with all this going on, and Mr. Cukor just barged right into my meeting with the police in the middle of Columbus Circle and said, 'Would you like to do *A Star Is Born* with me over at Warners?' And I said, 'Yes, yes of course, you arrange it.' And we finished the film and some time passed and he came to me and said, 'It's all set, you're going with me over to Warner Brothers,' and I had completely forgotten the incident." Bellamy, a Los Angeles native, had been in the business since he was eighteen. He recalls his days as an office boy in the production office: "I'd get in at four in the morning, check the weather, call the assistant production manager, and we would decide whether or not to send the companies out on location, gamble on it, or keep them in. If we kept them in, I would have to call every member of the crew by phone and say 'Forget the outside call, we're going to work on stage 8 today.' Then I'd call the assistant director and he'd have to call the cast and tell them. Later on I became a second assistant director. He's the one the assistant director turns to and says 'Will you go get Rita Hayworth?' At Columbia they had one production manager and an assistant production manager; and whatever show you were assigned to as first or second assistant, whatever you were required to do, you did it. You did everything. Oftentimes I would go ahead of the company on location, set up all the approximate locations that we might need, get permission to shoot in certain areas if that was needed, and then follow through with setting the rooms for all the crew and making arrangements for all the lunches and the lodgings; and then the company would come out, the director, the assistant, and they'd finalize the locations. After I'd worked for some time I made a five-year plan for myself—I said, 'In five years I want to be a first assistant.' I was lucky, I made it in four. When I became a first, I said, 'In five years I want to be a director.'

"The first time I worked with Mr. Cukor was on *Born Yesterday*. When you worked for him you really had your work cut out for you, because he relied very, very heavily on an assistant director. I would get everything organized for him, make sure that everything he might want was all laid out and ready, and he'd come on the stage in the morning and it was work, work, work. He was a very hard-working man himself and he expected the same from everybody, his cast and his crew—he expected them to be on their toes and to come in prepared. A very interesting thing with him—you could always go up and offer him a suggestion, which I did many times. You would suggest something about a scene, he would stop and rehearse it your way and either he accepted it and liked it or he would turn to you and tell you why he wasn't going to use it or why it didn't work. A good example of that was in *It Should Happen to You.* There's a great bit when Peter Lawford is nuzzling Judy Holliday, and she's trying to fend him off, but she takes off her earring so he can nibble her ear—that was an idea that came from the property man, Blackie, and Mr. Cukor thought it was great, so it's in the film. But that's the way he was, very receptive to people's contributions toward making a good film.

"After *Born Yesterday,* every time he would come to Columbia for a film he would ask that I be with him, which was very flattering. And then when we went to Warners to do *A Star Is Born,* I was still working for Columbia. They mailed me my check every week, which was kind of unique at the time, to be working at one studio but paid by another—at least for an assistant director it was."

Ray Heindorf, the musical director on the picture, had been one of Warners' major assets since 1932. In fact, his career had recently come almost full circle: one of his first jobs in Hollywood had been arranging the songs for the Eddie Cantor musical *Whoopee* in 1930; twenty-three years later he arranged the songs, wrote the background score, and conducted the orchestra for *The Eddie Cantor Story,* one of Warners' bigger (if not better) pictures of 1953. That year was also memorable for Heindorf because his hometown of Mechanicville, New York, had just celebrated his birthday, August 25, by declaring it Ray Heindorf Day. "Actually, it was three days," he recalled. "It was a very strange thing. They invited me back and they had this three-day celebration—it was quite a surprise. I mean, I used to play for silent pictures there when I was a kid; and I went back, and there was my old theater, the State—they were playing *She's Back on Broadway,* and my name was up on the marquee bigger than Virginia Mayo's!

"I'd begun playing piano there about 1922, when I was fourteen. We had a four-piece orchestra: piano, violin, trumpet, and drums. I wasn't interested in school; I was only interested in music. In those days we used to get orchestrations for some of the bigger pictures, for eighteen-piece orchestras, and I'd take the parts home and study them and see what the trombone played and what the horns played and what the instruments we never even saw played, and I'd break these orchestrations down for our four men. My father was very enthusiastic about this, and I'll never forget—in 1924 he took me to Saratoga Springs to hear Paul Whiteman's jazz band play Gershwin's *Rhapsody in Blue*. It had just been played in Carnegie Hall and really was something to hear.

"It was just about this same time that I began to study arranging. I was impressed with one man whose name was on all the important stock arrangements that they sent to the bands. His name was Arthur Lang, so I wrote to him in 1927, asking if he could teach me how to arrange, and he wrote back and said to look him up if I was ever in New York, so right away I went to New York. He had an office on Forty-fourth Street, and we talked and I got a job with him—I was sort of his utility man. I would copy his scores and proofread the printed copies and correct any mistakes. There wasn't any better way of learning to orchestrate than that."

Heindorf worked with Lang on several Broadway shows and in early 1929 accompanied him to Hollywood to oversee the music for MGM's *The Hollywood Revue of 1929*, one of the world's first "All Talking—All Singing—All Dancing" musicals. Heindorf went on to assist Alfred Newman on Eddie Cantor musicals; and by 1932 he found himself at Warner Bros., which prided itself not only on its introduction of sound but also on its use of music throughout a film. "Jack Warner was a great music lover," relates Heindorf, "and I remember he said to me once, 'Ray, you know how we use music here? I want it to start where it says "Warner Brothers Presents" and I want it to end where it says "The End." ' "

In his pre–*A Star Is Born* years at Warners, Heindorf had worked on practically every feature film involving music. His love and genius for music and superb musicianship had made him one of the most respected and able music directors in the business and had earned him a total of fourteen Academy Award nominations. He'd won twice: for arranging and conducting the George M. Cohan songs in *Yankee Doodle Dandy* in 1942, and again the next year for doing the same thing with the film version of Irving Berlin's wartime relief show, *This Is the Army*. His arrangements were brisk, robust, and exciting, with a syncopation and driving excitement that gave life and vigor to even the most lackluster songs. His work on quieter ballads and blues was characterized by a delicate, transparent sheen that subtly underlined the emotion and poignancy of both melody and lyric.

When Leo Forbstein—long in charge of music at Warners—died in

1948, Heindorf was elevated to the head position, which made him responsible for hiring musicians and assigning composers and orchestrators. He was efficient, businesslike, and outspoken in his determination that the Warners music department maintain its reputation as the best in the business—a position that was challenged frequently by his peers Alfred Newman at 20th Century–Fox and Johnny Green at MGM.

On August 13, *A Star Is Born* officially went into the works as production #386. On that day, in the "train shed" on the back lot, the dancers began rehearsing under the direction of Richard Barstow, who had won out over Michael Kidd to do the choreography for the film. Barstow was a specialist in big production numbers: he staged the musical interludes for the Ringling Bros. and Barnum & Bailey Circus, did the dance direction for the Broadway hit *New Faces of 1952*, and pioneered and developed the concept of the "industrial show," whereby a manufacturer would launch his product with a "by invitation only" extravaganza, most notably General Motors with its *Motorama*.

While Barstow and his sister Edith were working with a rehearsal pianist and a troupe of twenty dancers, Garland, still dieting, reported to the studio on August 21 to begin recording the songs on stage 9, the Warner Bros. recording stage, under Heindorf's direction and Cukor's watchful eye. The songs were being recorded with an expensive new state-of-the-art three-channel magnetic stereophonic system which Warners had first used in *House of Wax*, giving the sound a quality of astonishing richness, presence, and depth. Recalls Earl Bellamy: "The first song Judy worked on was 'Here's What I'm Here For.' In the film, she sings it on a recording stage, and then she leaves the microphone and plays the proposal scene with Norman, which unbeknownst to them is picked up by a live microphone and recorded. Now, Judy was very demanding, and she did the song several times, and each time she'd look at Mr. Cukor and he would tell her what he thought, and then they'd listen to the playback, and either she was right on as far as she was concerned or she wasn't and you did it again. Mr. Cukor would let her have her head in this, because he knew she knew best." Recalls Heindorf: "Working with Garland was just magnificent. It was the first time she'd sung in some time, and she was fresh. She knew those songs backward and didn't have to use any music, ever." However, the sessions were marred by a series of testy discussions with her vocal coach, Hugh Martin (who had written the lyrics for one of Garland's best MGM pictures, *Meet Me in St. Louis,* to music by Ralph Blane), over the best way to interpret the song.

Her disposition was not improved the following day by a late-night fire in her bedroom, caused by "faulty wiring," which almost got out of control, necessitating the evacuation of the house while the Beverly Hills fire department handled the situation. The next day she was back at the studio, recording "Gotta Have Me Go With You," the song which Esther Blodgett sings with the band at the Shrine benefit—a rhythm tune, and vocally very tricky. Garland was nervous and edgy from the fire and from the pills she was taking to help her lose weight; once again she differed with Martin over the manner in which the song should be sung. Voices were raised and remarks verging on insult were exchanged, according to the gossip columns in the trades.

On Friday, September 4, at three-thirty in the afternoon, Garland reported to stage 9 for the all-important rendition of "The Man That Got Away." Heindorf had spent several days and nights working on the arrangement with Skip Martin. An ex–saxophone and clarinet player for the Benny Goodman and Glenn Miller orchestras and a highly regarded arranger for Goodman, Charlie Barnet, and Les Brown, Martin had joined MGM in the late 1940s and worked on *The Barkleys of Broadway, Singin' in the Rain,* and *The Band Wagon.* He and Heindorf embellished Arlen's slow and steady beginning with a trombone playing a low blues phrase while Garland hummed. Martin had set the song for an on-screen jazz sextet— piano, bass, guitar, drums, trombone, and tenor sax—shaping the complex song so that it built properly to its climax. (He had written in solos for some of the best jazz talent in Hollywood at the time: Irving "Babe" Russin on tenor sax, Buddy Cole at the piano, and Hoyt Bohannon with the mood-setting trombone solo at the start.) Heindorf then gave the underlying orchestral track a throbbing, intense beat in the drums and the bass, played over an insistent rising and falling figure in the (off-screen) strings and woodwinds, with the full orchestra blasting out on the climactic phrases of the lyric; the entire piece builds to a pounding climax, with a diminuendo on the final phrase—the last statement of the title. The Martin/Heindorf version has turned out to be the best arrangement the song has ever received. Virtually every version recorded over the years has used it or a variation thereof, and Garland used it for years in her concert appearances; the first four bars of trombone solo never failed to evoke appreciative bursts of applause from audiences, who recognized what was coming.

"It was a difficult song to sing because of the range," recalled Heindorf.

"When you do an arrangement for someone, you have to take into account the lowest note that they can sing well, and the highest note they can sing well. No two people sing alike. Now, over the years, I'd heard Judy sing so much that I knew exactly how she'd sing: her phrasing, her intonation, where she'd take a breath. Any good singer will sing a lyric like they would speak it—where there's a comma, they take a breath—and that's just about what good singers do that ordinary singers don't do.

"On 'The Man That Got Away,' the arrangement was made in two keys, B major and D-flat major. It turned out that one arrangement was half a tone too low and the other was half a tone too high, so I transposed it to C and she sang it in that for the recording."

They worked for two hours and did four takes; once again, time was taken up by arguments between Garland and vocal coach Hugh Martin. According to Lawrence Stewart, who witnessed the scene, "She wanted to sing it loud and brassy, but Martin wanted it sweet and in a lower key. After much difficulty, the song was recorded both ways, and Judy's preference was adopted for the picture, because the lower and sweeter version lacked brilliance and all of those dramatic qualities which had to be developed in the song, not only in terms of itself but, more particularly, in terms of its function in the story." Martin was furious at Garland's insistence on doing the song her way, and their long-standing differences over technique and interpretation reached the explosion point. The next day *Daily Variety* reported that "a heated verbal hassle over the way [the song] should be sung resulted in Martin walking off the set in a rage. Later that night he was on a plane back to New York, leaving pic without a vocal coach."

By now, the announced start date of September 1 had come and gone, leading the proverbial "industry observers" to nod sagely and mutter "uh-huh." The incident with Hugh Martin only intensified the speculation that Garland was up to her old ways. When Warners announced a new start date of September 16, Mike Connelly, in his *Hollywood Reporter* column, remarked, "Write it in ice and set it in the sun."

The amount of work still to be done before the picture could begin photography was enormous, but Cukor, hard worker though he was, refused to be rushed into decisions until all possibilities had been thoroughly discussed and tested. Costumes were being designed by Mary Ann Nyberg, a new young designer who had impressed Cukor and Garland with her work at MGM on *The Band Wagon* and *Lili*. Cukor was looking at location photographs trying to decide on a suitable site for the wedding sequence;

he wanted to use real locations as much as possible instead of back-lot sets. Cukor had always liked the verisimilitude that actual places gave to the staging of dramatic action, but it wasn't until after the war that he'd had the opportunity to utilize locations extensively for his exterior shots. Beginning with *Adam's Rib* in 1948, he made it a practice to go on location whenever it would add to the impact of a scene. On *A Star Is Born,* twelve different locations had to be chosen, among them the studio itself, a Hollywood drive-in restaurant, the Malibu beaches, a Beverly Hills church, a cheap rooming house in downtown Los Angeles, the oil fields of Baldwin Hills, and the Lincoln Heights jail. Moreover, there were decisions on the interior sets, sections of the script that needed work, and the casting of the important subsidiary roles.

For the part of Oliver Niles, veteran actor Charles Bickford was signed in early September. Bickford, whom Cukor described as "a reasonable and intelligent man," had a career that dated back to the 1920s on Broadway; he had made his first film, *Dynamite,* for Cecil B. DeMille in 1929. Though Cukor felt that he had the strength and dignity needed for Niles, Bickford was in fact second choice. Efforts had been made to interest William Powell, free-lancing after twenty years as one of MGM's top stars; but he declined, feeling the part was not big enough. Because of his refusal, considerable discussion was given to the idea of rewriting the role to give Niles the Danny McGuire "pep talk" speech near the end, in the hope of attracting a big name for the role, but Hart quickly vetoed this idea: "I feel that it is more dramatic and unexpected if a minor character tips the scales at this point. It would be the normal and conventional way to have the head of the studio, her great friend, persuade her to go on. There is no excitement or surprise in this because throughout the picture Oliver has been functioning more or less in this way."

Several actors had been considered for the part of Matt Libby, the abrasive studio press chief, among them Howard Duff, Pat O'Brien, and Murvyn Vye, but the role finally went to Jack Carson, a former Warner Bros. contract player and an adept light comedian, who had reached fame of sorts co-starring with another Warners contract player, Dennis Morgan, in the *Two Guys from . . .* series in the late forties. After leaving Warners, Carson had starred on Broadway in an unsuccessful revival of *Of Thee I Sing,* then went on to great success in a production of *Girl Crazy* at the Dallas State Fair. Carson was known primarily for his considerable comedic talents, but his abilities as a straight dramatic actor had impressed Cukor as far back as *Mildred Pierce* in 1945. At work, he was a bright, funny man, always "on," but at home he was given to fits of moroseness, sitting for hours drinking, not talking to anyone. Jack Warner liked Carson and asked Cukor to interview him for the part, and afterwards Carson commented in an interview: "We found that we were both in agreement about what a press agent is really like . . . he's nothing more than a businessman . . . he has to be sharp, of course, but primarily he must be a level-headed businessman. Generally, he's a pretty solid individual who works regular hours, then goes home to his wife and kids. The first Matt Libby [in the 1937 version] was too tough to be believable; he was such a heel that all the press people were offended, but they've toned him down considerably this time."

Cukor had several choices for the small but pivotal role of Danny McGuire, the combination of Esther's best friend and her grandmother from the original. He had been favorably impressed with a young actor at 20th Century–Fox named Casey Adams (formerly Max Showalter), but he turned out to be unavailable. Moss Hart mentioned to Cukor that he "saw an actor in Rodgers and Hammerstein's musical play *Me and Juliet* by the name of Ray Walston . . . he's exactly the right age and has a wonderfully right face for Danny. He also happens to be one of the best young actors to have come along in the last ten years." But getting him released from his play commitment was too complicated, and Cukor decided to give the part to a young actor named Tom Noonan, who had just achieved a certain degree of recognition by playing Marilyn Monroe's nebbish boyfriend in Howard Hawks's film of the musical *Gentlemen Prefer Blondes.* Noonan was a nightclub comic who with his partner, Peter Marshall, had headlined such high-visibility night spots as Hollywood's Mocambo, Chicago's Chez Paree, and New York's Latin Quarter. In show business since the age of eleven, the young actor had been in only two films, and the role in *A Star Is Born* would be his first dramatic part.

One small role in the film was filled through a series of events that could have been lifted from Moss Hart's script. In the story, a young starlet evidently is living with Norman Maine; she chatters away while he is trying to distinguish Esther's voice in a television commercial. It's a tiny part, but important in pointing up Norman's appeal, his loneliness, and the vacuous world of film starlets. At Columbia in 1952, Cukor had tested a young actress named Sheree North; he later commented to Warners' casting director William Orr that "she is very attractive, amusing, and has personality. I was impressed with her possibilities . . . I think that properly handled, she could become quite a personality. She is an excellent dancer as well." But prior commitments made North unavailable, much to Cukor's disappointment.

At Warners, one afternoon in early September, Cukor was walking by a projection room with Bill Orr when he heard a voice singing. Orr told him it was the screen test of a twenty-year-old actress from the Pasadena Playhouse named Lucy McAleer. She recalls: "Bill Orr told me that Mr. Cukor looked in at the test and he said, 'That's the little girl I think we'll use for the starlet, Lola Lavery.' So he wanted to meet me. For the test I had done ''S Wonderful' by Gershwin; Merv Griffin was playing the piano and I sang and danced around the piano, ending up sitting on it for the finale.

"So Bill Orr sent me over to Mr. Cukor's home. It was a kind of walled villa above Sunset Boulevard, stucco white walls, and I walked into this heavenly patio. And there was a stairway that led up to the second story from the patio, and the first time I saw Mr. Cukor he was standing at the top of the stairs. He leaned over and said 'Come on up, little one, I'm George Cukor and I want to see what you can do.' So as I was coming up the stairs he said, 'So do you think you're an actress?' and I said, 'Yep, I sure do.' We sat for a few moments and he asked me if I would be willing to do a scene from *The Voice of the Turtle* with a young man who was going to have a screen test at Metro. Mr. Cukor was helping him. So in that room he coached us in *Voice of the Turtle,* and I'm giving it everything I've got, and he kept saying to me things like 'Now, don't give me any of that Pasadena Playhouse junk . . . I want to see what's in you come out.'

"So we worked a week together at his house, and when it was over I was thanking him because he told me I had the part, and I was so excited, and he said, 'Okay, where do you get it?' And I said, 'Get *what?*' And he said, 'It's in the blood, little one—you've got it in the blood. And I want to know, there must have been some actress somewhere in your family.' So I told him, 'Well, nobody you'd know. My great-aunt was an actress on the New York stage—her best friend was Ethel Barrymore.' Well, now, I didn't know that Mr. Cukor's best friend was Ethel Barrymore, so he looked at me somewhat suspect and he said, 'Oh really, who would that have been?' So I told him her name was Anita Rothie and he went, 'Oh my God, not Schatzi!' It turned out he knew her, very well. He said, 'That woman was out of her mind . . . she was crazy! If ever there was a ham, it was Schatzi.

So that's where you get it!' So we had a very nice feeling to start off with."
McAleer was given a term contract by Warners at Cukor's urging.

The same week that she was added to the studio's roster, Warners lost
one of its mainstays when Humphrey Bogart and Warners agreed to cancel
the remainder of their nonexclusive contract, thus putting an end to a
twenty-year professional relationship. There has been some speculation
over the years that Bogart was angry at not being given the role of Norman
Maine; but more than likely Bogart just wanted his freedom, and his
one-picture-a-year deal with Warners was interfering with his ability to take
on all the choice roles that had been offered to him since winning an
Academy Award the previous year for *The African Queen*. He was the last
of the major prewar stars to leave the studio, and his departure marked the
end of an era.

So did another decision made by Jack Warner that week. On September 16, he announced that the studio was cutting back on the use of
Technicolor in its productions and would henceforth concentrate on the
new Eastman single-strip method of color photography and printing.
Warners and Technicolor had an even longer relationship than Warner
and Bogart: the studio had first used the process back in 1928, when it
was still a two-color system. It had taken up the new Technicolor three-
color process in 1936 and had used it in a succession of beautifully colored films, carefully designed to take full advantage of Technicolor's advanced technology in both photography and printing. But it was an
expensive, cumbersome, and time-consuming system, requiring a camera
that exposed three separate strips of film, with a consequent increase in
production cost due to the additional raw stock and lighting expenses.
Also, it took several days for color "dailies" to be processed and returned
from Technicolor's lab in Hollywood. Over the years the company had
tried to simplify its technique, going so far as to develop, in conjunction
with Eastman Kodak, a single-strip color reversal film called Monopack
(which was nothing more than a 35mm version of Kodachrome), but the
results achieved with this were markedly inferior to the three-strip
method, and producers were loath to use it. Eastman finally introduced
its own single-strip color negative and print stocks for commercial industry use in early 1950. The results were still inferior to Technicolor; but it
was cheaper and faster, and Eastman had the marketing sense to make it
available to any and all comers, letting them process it in their own labs
if so desired and allowing them to give it any name they liked. Warners

first used the process in 1952 for *The Lion and the Horse*, giving it the imaginative name of WarnerColor. The process was not as versatile or as subtle as Technicolor; it gave skin tones a harsh quality and had an annoying predilection for the blue end of the spectrum and for reds that could be overpoweringly garish. These defects could be minimized, however; and Technicolor, seeing the handwriting on the wall, adapted its technology so that it could deliver to a producer release prints made on Eastmancolor stock, or use the Eastmancolor negative to make prints using its own fabled dye-transfer system. By September 1953, when Warner made his announcement, the studio was using Technicolor only for its biggest pictures and applying WarnerColor to its more modestly budgeted features, usually comedies and westerns. Another unspoken factor in Warner's decision was the discovery that the WarnerScope anamorphic lens could not be used with the Technicolor three-strip process; the resultant images were coarse, grainy, and poorly defined. This had been discovered almost immediately by Twentieth Century–Fox cameramen, who had the same problem with their first CinemaScope lenses: the studio had quietly switched over to an Eastman negative for *The Robe* and *How to Marry a Millionaire*, with exhibition prints made by its own Deluxe Color Laboratories. (Some prints had been made by Technicolor using the Eastmancolor method, so the films could still be advertised as being "in Technicolor.") Because of this, there had been a sudden run on Eastman's stock of color negative in early 1953, resulting in a considerable shortage for two months. By early September this situation had been rectified, and Warners announced that henceforth WarnerColor would be the studio's choice. This was just one more example of how the industry was shifting away from its long-established patterns.

Jack Warner made this announcement on September 16, perhaps trying to draw attention away from the fact that *A Star Is Born* had missed another start date. He needn't have worried, for on that day the industry's attention was focused on the Roxy Theatre in New York, where the long-awaited, much-ballyhooed premiere of the first CinemaScope picture, *The Robe*, was taking place. For three months prior to the picture's unveiling, 20th Century–Fox had mounted a massive promotional and advertising campaign to sell the CinemaScope process to the public and especially the exhibitors. Spyros Skouras was everywhere that summer and fall, demonstrating, selling the system, making speeches at theater owners' conventions, meeting with heads of theater chains, equipment suppliers, and bankers and financiers—anyone and everyone who could possibly be of any influence or importance in the task of persuading the industry to take up CinemaScope. The publicity and the coverage reached proportions unseen since the furor over *Gone With the Wind* back in 1939–40, climaxed by three separate pieces in *Life* magazine: one on CinemaScope, one on *The Robe*, and one a profile of Skouras himself. This had been preceded by extensive coverage in all the major news media except television, so that by September 16 more than twelve hundred theaters were equipped and eager to show *The Robe* in all its CinemaScopic, four-track stereophonic glory. This was a marketing feat of astounding proportions, even by the inflated standards of Hollywood: in less than seven months, Skouras, Zanuck, and Fox had organized, financed, and implemented a three-pronged program of film production, equipment design and manufacture, and theater conversion, all designed to change forever the shape and economics of making and showing films. Whether their efforts would be successful depended to a large degree on critical and public reaction to *The Robe* itself, and most of the New York critics were impressed with the film and the process, the New York *Daily News* going so far as to give the picture an eight-star rating—four for the film and four for CinemaScope. It was a relieved and jubilant Spyros Skouras who entered New York's El Morocco for the postpremiere party, waving the *Daily News* at everyone and shouting exuberantly and endlessly, "We did it! . . . We did it!" The debut was such a success that *Variety* editorialized: "Showbiz has reached the thrill-jaded end of a long series of near-miracles, including Cinerama, which pulled the chute . . . [The] business has gone a million light years since it was 'sensational' when the New York Hippodrome got twelve elephants in one scene. What'll they have to do in 1963 to blow off some eyebrows?"

One person in New York who had his eyebrows blown off was Jack Warner's taciturn elder brother Albert, vice-president and treasurer of the company. He was extremely admiring of not only the CinemaScope process but also the manner in which it had been packaged and sold; he was even more impressed as he watched the crowds form lines around the Roxy at all hours of the day and night. By the end of its first week, the picture had set a record for the largest seven-day gross in film history—$267,000*—and

---

*The old Roxy record had been set in 1947 by *Forever Amber*, which took in $180,000. The previous New York theatrical record of $184,000 was set by MGM's *Million Dollar Mermaid* during Christmas week at the Radio City Music Hall in 1952.

Albert, watching all the excitement and the money *The Robe* was generating, began wondering if WarnerScope might not possibly be crushed under the wheels of the CinemaScope bandwagon.

While Albert watched and pondered in New York, Jack, three thousand miles away in Burbank, was waiting for the new WarnerScope lenses to arrive from Germany while at the same time trying to speed up the preproduction work on *A Star Is Born*. Garland, recording the rest of the songs, was still trying to lose weight, under a doctor's supervision and with the help of her "diet pills"—Dexedrine, which kept her nervous and irritable. Luft had his hands full, trying to cope with her moods and juggling the various other problems that kept cropping up, not the least of which was Jack Warner's simultaneously telling him to speed things up and insisting that they wait for the new lenses. Cukor, Hoyningen-Huene, Allen, and the other members of the production team were continuing to test fabrics, paints, and lighting, this time to see how using WarnerColor would affect the look of the picture. The consensus, according to a letter Cukor wrote to Hart, was that "Warnercolor is difficult to control and is not true. It's all in such a state of experimentation that I think it will hurt the picture more than help. Judy's tests in Technicolor, however, are perfectly charming. She looks young, radiant, and alive. One thing we found from these tests is that a touch of color near her face, especially a light color, is very becoming to her."

In the same letter, Cukor brought up some reservations that Luft had about the dialogue in several early scenes, particularly the spoken asides as Maine, after waking up in the middle of the night, talks to himself, trying to remember the name of the girl singer and where she was singing. According to Cukor, Luft suggested that the dialogue be eliminated and the scene be played in pantomime. Hart agreed that this might make the scene work better and told Cukor to eliminate the dialogue. Luft was also troubled by the long dialogue scene between Norman and Esther in the "dive" after "The Man That Got Away," which Hart had set entirely in a booth in the club. It was an important scene, for it is the first time the audience learns anything of Esther's background and her yearnings, and it is the first time that Norman is shown in a sympathetic, human light. But Luft felt that the scene was long, static, and expository—a scene for the stage, not for motion pictures. Cukor evidently did not agree, for he did not mention Luft's reservations to Hart.

Instead, he asked Hart to rewrite the Academy Awards humiliation scene, which had remained largely intact from the original; Hart's only changes were in placing Norman at Vicki's table throughout the ceremony, instead of having him stagger in drunk midway through her acceptance speech, and in Norman's speech, which was contrite and begging as opposed to the original's anger, contempt, and ridicule. Cukor evidently liked the idea of Norman coming in late and asked Hart to reinstate this. He also asked Hart to rewrite the dialogue of the presenters, which Hart, largely unfamiliar with Academy Awards ceremonies, had lifted virtually intact from the earlier version. In his request to Hart Cukor wrote: "Here's the transcript of the last Academy 'do'. We might come in when the award is being presented for the best male performance. During this action, we cut to our principals, indicating—with your usual adroitness—that there is a place at table for Norman, but so far he has not shown up. We proceed as is, with the award being given to Esther, with the correct ceremonies. Then Norman (not in evening clothes, drunk) coming to the dais as in the old picture."

Hart rewrote the scene, but he didn't do his homework well, for he left the location of the scene at the Cocoanut Grove. The awards had not been given out in that type of setting since 1942, America's first year of active participation in World War II, when the Academy governors decided that a lavish banquet would be inappropriate and transferred the ceremonies to a theater—first Grauman's Chinese, then the RKO Pantages on Hollywood Boulevard. Strangely, despite Cukor's insistence on realism and accuracy in depicting Hollywood manners and customs, he did not suggest that Hart change the setting from the Cocoanut Grove to a theater. He may have figured that the public at large was not familiar with the circumstances of the presentation and wouldn't notice this anachronism; but by the time the picture was ready for release, television had covered the awards twice, and most moviegoers who saw *A Star Is Born* were puzzled by this jarring incongruity. (In Hart's rewrite, the only reference to the new reality of television at the awards was a descriptive phrase describing "a large television screen . . . on which is being duplicated the same action as is taking place on the little stage.")

Cukor was now writing Hart an average of two letters weekly, requesting new dialogue, asking his advice and opinions on staging the action and bits of business for the extras, and suggesting changes. Discussing a scene where Niles is called down to a set because Norman refuses to come out of his dressing room, Cukor wrote:

I think we have cooked up a very good pictorial ending for [this]. We will show Oliver driving on to the lot, an atmospheric view of the studio in the background . . . unfinished sets . . . streets, etc. . . . all very picturesque. The cast and crew, as you will describe them, will be sitting around waiting. The Company is presumably shooting a waterfront village some place on the China Sea, with a wonderful junk, sails unfurled, in the background. (This already exists—kindness of Warner Bros.) Oliver plays the scene with the director (as in the script), then, to find Norman, he walks behind a large plaster cyclorama—all these sets are on the exterior. Norman comes out of his portable dressing room looking like hell, a drink in his hand, dressed in trousers and in his own shirt. He should present a very discouraging picture, and look absolutely unfit for work, not drunk, however. (I am reminded of the time I took Oliver Messel [the costume designer] to the Wardrobe Department at Metro to meet Jack Barrymore. Oliver had designed a most dashing costume for "Mercutio," and when he saw a rather seedy gentleman, well past middle age with the suggestion of a pot belly, rather woozy on beer, his heart sank, he felt all was lost. Then Jack put on the costume. By some alchemy, he was now tall, slender, supple and young.) I would like to get some of that effect here, as Norman comes out of his dressing room—an insignificant, uninteresting little man. We play the scene with Oliver exactly as is, down to the very end where he says, "Why Oliver—you're really angry with me. Can't have that." . . . He suddenly rises, puts on a wonderful, colorful costume, a Marco Polo kind of pirate. A miraculous transformation takes place. He is young, vibrant, picturesque. He puts one foot on a rope and swings himself up to the deck of the junk. One should feel that in his slightly drunken state, this is a very tricky and foolhardy procedure. However, he makes it. We do a short bit of Douglas Fairbanks action, such as dueling and fade-out. All this would require just a slight change in the line, "Come to the set and watch me play a scene." He should, however, speak the speech, "You look like a crooked bond salesman when you're mad"—and then he takes off.

In the same letter, dated September 20, Cukor asked Hart:

What do you think of this bit of business for scene seven? In the Wild West Show, the star performer is on his horse, stage centre, and the cowgirls ride by him very rapidly from one side of the stage to the other. He ropes them as they cross in front of him. It might be amusing to have some attractive girls on their horses, waiting in the wings to make their entrance. Norman flirts and carries on with one of them. There might even be a suggestion of his threatening to mount—not the girl—but the horse, and ride on during the act. This could give a sense of danger during the scene with Libby, as though Norman might do something very foolhardy at that moment.

Cukor's constant worrying about the script and suggesting new ideas to Hart may seem a form of badgering, but they were simply his way of straightening out what he felt to be "kinks" in the screenplay. He remarked once:

> I rely a great deal on the script, perhaps because I came from the theatre. I have always had a respect almost amounting to reverence for the writer and his contribution. . . . If it's good, if it works, I stick with it, every comma, every pause. I have ideas about the script, of course, yet I would not call myself a writer . . . maybe what [stops me] is the physical writing of the thing. I could never undertake to write a scene.* I can only have suggestions that work or don't work. . . . Damn few directors can write . . . I have too much respect for good writers to think of taking over that job.

One of the main reasons that Cukor was writing to Hart so often, aside from his concerns about the script, was that preproduction on the film had reached the point where nothing more could be done until the new WarnerScope lenses arrived from Germany. This finally happened on September 20, and a series of tests with this "improved" lens showed that it could pass light slightly faster and had a greater depth of field (the distance from front to back in which a scene is in focus). But there were still distortion problems and a distracting horizontal curvature. Cukor and Luft thought the results not much better than with the older lenses, but Warner seemed resolute that they use WarnerScope on *A Star Is Born.* An impasse had been reached, and no one seemed able to convince Warner that the picture might suffer from using the anamorphic lens.

Cukor by now had almost resigned himself to filming *A Star Is Born* in WarnerScope and decided that a little homework was in order. The Hollywood premiere of *The Robe* was set for September 24 at Grauman's Chinese; at Cukor's suggestion, arrangements had been made for a Warner camera crew to cover the opening, in the hope that some of the footage—

---

*"Of all the films I have directed," recalled Cukor, "I can remember only one word of dialogue that I ever inserted into a film. This was Mary Boland's comment in *The Women* on the problems her latest marital breakup might cause. To the list of calamities that loomed, the scandal, the loss of money, etc., I told her to add the words 'La Publicité.' "

the crowds, the glamour, and the excitement—could be used in *A Star Is Born*. "We might get some interesting details," Cukor commented in a memo to Luft. "I think I might go myself to take a look at things." The event was every bit as spectacular as the New York opening—everybody who was anybody in Hollywood at the time was jammed into the theater to see whether CinemaScope was really "the new dimensional photographic marvel" that the ads and the New York reviews said it was. The consensus that evening was that it *was* a milestone of sorts; but Cukor had some serious reservations: "It is the most terrible shape. . . . There is hardly any cutting at all; much of the picture is filmed in long static takes, which could be good if it were handled properly. The screen is immense, and they hadn't really worked out what to do with all that space, so the composition was very awkward, very unimaginative."

The premiere was covered for Warners by cinematographer Winton Hoch, using the three-strip Technicolor camera and a standard camera equipped with a WarnerScope lens and Eastman Color film. Seeing this footage and comparing the two processes finally convinced Warner that Luft and Cukor were right. The WarnerScope images, even with the dozens of searchlights that were lining the boulevard for the occasion, were grainy, muddy, poorly defined, whereas the Technicolor footage was bright, sharp, and lush. Since much of *A Star Is Born* took place at night, it was obvious that photographing the picture with the WarnerScope lenses would detract from its effectiveness. For all the tests that had been made with the anamorphic lens, no one had thought to test it under nighttime conditions.

So Warner reluctantly gave in, and on September 30 Cukor exultantly wrote to Hart: "THE DYE IS CAST! We start shooting—willy-nilly—next Monday, October fifth, or very soon thereafter. I'm happy to say, no WarnerScope or WarnerColor—it's to be done on a large screen (not as hue-age as CinemaScope) and in Glorious Technicolor . . . Everything is going forward most satisfactorily . . . casting, the sets. . . . As you know, George Huene is our color co-ordinator. His ideas for the use of color are thrilling. We're all of us full of hope and confidence and excited. We'll do our best not to let you down."

In line with Hoyningen-Huene's ideas, Cukor sent a memo to Luft and the assistant directors saying, "I would like to make it a practice that we control the color of the clothes worn by the extras and bit players before we go into each scene. This should be co-ordinated with Mr. Huene."

Hoyningen-Huene himself expounded on this later: "Color pictures usually have too much color. Color should be disciplined and an emotional stimulant. A dramatic presentation selects only those events and characters that move it forward and keep it within boundaries. Extraneous incidents and people are left out. We tried to do this in A *Star Is Born*. Instead of permitting just any color to get into a scene and react on the consciousness of the audience, we selected our colors carefully, so that each had something to do with the mood or characterizations. Two basic things were considered in evolving the color patterns of scenes: (1) the mood, (2) the color of Judy Garland's costumes. Colors of everything else were designed in keeping with these rules." In line with this dictum, it was Hoyningen-Huene's responsibility, in Cukor's words, "to select every bit of material. . . . If we need a grey on a wall or a chair, anywhere, he looks it over, scrutinizes it, and if it's the wrong grey, too blue perhaps, he changes it. He edits color and nothing escapes him."

To edit color, of course, it must first be tested, and since the color of Garland's costumes was one of the primary factors in the color scheme, they all had to be tested, preferably while she was wearing them, as they might not work with her makeup and her complexion. Here Cukor et al. ran into their first bit of Garland temperament. She kept postponing the costume and makeup tests, and time was running short if the scheduled start date of October 5 was to be met. It may be that she was harried with too many details piling up on her at the last minute; or perhaps she was not in physical shape to be testing costumes—she was still dieting, and the somewhat too rapid weight loss was giving her a haggard look. Garland had always been sensitive about her looks, ever since she was described by a well-meaning Louis B. Mayer as "my little hunchback" in the early days of her career. In view of her lack of confidence in her personal appearance, the idea of photographic tests may have been nerve-wracking; also, the realization that the picture was about to go into production may have unnerved her. She was making her first film in four years—for her own company, true; but still, the pressure to prove herself all over again to Hollywood and the world must have been frightening.

Whatever the reasons, Garland kept delaying these all-important tests, prompting Jack Warner to send a memo to Luft: "I understand that Judy will not test any wardrobe until Monday or Tuesday. This means that you will not be able to get the film back from Technicolor until Thursday or Friday, and if we are going to find ourselves behind the eight ball again

. . . I am worried about all the delays and nervous tension, and we want to get this picture going."

Luft, as producer, was supposed to be able to control his star, but his star was also his wife. The upshot of Luft's persuasive attempts was that Garland refused to test her costumes until she felt like it, so the start date was pushed back once more, this time to October 12. This latest delay cost the picture the services of cameraman Harry Stradling, who had agreed to do the film based on the September start date and a three-month shooting schedule, after which he would immediately film the Warners epic *Helen of Troy* in Europe. With *A Star Is Born* now due to begin in October, Stradling bowed out and was replaced by Winton Hoch, who had already photographed the second-unit footage of the Hollywood premiere of *The Robe* which was to be used in the opening sequences of *A Star Is Born*, intercut with material that Cukor would film at the Shrine Auditorium, thereby giving an air of realism to the staged activity. Hoch was one of the pre-eminent Technicolor cameramen, having won three Academy Awards for his color work, most recently for John Ford's *The Quiet Man* in 1952. A former research chemist with Technicolor and a stickler for by-the-book shooting, he was notorious for refusing to shoot sequences because the conditions weren't "perfect" for Technicolor photography. Cukor probably knew of Hoch's reputation for stubbornness, but he always liked working with gifted professionals and so made no objection when Hoch was added to his staff. Besides, he had other things on his mind. In the week between October 5 and the new start date of October 12, Warner for some reason decided, as Cukor related to Hart, "to make the picture not only on the large screen in Technicolor but in WarnerScope as well. That means that your immortal prose will be played twice. The task looks formidable but . . . what *is* the Warner motto? Love conquers all?" This conceit on the part of Warner lasted only briefly, until it was pointed out to him that it would double both the shooting schedule and the budget; moreover, the studio had only three WarnerScope lenses, two of which were in use on a Guy Madison Western called *Rear Guard* while the other was scheduled for a Doris Day musical called *Lucky Me*, due to go into production within the month.* There was also Albert Warner's reservation, voiced earlier in the month, that he did not think it wise to use something as untried and

---

*Rear Guard was in production in the two-camera three-dimensional process using the WarnerScope lenses. It would have been the first anamorphic 3-D picture but was ultimately released in a non–3-D version as *The Command.*

untested as WarnerScope on a picture that looked to become an expensive prestige item. The process might work to the advantage of low-budget Westerns and musicals, but it would not necessarily be advantageous to the Garland film. As treasurer of the company, Albert Warner still was watching carefully the fantastic public and exhibitor response to CinemaScope, and he did not want to get into a marketing war with 20th Century–Fox by trying to introduce another new process that could only place second in the anamorphic sweepstakes. Indeed, he had tried to talk economic sense to his younger brother and convince him to take Fox's offer of a license for CinemaScope, but Jack was adamant about sticking with WarnerScope. He did, however, finally agree that *A Star Is Born* should be filmed in wide-screen only; so a press release, carefully worded to put the situation in the best possible light, was issued, stating:

> Jack L. Warner today declared that *A Star Is Born* will be photographed for general large-screen viewing and not in the proportions required for Warner-Scope projection. "We have been testing the WarnerScope lenses for the last two weeks," said Warner, "and are simply delighted with the taking and projecting results produced for us by the Zeiss Optical works. . . . [The process] right now exceeds in many respects the fine qualities we had looked for. But after two weeks of tests and careful re-examination of the many important values in the Moss Hart script we are convinced that the best results for . . . *A Star Is Born* can only be realized by not trying to stretch out an intimate story to meet the enormous area of WarnerScope. As we have often stated in the past several months, we will assign our . . . process only to those stories which are best adapted to the medium, such as *The Talisman,* * by Sir Walter Scott, *Helen of Troy,* and *Land of the Pharaohs.*"

This announcement brought a great sigh of relief from Luft, Cukor, and everyone else involved with the film, and it almost immediately unleashed the whirlwind of activity that would finally put the long-delayed production in front of the Technicolor cameras.

In late July, the latest approved script had been sent to the production offices of Warner veteran T. C. ("Tenny") Wright, eagle-eyed, tight-fisted, and one of Jack Warner's most valued servants. As general studio manager, he would be responsible for seeing that production #386 was brought in on schedule and on budget—no easy task. In his office, with the unit

---

*Released as *King Richard and the Crusaders* (1954).

manager, Robert Heasley, who would be his surrogate, Wright and the assistant directors broke the script down into a short synopsis of each scene, describing the set, the cast needed, including bit players and extras, and their wardrobe. From this breakdown, a shooting schedule was made up, estimating the number of days each character actually worked, how many days each would be "carried" (not needed for work but kept on the payroll for future use), the total number of days needed for the completion of each character's role, and the amount of time allotted for each set or location. This shooting schedule was then sent to the various departments involved in the film, where it was integrated into their overall work load.

The first and most important of these was the art department, where the thirty sets needed for the picture were in various stages of preparation, based on the production meetings, conferences with Cukor and the art director, and Gene Allen's rough sketches. The detailed blueprints drawn up here were then sent to the construction/crafts building (actually one of the old glass-enclosed silent stages), where they were built in the order in which they would be photographed. These sets ranged from the comparatively simple (a tunnel under the Shrine Auditorium) to the more elaborate (Norman Maine's home, the newlyweds' Malibu beach house, a detailed reproduction of the famed Cocoanut Grove, and an expanded, glamorized version of Jack Warner's personal office to be used as Oliver Niles's executive suite). Constructing, painting, and decorating these sets was one of the costliest items in the picture's budget. Even though sections of older, existing sets could be used, the costs of new materials, practical plumbing, plaster, floors, woodwork, iron works, rugs, paintings, furniture, etc. were enormous. Given Cukor's meticulous attention to detail, Hoyningen-Huene's unusual ideas for color, and Allen's modernistic interior designs, the problems of color, texture, wallpapers, paints, lacquers, and varnishes took on more complication and cost than was usual for a Warners film.

Further hampering the coordination of the sets and furnishings were problems in the wardrobe department, which was busy creating the costumes (including thirty separate designs for Garland), all of which, as pointed out earlier by Hoyningen-Huene, were prime elements in the overall color scheme of each sequence. Garland had finally shown up for her costume tests—at least for those costumes that had been designed and constructed. Garland had a difficult figure to design for. "She was heavy, she had no waistline, and her hips started under the bustline," recalled Walter Plunkett, who had designed for her at MGM. Mary Ann

Nyberg, who was designing her clothes for *A Star Is Born*, found her job made difficult by the constant revisions of the script and Garland's weight fluctuations and changes of mind. According to Christopher Finch in *Rainbow:*

> Never having worked with [Garland] before, [Nyberg] went into the project with some trepidation and a good deal of excitement. . . . She thought Judy one of the most delightful and charming people she had ever met. The star put their relationship on a chummy girl-to-girl basis. . . . For the Academy Award sequence, Nyberg had designed a . . . white dress—intended to emphasize the innocence of the character. When this garment was completed [Garland] loved it so much that she decided she must keep it for her personal use. Warning . . . Nyberg that she would hate her for what she was about to do, Judy proceeded to throw a tantrum for the benefit of Jack Warner and [Cukor]: "Look at this thing! How can you expect me to wear this! It makes me look like the great white whale." So the white dress was put away for Judy's future pleasure, and a new one—black with purple overlay—was made to replace it.

Apocryphal, perhaps, but there *were* two separate dresses made for the scene. And with the time involved, the design, the fabrics, and other materials to be used, and the salaries of dressmakers, pleaters, embroiderers, bead workers, and fitters, preparing the costumes could well cost thousands of dollars, even under the watchful eyes of Wright and Heasley.

While sets and costumes were being readied, the script was sent to the electrical department. Here the size of the sets and time allotted to each was computed, and from these figures was estimated the number of electricians and lights, the amount of electricity necessary, the time needed to light the sets, and the equipment that would be needed—what was at the studio and what would have to be rented from outside. Lighting a film is an exacting, time-consuming task, especially with a mood-conscious director like Cukor, who wanted to experiment with color and lighting effects on *A Star Is Born*.

While this was being worked out, the camera department was going over its copy of the script, assigning the necessary equipment and allotting the requisite amount of film, both negative and positive stock. The average footage for a feature at Warners was approximately 100,000 feet of negative, 60,000 feet of positive for the daily rushes, and the same amount for soundtrack footage. (Even though *A Star Is Born* was being recorded on magnetic tape, the editing of the track would be on photographic film.) Since the picture was to be photographed in Technicolor, the camera and the film would all be supplied by that company, boosting raw negative footage to 300,000, since the Technicolor camera exposed three strips of film simultaneously. Warner Bros. was a thrifty studio; under an order from Jack Warner himself, the camera and film departments were ordered to save all unused "short ends" of film for use by the laboratory when making dissolves and fades. Pat Clark, assigned to the picture to photograph stills of each scene for publicity, was also schooled in the Warner tradition of thrift—which in this case meant photographing only one still of each scene and not each separate camera setup, as was the practice at most other major studios.

Also assigned to the picture at this time was Alma D. Young as "script clerk"—the person (usually a woman) who sat beside the director on the set, timing the scenes, noting which lens was used, any changes in dialogue, how many takes of a scene were made, which ones the director wanted to print up and which to hold for printing later if something was unacceptable in the chosen take, what clothing the performers wore, what props they were using, and seemingly insignificant details such as the folding of a pocket handkerchief, the length of a burning candle or cigarette, and which hand the actors used when gesturing or the way their arms were folded.

This procedure in breaking down and estimating the script was carried out by every department that would have anything remotely to do with the production—special effects, process photography, editing, music, location, props, sound—so that by the first week of October, the sets, costumes, cameras, lights, technicians, and actors for *A Star Is Born* were ready and waiting for Cukor finally to begin photography on the second Monday in October.

Production

Monday, October 12—Columbus Day. Indian Summer was still keeping the Los Angeles basin pleasant: foggy in the mornings; warm, even hot, during the day. In Burbank, assistant director Earl Bellamy checked into the Warner Bros. studio at 6:30 a.m. and, along with the second assistant director, Warners veteran Russell Llewellyn, began coping with the first of the many crises that would plague *A Star Is Born* over the next nine months. The scenes prepared for the first day of shooting all involved James Mason as Norman Maine; Garland was not scheduled to work until the following day. As Mason recalled: "One constantly heard people saying, 'They're supposed to start shooting next week, but Judy'll never make it.' So it was ironical that I, whose reputation for punctuality was impeccable, was the one to hold up production for the first couple of days. My inner ear went on the blink, causing a chronic dizziness, so that if I turned over in my sleep, I would wake up with a sensation that I was about to tumble out of bed."

This had happened late Friday, and over the weekend Mason had called Bellamy, who informed Cukor and the production department. The schedule was juggled so that the first scene to be filmed would be that of Esther being a stand-in, waving her arm from a train window while snow whirled about her—the scene that Cukor had cooked up to replace a shorter, less satiric sequence in Hart's original. At 7:00, Bellamy and Llewellyn were on the train set—a permanent fixture on the back lot—checking the crew, the lighting, and all the necessary equipment and props.

Then the two men split up, Bellamy remaining on the set to attend to details while Llewellyn went to get Garland's stand-in. Llewellyn relates: "I'd take her over to the set so they could work out the lighting with her. Then I'd go by the casting office and get a list of the actors that were coming through—bit people and the like—and get them over to makeup, make certain they were all there and in the right costume. On that first day, for that scene, we had three bit players and twenty-six Central Casting extras and one automobile. The extras were all what we call atmosphere—they walked around in the back of the set, or in the foreground, or outside the stage door, so it would look like a busy movie studio. Then I'd get hold of a standby driver and tell him to go and stay by the makeup department or wardrobe department and make sure that our people were all brought out to the set on time. Then I'd go over to Judy Garland's dressing room and see how things were coming along there."

Jack Warner had given Garland Bette Davis's old dressing room, and on this first morning there was a memo from him on her dressing table:

Dear Sid and Judy:
Now that the picture is underway, we all feel, and I know you do too, that we are embarked upon a very important event, one of which we can all be proud. The culmination will tell its own story. Every good wish to you both.
Sincerely,
Jack

Garland was due on the set at 10:00, so she had been in her dressing room since 7:30, having her hair done and being made up by her makeup man, Del Armstrong, a free-lance who'd spent years at MGM, where he had specialized in working on Lana Turner. For *A Star Is Born,* he had been hired by Luft as an independent department head. "Gordon Bau was the head of Warners' makeup at the time," recalled Armstrong, "but Sid had told me, 'It's a big picture, and you're in complete charge.' So what I did was take a unit of the makeup department and I'd put in a request each day for what help I would need, through them. So I didn't take their power away.

"Now, on *A Star Is Born,* I'd get to Judy's dressing room around seven, which is when she's supposed to be there. And the hair stylist would be there with me, and we'd get ourselves some coffee and wait for her to come in. Nine times out of ten, she wouldn't be there at seven o'clock, but on this first day she was on time. We had the makeup set up in her room, as against the makeup department. She didn't want to go into the makeup department. That was a throwback to the old MGM days, because none of the big stars would go into the makeup department; we'd always go to them in their dressing rooms—they had very elaborate dressing rooms. So

Judy came in and we started. Usually the hair stylist would work on her first, put her hair up. While that's going on I'd sit in the other room and read the paper or have coffee. It could be an hour—just Judy, the hairdresser, and the wardrobe girl, and you could hear the three of them giggling and talking and visiting, comparing notes about what happened last night, or what didn't happen.

"Then I'd take over. The whole process shouldn't take more than two hours, even today. My approach to making up a star is simple: I make them up so that if they look good to you, to the eye, then there's no reason why they won't look good to the camera. With Judy, there was one problem—it was the same problem Lana had—no eyebrows. Because in the early days of glamour, they used to tweeze them quite a bit so they could make exaggerated shapes, and if you tweeze your eyebrows too much, then they just don't grow back. So I had some hair lace, like for a mustache or wigs, and I had some eyebrows made for Judy for this picture. You couldn't just pencil them in, because there's no dimension. A pencil is flat—pencilling is fine for a still picture, but for a motion picture people are turning their heads and you can see that it's flat. So I put these eyebrows on Judy."

While Garland was being made up, Cukor, Gene Allen, and Hoyningen-Huene had all arrived on the train set and were working out the blocking and the camera movements and fine-tuning the lighting. Cukor had been greeted on the set with two memos. One was from Jack Warner, telling him:

Delighted we are getting underway . . . and want to wish you every success and much happiness in the making of *A Star Is Born.* If there is anything I can do to aid you, just call me on 238 or 239, my office numbers.

Best wishes,

Sincerely,
Jack

The other memo was from the camera department, reminding Cukor and Winton Hoch that the image should be composed for the new 1:75 ratio, since the picture would be released in wide-screen. To facilitate this, a rectangular box had been etched into the camera viewfinder in the correct proportion, making it easier for Hoch to see where the top and the bottom of an image would be when the picture was exhibited in theaters. The memo reassured them: "Don't worry about the fact that the camera is picking up more picture than we need. This will be eliminated in the release prints as Technicolor will print the image to conform to this ratio."

It took nearly two hours to light the set. At 10:00 Cukor finished rehearsing action with the stand-in; the camera movements were all fixed, and the bit people and the extras had been rehearsed in their action. The time had come to film the scene. Bellamy sent Llewellyn to tell Garland that they were ready. She arrived on the set at 10:10, nervous but jovial, showing Cukor the bracelet that Luft had given her that morning, inscribed: "Columbus discovered America on October 12, 1492. Judy Garland began principal photography on *A Star Is Born* on October 12, 1953. With all my love—Sid." Garland wanted to wear it in the scene, Cukor agreed, and they began rehearsal.

The scene had been added to the script verbatim from Cukor's description to Hart, but it lacked details. So for the next half-hour, as Cukor rehearsed Garland, he also improvised dialogue for the bit players acting the parts of director, cameraman, assistant director, and wardrobe girl. Cukor elaborated on his working methods on a set: "The first three or four days on the set I'm rather shaky, but I plunge into my work just the same. . . . On those shaky first days . . . I'm not absolutely confident . . . everyone's nervous at first, I suppose. . . . When I work the atmosphere has to be happy, cheerful . . . amusing and funny. . . . That doesn't mean there aren't all sorts of crises, but I will not put up with strain—I can't think if I'm distracted. And I will not have unpleasant pressures on the set. Unless I'm sympathetic with people, I cannot function. The climate on the set includes relations with the actors, and with everybody, in fact. The hours are very long. You've got to be perfectly natural about the whole thing. No patronizing, no putting on airs. You're on the set under great strain from eight in the morning until seven at night . . . but you can't spend that long day with a cathedral hush over the whole place. I don't mind noise . . . I like everybody to be working in a perfectly relaxed manner. . . . All this looks rather permissive to an outsider, but there is great discipline behind it all. . . . That's the wonderful thing about a movie set—at one moment it seems pandemonium, then suddenly everybody is doing his job, and doing it very well, and it all falls into place. People know where they're supposed to be and what they're supposed to do."

This was exactly what happened on the set of *A Star Is Born*.

Rehearsal continued until 11:20; at 11:25, Cukor called "Action" and Winton Hoch guided the massive Technicolor camera in a dolly movement from a medium long shot of the exterior of the train to a close shot of the window, through which Esther's face is seen, thereby spoiling the shot—the joke being that stand-ins' faces are not allowed to be seen. This was photographed five separate times; various things kept going wrong. The fifth take, which lasted 44 seconds, was satisfactory, and the camera was shifted to another setup to photograph other angles. The scene took all day to complete; by 5:20, when Garland was dismissed, one minute and forty-nine seconds of film had been shot, in nine separate setups, covering one and a half pages of script.

When the scene was finished and the cast dismissed, Cukor and his staff moved to the next day's set, Esther's room at the Oleander Arms Motel. Here Cukor gave instructions to Hoch on the lighting and to Earl Bellamy on the staging and conferred with Hoyningen-Huene and Gene Allen on the color and mood of the scene. By the time these matters had been discussed and roughed out, and everybody had their instructions for the next day, it was close to 8:00. At the end of the first day of actual shooting on *A Star Is Born,* Cukor had filmed one script scene and Warner Bros. had spent approximately $25,000 for the day's work, an amount which it would continue to spend every production day until all 123 scenes of the script had been photographed.

Mason's illness was waning, but he was still in no condition to work, so the second day of shooting found the company working in the interior set of Esther's bedroom at the Oleander Arms Motel, a detailed copy of an actual structure on the corner of Crescent Heights Boulevard and Fountain Avenue in Hollywood. This set included Esther's room and an exterior terrace and stairs leading up to the second level of the building, where Danny McGuire and the rest of the Glenn Williams Orchestra were quartered. Later in the shooting, the company would go on location to the actual apartment building to film exterior shots of Esther's goodbye to the musicians after her decision to quit the band and take Norman up on his offer to get her a screen test with Niles. But on October 13, the only scenes to be filmed were short silent bits: one of Esther in bed, tossing and turning in the darkness and anguishing over what to do about Maine's offer; one of her getting out of bed and leaving her room to go upstairs to tell Danny of her decision to stay in Hollywood and try for a screen career; and shots of Esther later in the sequence, after the band has left, washing her hair while waiting for Norman to call.

Cukor wanted the early part of this sequence—Esther in bed—to be in almost total darkness, with only a glimmer of moonlight coming in through the window, just enough to illuminate Garland's face. Here, Cukor had his first bit of difficulty with Winton Hoch, who refused to light the shot as instructed, telling Cukor that the low level of light he wanted would never register with sufficient density to get a quality image with the Technicolor process. As Cukor later remarked, "some cameramen get into all kinds of habits and one has to watch them very carefully [so that they] won't put in all sorts of boring shadows and things like that. You have to give these men their head because they're artists—you have to stimulate them, not let them fall back on habits." Even with Cukor's prodding, Hoch ended up doing it his way, with the director's reluctant approval.

The sequence was complex only in the lighting, going from the dimly lit interior of the room to a combination moonlight/early dawn exterior as Esther leaves her room to go upstairs to the second floor. Cukor had staged it all in a single shot, and after spending almost three hours arguing about the lighting and setting the lights, he and Hoch took the first shot at 11:00, then did it twice more. After a break for lunch, they resumed work, this time shooting Esther washing her hair. This had to be shot in medium close shots, close shots, and close-ups of Esther's face registering anxiety at Norman's failure to call—all of which were necessary to give the film editor sufficient footage to build the sequence to Cukor's satisfaction. Each time one of these shots was taken, or retaken because of some technical or staging deficiency, Garland's hair would have to be rewashed and reset, which was done a total of eight times.

The sequence was finally completed at 3:20 in the afternoon, and the company immediately moved to the first of the many studio exterior locations. The Warner studio buildings, streets, back lot, and sound stages would all be utilized as the fictional Oliver Niles Studio. Cukor usually preferred to shoot his scenes in continuity—that is, as they occurred in the script—but Mason's illness precluded that, so a major jump in the story progression now had Esther on her first tour of the studio with publicity head Matt Libby after she has signed her contract. The script called for her to follow him across a high, narrow catwalk between stages into a projection room to meet Niles. Esther Blodgett—like Judy Garland—was terrified of heights, and Cukor had inserted this bit of business as Esther, not wanting to let Libby know of her acrophobia, grasps on to the side railings and, knees buckling, does a Groucho Marx–like lope out of the scene. It was the kind of self-deprecating comedy that Garland was so adept at; the catwalk itself was only about nine feet off the ground, but the photographic angle would make it appear thirty or more feet up.

For this scene, her first with another performer, Garland was joined by Jack Carson as Libby. The two had worked together once before for Warner Bros.: ironically, it was on stage at the downtown Warner Theatre in Los Angeles in the early 1930s, when she was still Baby Gumm of the Gumm Sisters and he was half of the comedy duo of Willock and Carson. After her hairstyle and her costume had been changed, Garland and Carson did two takes of the uncomplicated shot, and by 4:30 work had been completed for the day.

For Bellamy and Russ Llewellyn, however, work would not end for several more hours, as the next day's shooting was on location in Hollywood. After Esther has quit the band at Maine's urging, she waits for his call, which doesn't come; her money gone, she is forced to do the one thing she had vowed she would "never, never" do again—take a job as a waitress. Even more humiliating, she works as a carhop in a drive-in restaurant. For this, Bellamy and Cukor had chosen the real thing—Robert's Drive-In at the corner of Sunset Boulevard and Cahuenga Street, in the heart of Hollywood. Recalls Bellamy: "Mr. Cukor liked the naturalness—he liked to film the actual thing. He felt it gave reality to the situation. We went out there the night before we were to shoot: he would look over the place and give us a rough walk-through so that the cameraman could line up and light with the stand-ins; we would have discussions with the art director and the cameraman so that everybody had a chance to put in their suggestions as to how to make the scene look good—you know, take advantage of the way the place looked—as well as everybody tossing around ideas for staging. So that by the time we left the place the night before, everybody had a good clear idea of what we were going to be doing the next day."

The next morning, Bellamy was at the studio at 6:30, getting everything organized, seeing that the twenty-five trucks of equipment, which included portable dressing rooms, costume and makeup vans, and crew vehicles, were loaded and on their way by 7:00. "I'd see that everything was under control, then I'd leave one assistant at the studio to load the cast into cars, get them out to us by eight-thirty. I would go out there with the first car that left the studio and usually be there before any of the buses left the studio with the crew, so that I could see if the location was all set for us, see if the police had arrived. I would be there when Mr. Cukor arrived and I'd have the street ready, knowing what he wanted, and the location prepared and the extras would be there—they'd usually get there about the same time as the crew. While the crew was getting ready and the cameras were being set up, we'd get the extras in position and have the stand-ins rehearsed so that by the time Garland got there, all we had to do was walk her through the action, then rehearse it and shoot it."

Due to the professionalism of the crews and the simplicity of the scene itself, the master takes were done fairly rapidly—only eight shots were needed to set up the necessities of the scene. But when it came time to film Garland's close-ups as she recited the menu of varied hamburgers, fourteen separate takes were needed, due to flubbed lines, technical deficiencies, and assorted noises—Hollywood traffic, sirens, horns, the crowds who had gathered to watch the proceedings, and an occasional stray plane. Even with all the distraction and retakes, shooting was finished before lunch; and then the entire company—trucks, crew, extras—took the new Hollywood Freeway to downtown Los Angeles, 626 Spring Street, a seedy little dive called the Bomba Club. Here they filmed sequences of Esther unsuccessfully trying to get a singing job. By the end of the day, they had added another five minutes of film and had shot an additional three and a half pages of script.

While this was going on in Hollywood, Albert Warner in New York was reading the *Variety* headline that proclaimed a $3 million gross for *The Robe* after less than two weeks in release in fewer than two hundred theaters. This was an astonishing figure; nothing like it had been seen since the days of *Gone With the Wind* in 1939–40, and Albert Warner knew that *The Robe*, while a good movie, was no *Gone With the Wind*. It was the CinemaScope trademark that was the big attraction; it was a star in itself, like Cinerama: people were going to see *it*, and the picture was secondary. As the money continued to roll in on *The Robe*, Warner watched with dismay as the costs of *A Star Is Born* began to escalate far beyond what had been budgeted; the picture could conceivably end up costing 3 to 4 million dollars. Unlike his brother Jack, Albert Warner was no gambler. Nor was he convinced that Judy Garland's renewed popularity would carry over into films, filling movie theaters across the country to capacity for several weeks—and that, he figured, was what it would take to recoup the costs of *A Star Is Born*. In the technology-crazy movie market of late 1953, even the most atrocious little "gimmick" movies were outgrossing the best "flat" films. Warner decided to discuss the matter with his older brother, Harry, the president of the firm. The eldest Warner had little tolerance or affection for his younger brother Jack; their strained relationship was common knowledge. It was an old sibling rivalry: Harry resented Jack's being accorded favored status by his mother and father just because he was the youngest. Harry, dour, conservative, and withdrawn, was annoyed by Jack's flamboyance, his ebullience, his gregariousness, his love of publicity, and his reckless ways with the company money. Jack, for his part, respected and feared his eldest brother— feared him to the point that when Harry would journey from New York for one of his infrequent forays to the studio, Jack would not enter the commissary if he knew Harry was still dining. So when Albert brought up the subject of *A Star Is Born* to Harry, pointing out his reservations about the picture's cost and its potential popularity, Harry listened. He too had noted the amazing success of *The Robe* and CinemaScope. Early on, he had made inquiries about buying into it on behalf of Warners but had been dissuaded by Jack, who convinced his brothers that WarnerScope would deliver exactly the same results with less expense. Of course, that was before the well-mounted publicity campaign had made CinemaScope a household word; and now, in the light of the money CinemaScope was generating, Harry agreed with Albert: WarnerScope could not hope to compete. So just about the time that *A Star Is Born* was going into its fourth day of production, Albert Warner quietly set up a meeting with 20th Century–Fox vice-president Al Lichtman, head of distribution and, next to Skouras and Zanuck, the executive most closely associated with the company's efforts to have CinemaScope embraced by the entire industry.

By Thursday, October 15, James Mason had recovered sufficiently to be able to work on his first scenes. As he recalled: "I felt I was getting better. I was taking anti-seasick pills, but I remained unsteady for a long time— which was good, for it happened that the first set I worked in was Norman Maine's bedroom and the only sequence to be shot in it concerned his waking up in the middle of the night after having been put to bed a few hours earlier in an extremely drunken condition, trying to remember the name of the girl who had saved him from making a fool of himself. I could now use my dizziness for this." Cukor had devised an elaborate and imaginative addition to this sequence, as Mason discovered to his amusement: "On the way to the set I ran into a strange-looking girl in one of the corridors of the studio. She seemed to be dressed in a curtain of some kind, with bizarre red and gray body makeup on. When I commented on her appearance she told me that she was playing the part of a curtain. She seemed to think that this explained everything. George, aided and abetted by his friend Hoyningen-Huene, was trying to stylize the film, or parts of it, by relating sections to the work of some painter. In this case George had evidently thought of the drunken Maine waking in the night as a nightmare by Henry Fuseli (a.k.a. Johann Heinrich Fussli). The window drapes in the room were to take on the look of nightmare girls. Hence, the young lady as the curtain." Unfortunately, the better part of the day was spent trying to light and stage this so that it worked. After thirty-five takes, Cukor, Hoyningen-Huene, and Hoch gave up on the idea and shot the scene sans nightmare.

The rest of the day was spent filming the scenes with Matt Libby and Maine's manservant discussing the sleeping Maine (Manservant: "He'll smile in his sleep in a minute . . . like a child." Libby: "Like a child with a blowtorch. Mr. Maine's charm escapes me. It always has"). There were several plot points that this scene had to establish, including the fact that Norman had to be up and on his way to a mid-sea location by 6:00 a.m. and that he might be gone for several weeks. Libby instructs the manservant to "hide [Maine's] car keys . . . I've had enough of Mr. Maine for one night." The servant does this by dropping the keys into the glass containing his false teeth. When Maine awakes and decides to track down Esther, he finds the keys and takes the manservant's teeth with him, muttering, "I'll teach you to play fair, Graves."

The scenes were photographed in various parts of the darkened Maine mansion, a lavish movie-star home, tastefully and expensively decorated with a mixture of traditional and contemporary furnishings. The lighting and the camera movement were constantly fussed over and changed by Cukor, working with Hoyningen-Huene and Gene Allen. Earl Bellamy relates that "on any picture, but especially this one, lighting is your biggest time consumer, because it involves a great deal—your background, your foreground, and your principals. Mr. Cukor was a stickler for lighting effects. He had definite ideas and he would talk it over and explain what he wanted. He would lay out a shot the way he wanted it to move; then he would turn it over to the cameraman and let him do all the lighting.

But if he had something special [in mind], he would keep after them until he got exactly what he wanted."

Warners—indeed, the entire industry—was on a six-day work week; and after taking Sunday off, Cukor and crew on Monday moved onto the sanitorium set for the scene where Maine is visited by Oliver Niles. This was the scene that had been written into the 1937 script after Cukor had related to Selznick and Wellman the details of his trip to see John Barrymore, who was trying to dry himself out. Recalls Cukor: "Years ago, when I was going to direct *Camille,* I went to see Jack Barrymore about playing de Varville, the part Henry Daniell finally played. Jack had put himself into some kind of home in Culver City to stop drinking. . . . It was an old frame house that called itself a rest home. I went into some dreary, depressing room. Back of it was the dining room, and I noticed something that always strikes me as very shabby and sad—they hadn't taken away the tablecloths, and you knew they never changed them. Then Jack came in, with a sort of aide called Kelly. He took us into a gloomy sitting room and said, 'Can we sit here, Kelly? Nobody's going to come through and disturb us by pretending he's Napoleon?' " Seventeen years after the fact, Cukor found himself restaging this episode from his past.

Cukor's version is similar in outline to Wellman's; Hart lifted the dialogue intact from the original (including one pithy line from Dorothy Parker for Maine, "We dine at five-thirty. Makes the nights longer"). But the similarities are only surface. Wellman's version had a bluff, bonhomie bravado to it. It was external and superficial, with Adolphe Menjou, as Niles, playing smoothly and jovially while Fredric March as Maine was charming and unconcerned, with just a hint of hurt pride at the thought of being offered a subsidiary role in a big picture. Cukor enriched his version by concentrating on the gloomy, depressing aspects of the place, the melancholy quiet, and the awkward tension between Maine and Niles. Charles Bickford, whom Cukor referred to privately as "Old Ironpants," needed a great deal of work to loosen up and evince the kind of careful, caring warmth that Cukor felt was essential to the scene: the relationship between the two men is deeper, richer, and more poignant than in the earlier version. And Cukor added a short coda: with both men jockeying to sidestep the emotion of the moment, Maine sees Niles out, but just before the door shuts, he reaches out and grasps Niles's arm, saying quietly, "Thanks for dropping by, Oliver." When Niles is gone, Maine reverts to his old self, putting his arm around his "nurse" and saying, "Alone at last, Cuddles."

Garland was not needed for these scenes; instead, she had been working with Richard Barstow and the dancers, rehearsing the number to be performed at the Shrine Auditorium. In between, she had costume fittings and publicity photos while simultaneously trying to rest up for what gave every indication of being a difficult sequence: the scene in the after-hours club where Maine hears Esther sing "The Man That Got Away." This would be the first time Garland and Mason played together. It was a long, crucial scene; not only did it have to convince Maine (and the audience) of Esther's enormous talent, it had to set up the wary relationship between them, half bantering, half serious, and it was the first time that the real character of both was revealed. Additionally, it had to set the tone and the direction for the rest of the story, for it is here that Maine first convinces Esther that she is something unique, that she possesses "that little something extra" which is star quality. He gives her the beginnings of belief in herself and a sense of her worth and convinces her to try for "the big dream." It was a long, seven-page sequence in the script, and it had bothered Sid Luft greatly that all the dialogue between the two took place at a table in the club. He had asked Cukor to have Hart rewrite it, but Cukor was evidently satisfied with it: it lent itself to a favorite technique of his, a long single take in which actors perform an entire scene without stopping. Hart's description of this scene and its mood was most explicit:

INTERIOR OF THE DOWNBEAT CLUB. The word club is a misnomer. "Dive" would be more apt. It is a typical musician's hangout—a place where the boys feel truly at home—where they can play as they wish to their heart's content—not set orchestrations for smooth dancing—but improvising, "taking off"—the kind of place where a new sort of music is born or a Benny Goodman or a Bix Beiderbecke emerges, full blown. There are not too many patrons at this hour, but a number of the Glenn Williams aggregation are scattered among the tables, and on the little bandstand a foursome of the Williams Orchestra has taken over. Dan McGuire is at the piano, the drummer behind him, and on each side of him are the clarinetist and the trumpet. In front of them stands Esther. Her eyes half-closed, she begins to sing a low blues—first straight, then as she reaches the second chorus, a wild improvisation begins—throbbing and bizarre.

Norman Maine has entered as the number began. For a moment, he stands in the doorway, listening. Then he slides into a chair at the nearest table, his eyes never leaving Esther's face, a slow look of amazement and pleasure spreading over his own. As the number finishes, the effect on him is electric—he starts to applaud—then drops his hands in his lap and keeps staring at the bandstand.

According to Cukor: "What dictates your approach very often isn't you, but it's the situation—it's the text. It's what the play tells you. I envy directors who have everything written on a piece of paper and then just go on the set and do it. [I like to] do things simply. You just ride it . . . you do it naturally, I suppose." An approach like Cukor's takes much thought and preparation, and this scene had been on his mind for some time. He wanted simplicity, but he also wanted to experiment visually. "When you look at something," he later related, "you're used to seeing the whole of a thing—then suddenly you see a section, arbitrarily, not composed. Just a section of something cut off. In the David painting 'Sacre de Napoléon,' when the detail is reproduced in an art book, you see a head to one side, bits of other heads cut off here and there. And I thought, 'Why not do that in a movie?' So I decided that we could do that when she sang 'The Man That Got Away.' I wanted the camera to follow her, always in front . . . sometimes she would go to the side and almost disappear out of the frame . . . all in one long take, for the whole musical number. It isn't easy for an actor or an actress to carry a long take—you have to be strong. I wanted to do it with Judy because I knew she could sustain it." Long takes are much more complex than they sound, in that they have to be carefully worked out as to staging, camera movement, and especially lighting. The mood of this scene was particularly important, for Cukor wanted to convey Hart's description of a "dive" in an impressionistic fashion. Cukor, Hoyningen-Huene, Allen, and Hoch began working out the setup for this sequence after lunch on Tuesday the 20th. They worked for most of the afternoon, with Cukor becoming more and more irritated at Hoch's intransigence. The cameraman was adamant that the look Cukor wanted could not be achieved successfully; the low light levels, the impressionistic feeling of the musical instruments, Garland moving in and out of pools of light with the camera following. At the end of the day, they had not reached an agreement on anything and were still nowhere near ready to shoot the scene the next day. Cukor had very little patience with cameramen who, as he put it, "are great stars in their own right. Who refuse to listen, refuse to be influenced. . . . It's best to have someone with an open mind . . . I must have a cameraman who will listen." Cukor evidently relayed his displeasure with Hoch to Warner and Luft, for the latter relates: "I had hired Winnie

Hoch. He was a helluva nice guy and a goddamn good cameraman for outdoor stuff, but indoors his stuff was crappy. Lighting was bad—it just missed—and he did not understand what the hell we wanted to do with 'The Man That Got Away.' So I had to fire him."

This was not the only change in store for the *A Star Is Born* company. Late the previous week, Jack Warner had a lengthy telephone conversation with his two brothers in New York. The upshot of that call was that over the weekend he had been paid a visit by Al Lichtman of 20th Century–Fox, who had flown from New York specifically to convince Warner to give up his insistence on WarnerScope and to join the CinemaScope converts. Lichtman's arguments, as well as his brothers' insistence, evidently were more than Warner could resist, for on the Monday following the meeting he called Luft, who recalls: "Jack used to get to the studio about eleven-thirty, but this one morning we went over to Fox about ten a.m. because Jack had not seen anything in CinemaScope—nothing. So we went over and ran three pieces of three pictures that were being shot there, stuff with Tyrone Power and Victor Mature, and when he looked at it he agreed that it was great—much better than anything we'd been able to get with WarnerScope. So he made the deal with Fox. We had been shooting for about ten days and now we were gonna have to do the whole thing over from the start, so this changeover cost us a lot of goddamn money."

The switch to CinemaScope was not made instantaneously. It fell to Luft to break the news to Cukor, who remained unconvinced about the wisdom of the change. It was decided to film the next day's sequence, "The Man That Got Away," both in wide-screen Technicolor and in Cinema-Scope and WarnerColor and then make a firm decision after comparing the two. Hoch would continue to direct the Technicolor photography, while the CinemaScope camera was handled by Milton Krasner, on loan from Fox, one of the few men in the industry who had practical experience with the new medium. One of the arguments that Lichtman had used to convince Warner of the advantages of the new process was its economy: scenes would not have to be shot in multiple setups for editing purposes but could be photographed in one master shot, with the staging taking care of medium shots, close shots, and dolly shots. The theory, as propounded by Lichtman, was that CinemaScope was more like the stage—the action must be arranged so that the audience's attention is focused on the center of attraction. The proof of this would be in the filming of "The Man That Got Away."

Cukor and his crew were on the set by 9:00 working with Bellamy and Krasner. Cukor had worked out the action of the scene, which had Esther serving coffee to the musicians, sitting down, throwing a mute to the trumpeter, then standing up and singing as she moved among the men and their instruments. Because of the newness of the technique, and because Krasner had to be briefed on the lighting and photography Cukor wanted, the first shot was not taken until 2:30. After that, the lighting and the blocking had to be reset for Hoch and the narrower scope of the Technicolor camera. By 5:00, everything was set up and ready to go, but the first two Technicolor takes were spoiled by a malfunctioning camera, the second by Garland stumbling into a table; the third take was fine and was printed.

At 8:00 the next morning, everyone concerned except the cast and Hoch gathered in the screening room to look at the two versions. Even with the aesthetic imperfections of WarnerColor, the quality of the image and the staging in CinemaScope had an undeniable impact. After some discussion with Luft and Cukor, Warner made the decision: *A Star Is Born* would be started over, this time in CinemaScope. As Luft mentioned, this changeover was expensive; nearly $300,000 had been expended on the film so far, and all the footage was unusable. One thing everyone agreed on was that "The Man That Got Away" would have to be redone. The lighting was bad, the staging awkward, and it looked like the rehearsal that it was.

When the question of CinemaScope had been resolved, Cukor and his crew immediately began refilming, starting first with the scene between Mason and Charles Bickford in Maine's dressing room, where the actor tries to convince Niles to give Esther a chance in an upcoming film, and following with the scene of Niles being awakened in the middle of the night by a phone call from Maine, drunkenly raving about Esther, whom he has just heard sing. Neither scene needed any special adaptation for CinemaScope—the sets were still standing, the lighting had all been worked out beforehand, and there were very few problems caused by the switch to the new technique.

Milton Krasner, still on loan from 20th Century–Fox, photographed all these retakes. He and Cukor had worked together previously on *A Double Life* (1948) and *The Model and the Marriage Broker* (1951). "I thought he was very good," recalled Cukor. "He worked a lot with [Vincente] Minnelli. . . . I'm not so sure that I like his color work that much, though." Krasner could not stay on the picture permanently; he was Fox's resident expert on CinemaScope, and as such he was used to train cameramen at other studios in the vagaries of the process. The big problem now facing *A Star Is Born* was finding another cameraman, and quickly. Recalls Sid Luft: "I'd seen some stuff on television, in black and white—brilliant stuff—and I noticed who this guy was: Sam Leavitt. I was telling Judy about him and she said, 'You know, he was a camera operator for Harry Stradling.' So I thought, 'Let's get a hold of this guy—if he was with Harry for ten years or whatever the hell it was, he knows his stuff. He's the same thing as Harry Stradling.' Judy said he shot all the musicals, so I said, 'Let's hire him.' So I got him. His agent was Otto Preminger's brother, Ingo. It wasn't an easy sell, either, with Jack Warner, especially after he saw what Milt Krasner had done. And Jack had a thing about people who did television work. But in the end I got him and he started right in." Leavitt joined the *A Star Is Born* company on Friday, October 23, and was immediately at work on retakes of the sanitorium sequence, then on retakes of the scenes between Libby, the manservant, and the sleeping Maine.

The forty-nine-year-old Leavitt had been in the film business since the early 1930s, starting out as a camera operator at the Biograph Studios in New York. He moved to Hollywood in 1935 and had gone to work at Paramount, then moved to MGM, working as a camera operator for Joseph Ruttenberg and Harry Stradling. It was there that he had met Garland, who liked him a great deal. After becoming a director of photography on his own in 1951, he had specialized in off-beat, low-budget work for Republic and Columbia. His most famous work was *The Thief* (1952), a hard-edged near-documentary starring Ray Milland, filmed on actual locations in New York City and notable for the fact that though it was a sound film, only one word of dialogue was spoken. Leavitt was a facile, proficient technician; his work on low-budget films gave him an ability to light sets in the shortest time possible, and he was a fast, no-nonsense cameraman. He was unpretentious, loved his work, and was eager to please his director. He had just finished work on the 3-D *Southwest Passage*, which had also used Eastmancolor under the trade name Pathecolor, so he was familiar with the process's strengths and weaknesses.

That all these factors made him an ideal choice for the troubled *A Star Is Born* soon became evident on the first major scene he shot for the picture, the retake of "The Man That Got Away" on Tuesday the 27th. In contrast to the lengthy setup and lighting time on the earlier attempt, Leavitt was given the camera setup at 9:00 a.m., started lighting the set at 9:10, and was ready to shoot by 10:45. Leavitt later recalled: "Cukor had ideas about this number and his ideas were kind of scrumbly. He told me, 'I want to shoot this sequence with Judy singing in this barroom. I want her to sing this number and walk around these musicians, about seven or eight of them, and sing the number in between them, go around them and then come back and go around the room.' This is where the intricate part came in. He said, 'I want to see her, but I don't want to see the musicians. I don't want to see their instruments, I don't want to see their faces, I don't want to see anything about them. I just want to see her alone.' That was the hard part, because when she went in between these people, she was lit from one direction. When she looked over in another angle, she was lit from there, but when she walked over a ways, she got in the way of a musician, and every time she did that, the wrong light hit her, and I had to take the light off her. I had a helluva time trying to cut one light off her and put one light on them, and that was tough because here she is in a place where she was definitely lit right, and then she'd move over here and she'd get into this light here, that would hit her on this side, and the light didn't make her look good. The toughest part was getting her out of all the lights that she wasn't supposed to be in. I took a little time and I asked her where she thought she was going to sing, and I mapped it all out in my mind, then I had the stand-in walk around. After I lit it with the other girl, then I had her go through it for me to see if I got it right. A couple of spots I had guessed wrong with the lights, and Judy showed it to me—she knew her lights, knew where her key light should be, and could tell if it wasn't hitting her right, so then I'd move the light to make her look good. It was a tough hombre to do, you know. I think in all my career, this was the toughest lighting problem that I ever had. I should have had a week to piddle around with it, but I couldn't because there was too much money involved. The musicians—these guys didn't know what the hell I was doing; they didn't give a damn about the lighting. All they were concerned about was going through their musical score and playing right."

Cukor kept the staging much the same as he had devised for the first version, so there was very little change in the way of blocking. But Gene Allen and Hoyningen-Huene, after seeing the first version, had redesigned the look of the set. Recalls Allen: "The first time it all looked as if we had painted a set to look like a bar. It needed to be softened up some way, because it looked a little garish. So to give it a slightly impressionistic look, I convinced Sam to let us put a scrim between the musicians and the back bar. If you look very carefully at that scene you can see the scrim nailed down on the floor; of course nobody notices it, but it's there and it gives a soft tone to the back, and we had some of the grips with bee-pots smoking it up a bit, and it looked a lot better."

Shooting "The Man That Got Away" was an exhausting ordeal, and not just for Leavitt and the crew. Earl Bellamy remembers: "We had the playback machine there with the recording of the song; and, you know, most singers just mouth to the playback. Not Judy. When she sang to a playback, you couldn't hear anything. That playback was turned on to its peak, but you could hear Judy above it. She was unbelievable when she sang to a playback. She wanted me to start it full blast and then she started singing and she topped it. You could stand anyplace and you could hear that playback, but you could hear Judy just as clear as a bell, and she sang right with it and everything was right on. It was just absolutely beautiful; she put everything that she could possibly put of herself into a song, and as a result, she's really down for the count for about ten minutes. When we finished the number, she took me aside and said, 'Earl, give me a break before the next take,' and I said, 'Fine,' and she went to her dressing room, and we waited about fifteen minutes, and she came back fine and did the whole thing again. Each time she was just as tremendous as she ever was. She never varied when she sang, and she never missed." According to the production log, because of technical problems, staging, lighting, or play-back problems, Garland did twenty-seven takes of this number over the next three days, both partial and complete, so that by the end of the third day she was emotionally and physically exhausted. In watching the rushes, it was found there were three good takes of the number, but everyone had reservations about the scene itself. Recalls Bellamy: "Mr. Cukor had her doing bits of business before she sang, and all of that action didn't really fit the song. In my opinion, thinking back on it now, it destroyed the song, it didn't have any meaning—it was just too busy." Gene Allen remembers other problems: "We all had the same feeling: The color wasn't right. And she didn't look good—her costume was wrinkled, it didn't fit right. Judy would put on some weight, as some of us are apt to do, over a weekend and be a few pounds heavier than she was when they first made the dress. So that didn't look good. And even with the scrim and all, I still didn't like the look of the bar. But even with all that, it was still an exciting number."

As the company finished shooting this sequence, Warners made official what heretofore had been industry gossip. A lengthy press release from Albert Warner's office in New York announced that Warner Bros. was taking up CinemaScope and that *A Star Is Born* would be the first Warners film to use the Fox process. "This is being done," it was explained,

> to clarify and standardize for exhibitors and the public a single process, thus eliminating any possibility of confusion. We are happy to pool our technical and engineering know-how with 20th Century–Fox in an even greater development of the CinemaScope system, which we feel is best suited for many of the important productions we plan to bring to world audiences in the future. We believe the industry can best be served by leading producers collaborating and cooperating in technological advances for the best interests of the business.

Significantly, no mention was made of the WarnerScope process; and even more significantly, the announcement came from Albert Warner, not from Jack as it would have under normal circumstances. The ever-vigilant *Variety* quoted industry rumor that the first shipment of lenses to Warner Bros. from Zeiss was inferior because the optical company had been supplied with the wrong specifications by the studio. In a separate editorial, the journal made oblique references to the Warner-Zanuck standoff: "Warner Bros. is to be commended for unbending from what is known in the trade to have been a pretty firm and sensitive earlier emotional as well as technological conviction."

The studio's capitulation was a triumph for Zanuck and Fox but a galling defeat for Jack Warner personally. Being a seasoned gambler, however, he shrugged it off with seeming good grace—not an easy thing to do, as he had lost nearly $400,000 of the firm's money in his battle to combat Zanuck and establish WarnerScope. In a privately negotiated face-and-money-saving gesture, Fox agreed to take over Warners' contract with Zeiss, which had been primarily for the manufacture of projection lenses. This worked to Fox's advantage, as Bausch and Lomb were having difficulties turning out enough lenses to supply all the theaters that wanted the anamorphic device. Enabling Warners to keep its promise to exhibitors that they could rent the new lenses instead of being forced to buy them, Fox gave Warners' distribution arm three hundred lenses. Additionally, Fox agreed to sell CinemaScope equipment to all the Warner-affiliated theaters at the same reduced price it was offering its own former subsidiary theaters.

This was a major victory for 20th Century–Fox in its effort to sell the new technology to the industry and to the moviegoing public. It now had every studio except Paramount, and virtually every major theater chain in the country (and abroad), producing and exhibiting films in CinemaScope. Almost literally overnight, Spyros Skouras and his band of unlikely revolutionaries had succeeded in sweeping away almost all opposition to the new process. By the end of 1953, CinemaScope was firmly established as a viable economic and aesthetic force; the new shape and sound would dominate Hollywood film production for the next two decades.

Starting Over

Now that CinemaScope was officially the order of the day, Cukor and his collaborators were faced with the problem of filling the vast expanse of screen. "It is the most unfortunate shape," remarked Cukor, "like a mailbox . . . the problem is, you can't get any height in the thing." Milton Krasner and another Fox anamorphic expert named Rosenberg had given Cukor and Leavitt a set of rules that had to be adhered to when working in the new process: "We couldn't move the camera up or down, because of distortion, and we couldn't move back and away from the camera," recalls Cukor. "Everything had to be played on a level plane—if someone were too much upstage, they would be out of focus. And you weren't supposed to come in really close on faces. It was rather like what happened when sound came in—you were supposed to forget everything you'd learned. Well, we shot like that for just one day—and then, with Gene Allen and George Huene, we said, 'To hell with it.' We just paid no attention to that unfortunate mailbox shape, we ignored all the rules."

Gene Allen remembers this period of change very distinctly: "We had to learn on the job. Fox had given us a whole list of rules, like lining up your actors in a straight row, because of perspective problems, focus problems, and all. Well, Cukor said, 'I don't know how the hell to direct people in a row. Nobody stands in rows.' And as he said, you couldn't get height. So we were constantly on our toes about designing. We found that we would have to jack up tables and chairs to get a plane representing the floor plane, because in CinemaScope you just didn't get floors or ceilings in. Then we had to find ways to bring ceilings down into the picture, so that you got some feeling of where walls were in relationship to the actors. So all of these things were going on at the same time: how do you stage a scene that was shot in the old three-by-four proportion, and now suddenly you have to redo it and you have a few feet on each side left over? Well, you

had to redesign, you had to move people apart, you had to fill the screen
very carefully. We were trying to watch the schedule; we had the problem
of shooting and reshooting—I don't know of any other film that suddenly
had all these problems dumped on it. Cukor never spoke much about it,
but he had to be terribly nervous about putting his reputation on the line.
George Huene and I began working with him on every shot, every angle;
we were always right there. And we were all learning. For every setup, I
looked through the finder with the permission of the cameraman and the
operator—I found a way to work with them instead of against them. You
had to be a diplomat, because you're dealing with great temperaments; but
I had a lot of enthusiasm, and they liked the idea of the team, the concept
that we were only doing something to make it all better. And when they
found out that we didn't do things to make them look bad, and that they'd
get credit for any great ideas we might have had—well, then it turned out
all right."

"It really was a group effort," remembers Leavitt. "We all got together
on it. There weren't too many problems as far as I was concerned; I just
went with what the art director and the designer thought. Cukor was
number one, naturally—he was the guy who thought up a lot of wonderful
ideas. Working with a man like that was a great feeling—his ideas were
usually unusual. Since none of us knew anything about CinemaScope, there
were some problems that we had to straighten out, and that's where the
group effort came in. No kidding around there—whatever happened, the
other man took over and helped you out. Gene Allen was the biggest help
to me. He was a very fine art director; he and I always worked together,
talking about compositions and color. This being my first picture in
CinemaScope, it didn't even give me a chance to breathe—it was like being
pushed into a fire. I had to find out about the lenses. I had a lot of problems
with those lenses; I didn't even know what they did. With CinemaScope,
you'd use a two-inch lens for crowd scenes, which brings everything in
closer to the audience. Now in ordinary film photography, you'd use this
lens only for photographing close-ups. Much of the time, I'd find out what
these lenses did just by seeing it on the screen in the rushes. That's what
I mean by being pushed into something that you weren't ready for. I had
to learn to be a photographer all over again. Without Gene Allen and all
these other people working with you, it never would have come out as good
as it did."

If the new shape of CinemaScope pushed the imaginations of Allen,

Hoyningen-Huene, and Leavitt into new areas, the use of Eastmancolor taxed their combined ingenuities to the fullest. The wide range and delicacy of color available with the sophisticated Technicolor three-strip method were replaced by the more primitive and garish effects of single-strip WarnerColor, with its much more restricted palette. Allen relates: "It was a new system with all of its built-in problems. You didn't have the separation of colors we were used to. We didn't have the grays and the interesting rich blacks and darks. It was kind of muddied up: darks were too dark; where light faded off, it went to green; blues would pop through, so that even on the grayest day the skies would be the brightest blue. Anything that was a cool gray turned blue. And the color was hard—it didn't have the richness and the softness that Technicolor had. If the exposure wasn't absolutely right on, everything would go red. We really had to control what we did and be very careful. It was a moody picture at times, and Cukor wanted to play it for mood. But when you did, the light fell off in the dark; instead of going to rich darks that you can control, they became shadings of green, and this was a problem.

"Then we found that the film, even with all our efforts at controlling the color, was just too overcolored, because the Eastmancolor was erratic. So Cukor, Huene, and myself started a process right then of eliminating color; we damned near did a black-and-white picture, except for little accents of color. But then when we did color scenes, where there had to be a lot of color, then we did great color, all controlled and related and in good taste."

For Leavitt, who was used to the idiosyncrasies of Eastmancolor, there were fewer problems: "As far as the colors were concerned, they took care of themselves—all I had to do was light it. I went with the designing and the art direction. But they can't help you on the lighting; that you have to do yourself—as far as the cameraman is concerned, the lighting is your own, nobody takes that away. Like the art director—nobody takes away his sets—or the designer—you can't take away his colors."

On this latter point, Leavitt was evidently unaware of an incident that occurred just about this time, as the changeover to CinemaScope and WarnerColor was getting under way. The shooting schedule called for a sequence in which Esther reports to the publicity offices of the Niles Studio on her first day under contract. Sid Luft relates: "Judy was in a red dress, and they had the interior of the hallway painted red, and I saw this and I said, 'I don't give a goddamn what Gene Allen or George says—it won't work. Judy in a red dress going through these halls—you'll have the red mixing with the red—it won't work.' So I ordered the wall repainted. The next morning George calls me up and says 'What the hell is going on? The walls are gray.' I said, 'George, you've gotta shoot it that way, I ordered it done.' He says, 'You did.' 'Yes, I did. I didn't want to take the risk of a whole day's shooting, of having the red bleed into the red—it would've been a mess. That's the way it is, George' And I hung up. We worked it out later, because it turned out great anyway."

Evidently Warner, nervous at the amount of time and money being spent on reshooting and the expensive experimentation that was being conducted at this point, told Luft to exercise his powers as producer and watch the costs, not let the experimenters go overboard. "I do remember that incident," relates Gene Allen. "I can't remember the details, but I do know that *nobody* changes the color of the set—no producer, no Jack Warner, anybody. If they're going to do it, they do it through George Cukor, and then down through his art department. And that's who would make changes. So I think the set was repainted back the way it was." The evidence in the finished film, however, indicates that Luft had his way, for the hallway walls in the scene are gray.

Luft's seeming high-handedness in this could not have endeared him to Cukor, nor did Luft's interference in what Cukor felt to be his own area of expertise: the printing and viewing of the daily rushes. Cukor's directorial approach was to shoot a scene as many times as he thought necessary to obtain the nuances, the details that might make it a little better each time it was done. This might mean twelve or more takes before he was satisfied. The problem then was in trying to decide which take was best, and the only way to do that was by looking at them. Normal industry procedure was to decide on the set which two takes were to be printed for viewing in the rushes and which were to be held to be printed later, in the event that something was not quite right with some aspect of the chosen takes.

"I had a number of run-ins with George," recalls Luft. "He was printing up too much film, and Jack would complain to me, 'Jesus, he's gonna bust you—print this one, print that one.' So I said to George, 'You can't do this—we're gonna go way over budget.' He said, 'I must protect myself.' I said, 'I know, George, but don't ask them to print it; hold it. If we don't like what we've got, then we'll print it.' He was just protecting himself too goddamn much."

Russ Llewellyn recalls the upshot of all this: "Cukor walked into the projection room [to look at the rushes] and we rolled the film—he'd see it. The next one came on—he'd see it. Then the lights came on. Cukor says, 'Where's the other one?' 'Oh,' I'd say, 'we haven't got it.' 'You haven't got it? Why?' 'Well, the production office wouldn't okay it.' And he said, 'Get all of my dailies in here or I won't be back to see them.' And he walked out. They were trying to cheat on him, thinking he'd forgotten about it. But, by God, he went out and he got everything he wanted."

Luft's attempts at trying to keep a firm hand on the film were not helped by the prevailing attitude toward him by the production crew, all of whom were professionals and loyal to Cukor. It was an attitude that emanated from the very top echelons of the studio, starting with Jack Warner, who had unkind words for Luft in his autobiography, *My First Hundred Years in Hollywood* (for which Luft later sued Warner and claims to have received a substantial settlement). According to Russ Llewellyn, "the only contact I'd ever have with Luft was when I'd run into him at the racetrack all the time. But never on the set. No. He was scared of Cukor. Cukor wasn't going to take his advice on anything. He knew nothing about pictures . . . he didn't know a camera from a dissolve." The unfortunate and inaccurate perception of most people involved with the film was that Luft was producer by virtue of the fact that he was Garland's husband, and as such he was not considered a creative individual, not a full-fledged member of the closely knit, inbred little community that Hollywood really was. He was reviled, condescended to, and generally politely ignored, though never to his face—this despite the fact that the entire project was his idea, and despite the fact that he was the only person who was able to exert some kind of control over the mercurial and temperamental Garland.

Lauren Bacall, who knew them both at this period, is one of the few people in Hollywood who saw Luft honestly: "Sid was a wheeler-dealer, but not a bad guy. He and Judy were crazy about each other. He was very good for her; he gave her a reason to get it all together. He gave her a semblance of family life. And he always took care of his children—he was devoted to them. Judy had a hard time dealing with life. She was, God knows, talented—fun to be around, bright and witty, very funny, very smart—a little cuckoo, but who isn't? She had lots of fears—she was terrified of going on stage; she was ruthless sometimes in her dealings with people. But she needed constant reassurance; whatever quirks Sid may have had, he was the one who helped her get through. He took care of her through some rough times that could not have been easy for him."

It wasn't until mid-November that the production had absorbed the changes, the clashes, and the uncertainty and found its momentum. In rapid succession Cukor led his people all over the Warners studio and the Los Angeles locations, filming the early part of the story, dealing mainly with Norman and Esther's initial scenes together—largely the medium shots and close-up work for the Shrine Auditorium dressing rooms at the benefit. The art department had decided to make the studio itself double for Oliver Niles Studios, and Cukor was able to use the actual buildings and grounds of Warner Bros. to good advantage, contrasting the intimacy of the Spanish-style office buildings with the massive, all-encompassing sound stages. Instead of using the departments as they actually were, he found aspects of the decor that suited his ideas for the script. The wardrobe building, with its revolving iron gate, became the publicity headquarters because Cukor liked the idea of Esther spending her first twenty minutes at the studio being hustled through a series of encounters with the ladies in the publicity department ("Oh, hello, dear. I was expecting a blonde. I don't know why—glad to have you with us"), in the photo gallery ("Get out of the way!"), with Matt Libby in his office ("Um. Glad to have you with us. Would you like to meet the big boss? Probably the only chance you'll get"), and with Oliver Niles himself in his projection room ("Oh, hello, dear. Glad to have you with us. Good luck to you, dear"). At the conclusion of all this, Esther finds herself descending the staircase outside the projection room, ending up exactly opposite the same flight of stairs she had entered by. Shaking her head in exasperation, she turns to leave and finds herself caught in the revolving iron gate.

A warehouse opposite the commissary was redesigned and became the payroll window wherein Esther Blodgett first learns her new name from a payroll clerk. "New here? Okay, let's see. Oh, yes. Your name is Vicki Lester—V-I-C-K-I L-E-S-T-E-R. Move on, please." Esther's stunned reaction to this originally gave way to bemused acceptance: "It could have been worse—could have been Beverly Wilshire." But Cukor deleted the gag, preferring to concentrate on Esther's appreciation of the nonsense of the situation ("Vicki Lester??"), her reluctant acceptance of it ("Vicki Lester . . ."), and, finally, her insouciant shrug of resignation. The progression showed Garland at her light-comedy best—her facial expressions, her inflections, and her body language are superb at revealing Esther's naivete, her bewilderment, her momentary outrage, and her sense of humor.

The sound building became the Niles projection booth, where the great man is watching one of his studio's latest—a Western. (The actual film Bickford was watching was *The Charge at Feather River*, the second Warners 3-D adventure starring Guy Madison.) One of the executive offices stood in for Norman Maine's dressing room. Several sequences took place here, but perhaps the most important was the scene where Norman sees Esther made up as a glamorous floozie for her screen test, hurries her off to his quarters, and in a light and tentative manner eliminates all the artifice the studio has loaded her down with to make up for her alleged shortcomings ("My ears are too big and my nose is all wrong and I've got no chin"). Slathering gobs of cream on her face, he begins transforming her; and as the end result of all his labors, Esther takes on a wholesome twenty-five-year-old's radiance. To get this effect with Garland, Del Armstrong lightened her face, widened her eyes, and gave her a full-lipped look that made the actress look truly lovely. The effect was completed by Hoyningen-Huene, who devised a light-pink key light which he mounted three feet away from her face; this smoothed out the lines around her nose and filled in the hollowness of her cheeks, giving her a soft, virginal quality.

In the third week of November, while a second unit filmed the action for the puppet commercial, Bellamy and Llewellyn led twenty transportation units to the seedy Bunker Hill section of downtown Los Angeles. In the script, Esther, having left the band and unable to find a singing job, goes to work as a carhop and moves to a dingy rooming house in a decaying area. This would be the first of two trips the company would make to this location. Today would be spent filming scenes of Esther's dejection and Norman's search for her throughout the building while she is on the roof drying her hair. Throughout the film Norman is seen driving a 1953 Lincoln Capri convertible, but for this sequence he was fitted out with a silver Mercedes-Benz, befitting a star of his stature, and also for script purposes, so that the neighborhood children could swarm all over it, blowing the horn, arousing Maine's anger and Esther's attention. Fog and heavy smog prevented much exterior work, so the company was compelled to pick up the necessary shots when it returned for the scene of Esther and Norman's awkward reunion. The landlady, her friends, and their children disrupt the two with their demands for autographs and photographs, and when Norman becomes angry, the pack turns on him and becomes indignantly nasty ("Say, just who do you think you are, Mr. Norman Maine?").

As Bellamy recalls, the production had begun to hum along quickly and efficiently when suddenly, just as work was finishing at the downtown location, "I got a call about two or three in the morning and it was Judy and she said, 'Earl, I don't feel well and I won't be able to get in tomorrow.' I said, 'Fine,' and then around six-thirty or seven I called James Mason and told him that Judy was ill and that he'd have to come in and start the day and work the whole day. I must say, he was absolutely a perfect gentleman every time this happened; he never quibbled about it at all. He said, 'Fine, I'll be there,' and he was always there on time, always knew what he was going to do. You never heard any complaints from James; he was very receptive and very happy to do it. So, as a result, it was smooth and we kept right on shooting without any delays."

During Garland's absence, the company reshot much of the material that had been done earlier, before the changeover to CinemaScope, then moved on to new sequences that did not need the actress. These included the expensive setup wherein Niles is called out to Norman's set because of the actor's drunkenness. To film it, as before, Cukor and crew made use of the standing set of a Chinese junk on the Warner back lot, peopling it with seventy-five Oriental extras and a small number of actors playing technicians and other film personnel. The scene involved a long traveling shot of Mason and Bickford talking as they walked to the set, whereupon Norman went into action as a swashbuckling pirate swinging across a group of extras with a cutlass between his teeth. The shot was made even more complex by the extras and the other actors, who were disoriented by the presence of two camera crews, one real, one fake. With two cameras, two sound booms, and two groups of technicians rushing about, the extras and the crews began straying into the picture, much to everyone's confusion. After some brainstorming, it was decided to simply mark off the boundaries of the set with white tape and to tie colored markings on the real camera. This idea was used throughout the rest of the picture whenever there were sequences involving moviemaking.

Garland was ill for four days; on her return, she refilmed the scene in Esther's room at the Oleander Arms. This time Leavitt assured Cukor that it could be done his way, but it still proved difficult. Work started at 10:00 a.m. and finally finished at 5:45. Even with the lower light levels that could be used with the single-strip WarnerColor negative, the photography was exceedingly time-consuming and exacting because of the restricted color sensitivity of the color negative, especially in areas of dark and shadow. It was like driving with your eyes closed, as there was no accurate way of telling what, if anything, would show up on the film. According to Earl Bellamy, "Mr. Cukor wanted the scene lit just like it was candlelight. I never felt so sorry for Sammy as [when] he tried to light the thing; you could see the beads of perspiration start out on him. It was the lowest key that color could be exposed in—a really very, *very* low light level—and he turned to me at the end of the day and said, 'All I can tell you is I hope we've got an image.' He was at the lab the next morning when it opened and he ran the scene before he ever came to the set; I was waiting for him when he walked in, and he said, 'I think it's gonna work, Earl.' That night we ran it for Mr. Cukor in the dailies, and it was beautiful. To this day it's one of the most gorgeous shots I've ever seen."

The next day, the company moved back to the apartment motel at Crescent Heights and Fountain which would be used for exteriors of the Oleander Arms. Here were shot Esther's farewell to the band, Esther waiting by the pool for Norman's call, and a later sequence in which Norman, returned from his six-week location jaunt, quizzes the landlady, trying to find what has become of Esther. Then, cast, crew, and equipment moved back to downtown Los Angeles to complete the sequence of Norman and Esther's reunion on the rooftop of the boardinghouse. This was a particularly grueling day of shooting: Cukor had done seventeen takes of the scene between Norman and the landlady and thirteen of Esther saying goodbye to the band; the relatively uncomplicated scenes on the rooftop required fifty-three takes to satisfy Cukor. The day had been chilly, and Garland had to play her scenes on the rooftop in a bra and shorts, as it was supposed to be a warm summer day. Not surprisingly, Bellamy received another middle-of-the-night call from the actress, saying she was not feeling well and would not be in the next day.

Fortunately, the schedule called for filming scenes on location at the Santa Anita racetrack, and Garland was not needed. Once again, Bellamy dispatched a caravan of twenty-six trucks, vans, and cars from the studio at 6:00. The production staff followed at 7:00; James Mason and Jack Carson, the principal actors for the day's scenes, left at 7:45; and the bit players and seventy-five extras from Central Casting left the studio at 8:00.

On the casting of these smaller parts, Earl Bellamy relates: "At the start of shooting, Irene Burns, Mr. Cukor's secretary, would give me a list of names and say, 'Earl, these are some of Mr. Cukor's friends, and if you could use them, he would appreciate it,' so whenever I had a small part that needed a good face or a good character bit, I would just see to it that Mr. Cukor's friends worked." In the case of *A Star Is Born*, this was to the picture's advantage, for, as Cukor explained in a memo to Luft and the assistant directors, "I would like to make it a practice [with this film] to cast some players both in bit roles and in crowd shots . . . to create the impression that studio life in Hollywood is made up of a comparatively small group of people who constantly cross paths in both business and social activities." Many of Cukor's friends were actors, frequently older performers whose careers had peaked long ago and who were now relegated to doing bits or "atmosphere" parts or an occasional speaking role. For the Santa Anita sequence, Bellamy gave small parts to Gertrude Astor, one of the great beauties of the silent screen, and Pat O'Malley, who had started his film career with the Edison stock company in 1907, rising to become a prominent leading man in the 1920s. Cukor took care not only of his old friends but of their children, too: Ethel Barrymore's son Sam Colt (grandnephew and namesake of the Samuel Colt who invented the Colt revolver) had been working in small parts for most of his career—a career that he had gone into against his mother's wishes and which was largely undistinguished. He and the two other veterans were given "speaking bits"—bit parts with a line or two. In this particular scene, they played people who either had worked with Norman Maine or knew him socially but were now snubbing him or brushing him off after his humiliation at the Academy Awards ceremony.

The scene itself involved physical violence, rare in a Cukor film: Libby, encountering Maine at the bar, insults him, finally pushing Norman's pride too far when he sneers at him, "You fixed yourself up pretty well—you can live off your wife now." Norman lashes out at him, and Libby punches him, knocking him down, at which point a crowd gathers, commenting in disgust, "Oh, it's just Norman Maine" . . . "He's drunk again" . . . "He's been drunk for years" . . . "How does Vicki stand him?" . . . "She must feel sorry for him." As the next race is announced, they disperse, Libby nonchalantly strolls away, and Norman, left at the bar, orders a double scotch, his first in months. As he downs it, the physical and mental turmoil of what he just experienced makes his entire body shake and cringe in humiliation and revulsion. All of this had to be carefully worked out—action, staging, camera movement, and timing—with both principals and extras.

Norman's entrance down the grand staircase and his scene with Colt, Astor, and O'Malley was filmed twelve times before Cukor moved on to the next and most crucial part, the confrontation between Maine and Libby at the bar. This involved a delicate bit of timing, as the camera was behind the bar, shooting out toward the lounge. The action called for Mason to walk over to the bar, sit down, order a ginger ale, and have a short bit of dialogue with the bartender, then turn just as Libby sits down next to him. It was delicate because Carson walked into camera range as Norman began his conversation with the bartender: Mason's back was to Carson, and he was far enough away so that Carson could not hear what was being said and, without hearing the dialogue, could not time his arrival to coincide with Maine's turning around. "We'd use cue lights for a situation like that," relates Bellamy. "Normally the director would cue the actor, but Mr. Cukor would get so involved in the scene that he would forget to press the cue light, so it was up to me to work it out. I remember I had Carson stop midway in his walk and look at something he was holding; when the dialogue reached the point where Jack should start walking, I'd push the button, he sees the light, puts whatever it was back in his pocket, walks to the bar and sits down just as Mason turns around."

After two days away, Garland returned and recorded the songs "It's a New World" and "Someone at Last." At the same time, on a set duplicating the famous Cocoanut Grove nightclub in the Ambassador Hotel, Cukor filmed a scene that was both lavish and intimate—intimate because it was basically a duologue between Norman and Bruno, the maître d', as Maine tries to find "the little dark girl who sings with the Glenn Williams Orchestra" who saved him from making a fool of himself earlier in the evening.

"The Williams Orchestra finishes at one o'clock," Bruno explains. "They finished about an hour ago. Then the rhumba band takes over." But he does give Maine a clue: "The bands that play here, the musicians, they go to a little place on Sunset Boulevard after they finish here. Maybe she's there. Crazy people, Mr. Maine. They blow their heads off here all night and then instead of going to bed they go to this place and blow their heads off for themselves—for nothing."

As the scene continues, Maine asks, "Is there anyone here I know?" and Bruno, who obviously knows Maine and his tastes well, proceeds to call his attention to some of the more available ladies in the room: "There's a new little girl from Paramount—very pretty, Mr. Maine."

"She's with someone."

"Only her agent. He'll be glad to leave."

"Too young, Bruno. I had a very 'young' week last week. Not worth it. Anyone else?"

"Miss Sheldon. She's very beautiful tonight, Mr. Maine."

"No. She hit me over the head with a bottle."

"Yes, I remember. It happened right here. But I thought everything was all—"

"No. They only hit me once. . . . Who's the little girl in the green dress over there?"

"*No*, Mr. Maine. Pasadena. Let it alone."

It was one of Moss Hart's finest creations: a sharply observed, witty, and sophisticated little gem of a scene that subtly pointed up Norman's womanizing, his loneliness, and his boredom while simultaneously giving a quick and amusing glimpse into the flesh-market aspect of the Hollywood social and nightlife scene. Cukor staged it in one long, continuous moving shot, as Norman and Bruno move among the trees edging the dance floor, with the orchestra and the dancing couples in the background, and the foreground peopled with isolated groups of diners, drinkers, and talkers. Cukor had picked a little-known character actor named Frank Puglia for the part of Bruno, and he and Mason rehearsed the scene while Leavitt and his crew lit the set, which took almost an hour, because the palm trees kept getting in the way of the actors and the camera. Another half-hour was spent moving some of the trees, then relighting the set, placing the bit people, rehearsing them in their action, and getting the dancers to stay within camera range as the camera movements were set and the blocking for Mason and Puglia was worked out, so that their dialogue was carefully and naturally delivered as they moved across the room, weaving in and out and around the palm trees. The rhumba band had been recruited from the local Zenda ballroom and was playing live music instead of prerecorded as was the usual custom. This led to further complications, as the music tended to drown out the dialogue, so some time was spent getting the band to play down to an acceptable level. By the time more trees had been added, and all had been repainted, the ninety-five extras carefully placed and rehearsed, then more lighting and camera adjustments made and a break taken for lunch, it was three p.m. before Cukor and Leavitt took the first shot. After that, the scene was retaken fifteen times, mainly because Frank Puglia had so much difficulty with his lines, coordinating them with his actions and the bits of business that Cukor had devised: unobtrusively producing a lighter for Maine's cigarette while simultaneously scanning the room to try to find him a suitable companion. Cukor wanted a specific kind of smooth, near-obsequious performance from Puglia, and the veteran actor was having trouble achieving the shadings and nuances that Cukor kept urging him to strive for. Finally, the thirteenth take was completed with no mishaps. The scene was done twice more, and Cukor finally was satisfied with take 15. By the time they finished, at 5:00, almost two pages of dialogue had been filmed—three and a half minutes on screen.

The next day was Thanksgiving, and the holiday marked the end of the first complete month of shooting on *A Star Is Born.* In thirty-five days of filming, the production was nineteen days behind schedule, and Warners had spent nearly $1 million in filming 33 of the script's 123 scenes, just over an hour's worth of usable footage, with roughly three quarters of the script still to be photographed.

The next major sequence found Cukor, Garland, Mason, and company traveling ninety miles north of Los Angeles to the tiny town of Piru to film the elopement and marriage of Norman and Esther and their pursuit by Libby. Once again it was Cukor's request for the offbeat and the realistic that led them on location when the scene could easily have been done on the back lot at the studio. Relates Bellamy: "Mr. Cukor wanted to go away, far away from Los Angeles, because it was kind of a secret affair, their marriage, and we needed a town that was so small that nobody in the place would recognize them, nobody would even know they were there. During preproduction, the location manager would go through the script with us, and we'd all decide what should be done on location. In those days, the location manager had photos of places, arranged by category—you know, restaurants, hotels, small towns—and he'd bring in pictures of all these different locations that might be what we wanted. He came in and showed us this little street in this little town. Mr. Cukor liked the look of the place, so before the picture started, Mr. Cukor, Gene Allen—everybody—we all drove out there. Mr. Cukor liked the naturalness of the place, he felt it really added to the situation, so we decided that was it, what we had to do, and how to do it, and that's where we shot it."

. . .

Location filming of another sort was used for the next major musical sequence: the song "Here's What I'm Here For" and the scene of Norman's marriage proposal to Vicki were to be photographed on the actual studio recording stage. The scene was photographed over the next two days, with twenty-five musicians, sixteen singers, and three actors playing the sound recording engineers who perpetrate the joke of taping Norman and Vicki's conversation. Tom Noonan, playing Danny McGuire, now Vicki's musical arranger, was supposed to lead the orchestra; but Cukor decided that for the actual conducting of the orchestra he needed a real conductor. So Ray Heindorf, for the second time in his career, went before the cameras to play himself, albeit anonymously. (He had played himself in the 1949 film *It's a Great Feeling*.)

The scene was designed to be taken in fourteen separate shots; and while they were relatively simple, setting them up, with lighting, camera positions, and the complexities of the music situation, exhausted almost all of the first day. Cukor spent very little footage on Garland singing; all of the shots of her with the orchestra were done in one or two takes. The scenes between her and Mason, however—especially the two of them listening to the playback with the musicians—were done over and over again, as many as thirteen times, to achieve the delicacy and charm Cukor wanted.

On December 15, the company began working on one of the more complicated and expensive sequences in the script. At seven that morning, 257 extras from Central Casting arrived at the studio to be made up and costumed as the hierarchy of Hollywood for the Academy Awards presentation. As mentioned earlier, the scene was not accurate for the time period it represented, since the Academy Awards were no longer given at the Cocoanut Grove. In all probability, Warners wanted to save money by not having to build another set; moreover, from the standpoint of staging, it would be easier and simpler to set the scene up at the Grove rather than on a theater stage, where it would be more difficult for Norman to make his way to Vicki's side. Whatever the reason, the scene went ahead as written by Hart. Cukor, as he himself pointed out, was a fanatic about sticking to what the author wrote. "He worked hard on his scripts," recalls Gene Allen, "but once they were written, there were not a lot of changes. I heard him tell more than one actor or actress, 'Yes, that's where I want the period. And, yes, that is a comma, and yes, those dots mean pause. And read it that way.' Once he worked hard on a script and thought that was it, that's pretty much the way he shot it."

Cukor had been attending Academy Awards ceremonies since 1931, and his shrewd observations and sharp eye for details had to be held in check by him as he sought to conjure up the atmosphere, the excitement and tension, and sketch in the background and the dozens of little bits of emphasis with which he wanted to highlight the scene itself. Allen recalls: "Mr. Cukor and I would rehearse the next day's scene. I would play parts and he would play parts. I would be the camera, and we would lay out all the blocking, the action. And then he'd give all this to the cameraman, and while the crew were lining up and lighting, he would work with the actors." Cukor later commented: "The curious thing when you're making a picture . . . you've got this piece of paper in front of you . . . and the actors . . . and that's all. . . . I really don't know what the process is [that makes it all work], I choose to say it's style. You make big decisions, small decisions and decisions you aren't even consciously aware of. You do unexpected things on the set. Making a picture is enormously important to me and the experience is a joyous one. . . . You can do all sorts of preparation but nothing can be planned out perfectly ahead of time. . . . My first reaction to a scene is always emotional. Even when I describe scenes I describe them emotionally. I don't weep or anything, but there's always some part of me left bloody on the scene I've just directed. That's what gives it intensity. Then there are technical things—I may change the lighting or tell an actor 'You were slow on that,' but it's always the emotional impact first. Also, a director has to be able to solve certain things, to see what's wrong. He has to be constantly improving, refining and to do this properly, he has to know the people with whom he's working. Some people require a very light touch, others need coaching."

"Cukor was always totally faithful to the subject matter that he planned to convert into film," recalled James Mason, " . . . and when I started to work with him I [sometimes] found it rather hard going. . . . Here was George talking at me, talking, talking. I submitted to a nonstop flow of talk . . . he was leaning over me all day with his chin thrust out. He had a funny way of directing, of kind of translating the lines into vivid modern terms— 'This shit,' 'What the fuck.' He had a keen image of what he wanted, the way he wanted Norman Maine to behave. I believe what he really wanted was a sort of mimicry of John Barrymore; the only actor he ever talked about was John Barrymore. In the long run I regret that I could not do just what he had wanted. The image I was creating was not Barrymore-esque at all—it was based on some of my own drunken friends. In fact this was the best that I could offer him. Stylistically, a Barrymore figure might have been preferable; but I never had liked what I saw of Barrymore, at least in most of his old movies."

While Cukor and Mason tried to mesh their conceptions of Maine, Earl Bellamy and Russ Llewellyn were working out the background action of the scenes, rehearsing the extras and bit players. The scene had been set up to start on a medium shot of Jack Carson as Matt Libby in the jammed press room as the Best Actor award is presented. As the camera retreats in front of him, Libby makes his way out to the floor of the main ballroom, walking past a battery of newsreel and television cameras; as he does, the point of view shifts to a long shot of the room itself:

> Men in dinner coats and women in elaborate evening dress crowd the tables to the farthest corners of the room. A large television screen is in evidence on which is being duplicated the same action as is taking place on the stage. At the moment, the entire room is applauding and a band is playing as Raymond Wallace, a youngish man, but not a youth, mounts the stage from the audience to be greeted by Susan Ettinger, last year's Oscar winner, who shakes hands with him and presents him, this year's male winner, with the Award statuette.

For the part of Miss Ettinger, Cukor had picked a young red-headed newcomer named Amanda Blake. Her part consisted solely of announcing the winner, presenting him the award, listening to his speech, and then exiting with him. It was what was known as a two-line bit. Richard Webb, playing the winner, had done featured roles in several Warner Bros. and Columbia B pictures; Rex Evans, playing the emcee, was a veteran character actor, while Steve Wyman, playing Nigel Peters, who presents Vicki with her Oscar, was a good-looking newcomer whose only previous work had been a tiny part in a Universal Western. With all of them Cukor worked quickly and carefully.

While the action was being worked out and coordinated with the camera crew, the special-effects camera crew was working out an ingenious split-screen effect that would take advantage of the huge expanse of CinemaScope screen in an innovative manner. As Vicki is presented with her award, the main camera would hold on a long shot of the entire room, with Vicki a tiny figure on the stage. On the right side of the screen, however, was the large television screen that Hart indicated, and on this would be repeated the same shot. But as the television camera crew was seen to dolly forward in the action of the scene, the figure on the television screen was enlarged until the entire television screen was filled with a close-up of Esther giving her acceptance speech. It was a unique and effective method of filling the large screen with the spectacle of the scene while simultaneously concentrating on the intimacy of the moment.

Because of the complexities of the sequence, the first shot was not taken until 12:40 p.m., and the shot was retaken seven times; the rest of the day was spent on the crowd's reaction shots. All the while, Mason waited for his scenes to be readied; he left at 4:30 without having worked in front of the camera. It was the same the next day: six shots were taken, none of which involved Norman.

But on the third day, Mason gave one of the most poignant and subtle performances in the entire film. As Vicki is making her acceptance speech, wrote Hart,

Norman enters, drunkenly applauding, stunning the crowd and Vicki into silence as he mounts the stage, congratulates her, and tenderly kisses her on the forehead, asking: "May I borrow the end of your speech to make one of my own?" Addressing the audience, he says:

My method for gaining your attention is a little unusual, perhaps, but hard times call for harsh measures. . . . Had my speech all prepared—but it seems to have gone right out of my head. Let me see [*he laughs*]—silly to be so formal, isn't it? I know almost all of you sitting out there by your first names, don't I? Made a lot of money for you gentlemen through the years, haven't I? Well, I need a job now! That's it! That's the speech! I need a job . . . simple as that . . . I need a job . . . that's all. My talents, I might add, are not strictly confined to dramatic parts—I can do comedy as well. Play something, boys.

He gestures to the orchestra in back of him and inadvertently strikes Vicki sharply across the face. He stares at her wildly, his eyes not focusing, and starts to sway slightly. He is beginning to come apart. He makes no effort to resist as Vicki pilots him from the stage and through the shocked crowd. Oliver pulls out a chair for him and he almost collapses into it. His hands go over his eyes as the realization of what he has done begins to come over him; in anguish he begs, "Somebody give me a drink . . . please. . . ."

Cukor filmed Mason's scenes in six setups: two alternate versions of his entrance, two different angles of the bulk of his speech, one long take on the entire speech, and a close shot of Norman at the table asking for a drink. The difficulty with doing this kind of delicate scene over and over is, as Cukor pointed out, "to make it fresh, give little changes each time . . . if you have too much rehearsal (or many takes) it becomes mechanical. Good people will vary it every time, for every take." It took twelve complete takes of the scene of Norman's speech before Cukor was satisfied.

The dramatic core of the sequence, what made it so effective, in Cukor's view, was "seeing a proud man humbled." Mason utilized a bit of business that he devised himself: having Norman step alternately up and down the dais as he makes his plea. "It was something I'd seen a little child do once, as he was being scolded for something—he shifted up and down on each foot. I thought that Norman was very childlike, and it seemed like a nice bit, so I just put it in."

The next day, after looking at the rushes, and not seeing everything he wanted in the okayed takes, Cukor wrote a note to Warner:

Dear Jack:
I saw the rushes on the Academy Award scene. They are powerful and moving. As I suspected, the action is pretty slow in spots. I think that in some of the other takes there are parts that probably are more effective, so I would like to see them as well. Dealing with a drunk is always a pretty tricky business; you have to tread a fine line. I'd like to be as sure as one reasonably can about avoiding any of those bad laughs.

That same day, while Cukor was diplomatically confronting Warner on his "no excess printing" edict, the company had begun shooting scenes in the Malibu home of Mr. and Mrs. Norman Maine. The sequences scheduled for the day's work involved a gala housewarming party thrown by Norman and Esther for their friends and co-workers. The day before, Bellamy had sent out a request for twenty-five dress extras (including, at Cukor's request, Mae Marsh, the star of D. W. Griffith's *Intolerance* and other silent classics). However, in being fitted for Mary Ann Nyberg's costume for this scene Garland, for whatever reason, was "displeased with the dress made for scene 80," as a note in the production log indicated. The call for the extras was canceled, and instead Cukor filmed a later scene on the same set, in which Niles tells Norman that the studio is dropping him. Even this fairly simple effort was sabotaged by camera trouble. Thirteen takes were marred by the malfunctioning camera, and the company was dismissed at six-thirty without having accomplished anything.

The next day, while Cukor, Mason, and Bickford filmed the scene, Garland, trying on the altered costume, still considered it "unsatisfactory" and evidently ripped it in a rage and left the studio at four, either furious or exhausted. According to Del Armstrong: "Judy was nervous and distraught at times—some slight little things would irritate her. She would throw tantrums every now and then, but not without provocation. She would never purposely hurt anybody; she was too much of a trouper for that. She spent too many hard years at MGM being stepped on. Wardrobe designers, as a whole, want to impose their will on the other person, saying, 'Wait a minute, this is what you're going to wear.' They're a strange lot, wardrobe people, because they have delusions of grandeur. They think the picture rises and falls on their contribution to it, never realizing that a lot of other ingredients go into it too, not just a pretty dress. So I've seen these confrontations with Judy, and with other stars too. Judy stood up for herself—it wasn't just because she was extra-emotional or showing off or being difficult. I don't think she ever showed any hostility unless she had a good cause."

Earl Bellamy concurs: "Judy was demanding from the standpoint of wanting things right. She was very demanding of herself, basically; but she was demanding of others too—like wardrobe, for example. She didn't like [that dress], and they tried; [but] the ultimate result was no, it didn't work, and we shut down until we got things organized."

Getting things organized meant bringing in a new costume designer—in Allen's words, "to try to give her a figure . . . she was difficult to dress." The person chosen to do this was Jean Louis, Columbia's ace designer, who had created glamorous images for Rita Hayworth, Rosalind Russell, Lucille Ball, and Judy Holliday. He was exceedingly busy, and it took the intervention of Cukor himself with Harry Cohn, head of Columbia, before the designer agreed to do it.

Garland's personal problems were intensified by the fact that Luft, whom she depended on for support and reassurance, was gone for several days to attend his father's funeral in New York. When he returned on December 21, he found the production in a near shambles. Garland had been unable to work since the 18th; while she was out, Cukor and the rest of the company had shot various bits and pieces of retakes and journeyed down the coast to Wilmington to film scenes of Norman on location in the early parts of the story. The day before Christmas was spent looking for suitable locations in Laguna Beach to double for the location of Norman's suicide in Malibu, which was not considered isolated or dramatic enough. These shots were filmed late in the afternoon the day after Christmas and were completed relatively smoothly and quickly.

With Luft back, Garland was able to begin work again. Everyone was now keyed up and ready to start one of the most spectacular of all the sequences in the script—the crucial and expensive Shrine Auditorium benefit.

As noted earlier, Cukor had taken Hart's one descriptive paragraph and expanded it into an evocation of the confusion, hysteria, and glamorous razzle-dazzle of a big, important Hollywood opening night. Cukor had been to many such events, but with the exception of *The Robe* opening he had never studied them in detail. As he later stated: "When you know you are going to do a film, you look at things with different eyes. I delve into the texture of life and reality and then recreate the whole thing. Reality must be observed, then transmuted."

Once this particular reality—the theater, the crowds, the excitement— was established in the opening sequences, Cukor, as per the script, had to introduce the principals, make story points, and stage and photograph the first musical numbers. To achieve all this would take, according to the production office, approximately eight days, twenty-two transportation units, 496 dress extras, sixty-eight additional extras for small speaking parts, five stand-ins, eight limousines, three yellow cabs, five portable dressing rooms, a thirty-six-piece orchestra with instruments, five television cameras, four actual film cameras, sixty-five separate pieces of lighting equipment, eight horses, and two animal wranglers—the latter because it had been decided to use Monte Montana's entire Wild West Show as the opening number of the benefit show.

The venerable Shrine Auditorium lent itself perfectly to the scale of this sequence. Built in 1926 from a design by architect G. Albert Lansburgh, it was a Moorish fantasy of domes, turrets, and arches; with its 6,700 seats, it was the largest theater in the world. Its vast stage and cavernous auditorium had been seen only once before on film, for the New York debut of the giant ape in 1933's *King Kong.* The stage was one of the largest in existence; wing space was equally large, and Cukor intended to take full advantage of it in the tense scenes showing a drunken, riotous Norman creating havoc amidst the already frantic backstage activity of the benefit.

For Bellamy and Llewellyn, the organization of such a large sequence was a matter of scheduling and keeping track of literally hundreds of details. The makeup, dressing, and feeding of the extras and bit players was a mammoth job, but fortunately the Shrine Auditorium had a sister structure in the back: the Shrine Exposition Hall, which could comfortably accommodate several thousand people, dining tables, makeup cubicles, and costume racks; food could be prepared and served from the in-house kitchen.

This was the first time that Richard Barstow's dancers would work in front of the camera. Barstow had been hard at work on the back lot since August, devising routines for the four songs that would be full-fledged production numbers in the film. Bellamy had alerted him that the first song, "Gotta Have Me Go With You," was scheduled for photography on the Shrine stage on December 28; Garland had begun working with Barstow and her "dance-in," Gloria DeWerd, on the movement for this first number whenever she could get time away from shooting. The script called for Esther and the Glenn Williams Orchestra to go on in place of the drunken Maine. He, however, will not be kept off, and lurches onto the stage and into the song and dance. Esther quickly averts an embarrassment by making him seem part of the act: she works him into the dance, and he, realizing the situation through his alcoholic fog, rises to the occasion, does a little step with her, exits in a very showmanly fashion, and then brings her back on again for a bow, as if it were all preplanned. Barstow had to work all this out, devise steps for Garland and the two male dancers who accompanied her as she sang, and incorporate Maine into the action.

Staging musical numbers was a new experience for Cukor, although he had done some similar work in the music-hall sequences of *Zaza* in 1939 with Claudette Colbert, with Fanny Brice as technical advisor. "I try to think everything out ahead of time," Cukor commented. "I feel my way around a long time ahead to see how these things can be managed; everything has to be planned ahead for these big numbers. . . . In this respect . . . I have working with me one of the most talented art directors in the world, Gene Allen. He is the greatest help to me . . . he's an art director who does everything"—including working out every angle of every shot in the film. "I was feeling my way on this picture," recalls Allen. "I got to work with him an awful lot on setting up shots, and more and more he turned that over to me. I always did tell him what we were going to shoot next and how we could do it. 'We can do it this way—they run out of the shot and we can [change the angle] over to here and we can pick that up and all.' Then I'd do a quick thumbnail sketch for the cameraman so he'd know how we wanted it. Then Cukor'd send me off to work with the choreographer so I'd know the numbers. Barstow would show it to me and I'd be working out in my mind where the cameras would be, how it could be shot. Then Mr. Cukor would come in and look at it and I'd explain what I thought; he might make some changes—you know, with the camera, place it differently. So that when we come on the stage and they'd do it, I'm standing there with Mr. Cukor by the camera as the dance goes on, so there were no problems between any of us—Cukor, the cameraman, George Huene—we really had a nice time shooting this stuff."

While these details were being worked out on the stage of the Shrine and the lineup and lighting were being attended to, Del Armstrong was overseeing a squad of makeup assistants who were readying the seventy-five extras playing dancers, jugglers, English buskers, ballerinas, and cowboys and Indians for the Wild West Show, and the hundreds of others who had to be ready for the nine a.m. shooting call. "When we were filming down at the Shrine, it was one of the few times I had to use makeup charts on the picture, because there were so many people to worry about. I had all these assistants and I'd make up some drawings and put them up on the wall to have them all thinking in terms of the same look—that is, a different look for the audience, a different one for the performers on stage and the musicians. The principals, of course, are supposed to be pretty normal, but for the backstage stuff, I made up some harlequins and mannequins, clowns, ballerinas, things like that—background stuff."

While Armstrong made up the performers, Bellamy was working out the action for the extras and the bit players. "On the backstage stuff," he recalls, "Mr. Cukor let George Huene really have his head on this, and I worked very closely with him. He'd say, 'Now here's the idea, Earl,' and then it was up to me to get what his idea was and then show him the standpoint of the staging to see if that's what he had in mind. Now, I had worked on a lot of other shows before this; I'd familiarized myself with some of the stuff that Western Costume had, so he and I went over there and selected a lot of costumes for the Shrine sequences. The button men in the button suits—the buskers—that was something we added."

An interesting example of the details that a creative assistant director can add to a scene: As Norman is drunkenly making a nuisance of himself backstage, he is confronted by Libby, who tries to talk him into a phony press conference to keep him from going on. Norman is engaged in conversation with the English buskers and has donned one of the button coats that Bellamy refers to. As Libby pulls Norman away, one of the buskers (played by ex–Keystone Kop Heinie Conklin) moves in swiftly to pull the coat off Norman, who is so drunk he hardly notices it. "That was just something I added—I thought it would work, and it did, and Mr. Cukor liked it. What was so super about the entire film was that so many people, like George Huene, Gene Allen, and myself, we would all work together for ideas to present to Mr. Cukor to get the best out of the film. As a result, I think the stuff at the Shrine—I'm really proud of that, because . . . it has so many things, so many interesting things going, and it really shows what we could do with CinemaScope."

Hoyningen-Huene was responsible for most of the stunning imagery of these backstage scenes. He brought in reproductions of paintings by Degas, specifically "The Dancers" and "The Dancing Class," showing them to Bellamy and Leavitt, who would thereupon set up the staging and photography to suggest the paintings. "Gene Allen would sketch it out," relates Bellamy, "and we'd show what could be done. I remember Huene wanted a long, transparent gauze-type thing stretched across the backstage area at one point. Then he put a pink light on it and we had horses and people moving behind it and it gave a wonderful effect, especially when Norman staggered through it . . . I thought it was just outstanding. He had marvelous ideas for background, tremendous ideas about shadows, about light: there's whole areas of the screen that he kept dark. It was very exciting." Hoyningen-Huene elaborated on his work on these sequences later, in an interview: "It is in the Shrine Auditorium scenes that color really plays its big scene. Nearly 800 extras in the theatre are grouped in accordance with the color of the women's evening clothes. We put the women in yellow in one part of the auditorium, those in gray in another. People formed blocks of color which blended into each other without that restless, dispersed look usually seen in crowd scenes. . . . We tested the color of the theatre program four separate times before we decided on the final phosphorescent pink. In the picture, the programs will appear as pinpricks of red, accentuating the excitement of the crowd pushing their way into the auditorium."

All of the first day's work at the Shrine was devoted to setting these details, working out lighting, staging, groupings, and bits of business and setting up multiple cameras. "We had three or four cameras," recalls Gene

Allen, "and everything was on dollies and moveable. . . . It was exciting and everybody was cooperating. . . . Cukor wanted to get all the footage he could so that he could play with it in the cutting rooms. He wanted to do things he never did before, things he always wanted to do . . . lights flashing, shining right into the lens . . . for years that was a no-no. . . . Huene was running all over the place. . . . He would go and find these bits of gauze and cloth and put these on the extras to make sure the color was all co-ordinated."

Finally, mid-morning on December 29, everything was ready for the first shots to be taken. These primarily involved Bickford and Carson conversing about Maine in Oliver Niles's box while in the background the Wild West spectacle is played out on the stage. Also filmed that day was much of the backstage action, with Sam Colt playing the harassed stage manager trying to cope with Norman, who insists on riding a horse onto the stage. Finally, the next day, Cukor shot the opening musical number with Garland, two dancers, and the Glenn Williams Orchestra: the lively, uptempo "Gotta Have Me Go With You." Hoyningen-Huene related that "at this point in the story, Miss Garland is a band singer of no importance, so her entrance onto the stage is painted in subdued and neutral tones . . . the background is an unimpressive gray." Garland was also wearing the first of the several costumes that Jean Louis had designed: a navy blue top and skirt, split up the side to reveal her black-stockinged legs. The only bits of color on her were her lipstick and the red carnation in her lapel. It took the better part of two days, and more than forty takes, before the number was completed with all the necessary angles and "protection footage" that Cukor felt was necessary.

After a break for the New Year's holiday, the company shot for the next six days at the Shrine, filming the scenes between Niles, Libby, and Lola Lavery, the starlet who is one of the studio's "hot properties" and Norman's inamorata. This was Lucy McAleer's first taste of big-time moviemaking, and it was during the shooting at the Shrine that her name was changed to Lucy Marlow. She remembers: "The studio sent me three pages of names from which I was to choose. My mother said there had been a Julia Marlowe on the New York stage who was very famous, and she thought that might bring me good luck—so we took the 'e' off it to make it a little more distinctive, and that became my name."

Lucy Marlow's first day as a professional actress was memorable to her for several reasons. "In the scene where I walk into the theater with Charlie Bickford and Jack Carson, I had on this beautiful dress with a huge flounce on it from mid-calf down, so that I couldn't see the white tape mark on the floor, where I was supposed to stop. I kept missing my mark. I did this about three times, and after the third time the extras—the Shrine was full of extras, there must have been six hundred or so in the background—began to titter a bit, which made me all the more nervous. So Mr. Cukor said, 'Would you go have your makeup checked, little one? We need to do some setup here.' So I went off to the makeup area. I found out later from a wardrobe lady that Mr. Cukor announced to the extras: 'Miss Marlow is having a problem hitting the mark because of her costume. We're going to remedy that; that's easy to do. What is not easy to do is to handle the likes of you'— with some of his adjectives thrown in—'making it uncomfortable not only for her but also for the rest of us who are trying to do our best for the film. If I hear one more titter from any one of you, I'm firing the whole lot.' That's what he said, for a little starlet. I adored him."

Cukor evidently trusted Marlow enough to let her do what she wanted as Lola Lavery. In the scene with Bickford in the box when Libby announces that Norman is drunk and shouldn't go on, Marlow relates, "Mr. Cukor kept photographing . . . and I'd ask him, 'What do you want me to do?' because he kept taking more footage. Finally, in between takes I said, 'Please, Mr. Cukor, is there anything else you want me to do?' He said, 'No, whatever you want to do.' I had figured out from the script that Lola Lavery was probably not a very intelligent girl. She had probably been kept or was being kept by Norman Maine; consequently, she wasn't at the premiere for any other reason than to be seen. When somebody wants to be seen and is that self-indulgent, they preen, so that's what I did."

Marlow recalls another singular experience later on in the shooting: "I was talking to some of the gypsies, some of the dancers, and suddenly everybody broke for lunch. Well, everybody could go to lunch except me, because I couldn't sit down in that black dress I was wearing. I used to rest on what they called a 'slant board,' where you sort of leaned back and rested your hips. So I ran back to my little portable dressing room, trying to find the wardrobe lady or someone to unhook me so I could put on a smock and go in and sit down and have lunch. I couldn't find her, she had gone off to lunch, so I was going around asking everybody I met to unhook my dress. And everybody I asked said, 'We can't, we're not in that union.' I didn't know what that meant, and they told me that if they unhooked me they could get fired or the wardrobe lady could get fired.

"So I was going around almost in tears and I was almost by myself in the Shrine, behind the curtains—I was standing there looking around when I heard someone say, 'What's the matter, kid—you lost?' and I turned around and there was Judy Garland. Now, I had not met her—all I heard was 'In heaven's name, don't say anything to her until she says something to you!' There was talk that she was drinking heavily, that she was on drugs, and she was very, *very* difficult, so the best thing to do was to stay out of her way. And then here I was, all alone with this monster I had heard about. But I had adored her all my life and had used her as one of my standards when I had to sing, so I stuttered, 'Oh, Miss Garland, I can't get out of this dress and the wardrobe lady has gone off to lunch and nobody can undo it because—' And she said, 'Oh, knock it off, to hell with it, I'll undo the dress! If you don't tell anybody, I won't . . . Just don't tell anybody I'm smoking!' She had a cigarette hanging out of her mouth while she was unbuttoning my dress—she told me the fire hazard at the Shrine was something else, nobody was allowed to smoke, so everybody was going bananas, running out the side door to have a cigarette whenever they could.

"As she was undoing my dress, I was reaching out for some kind of conversation, and I asked her if she was pleased with what she was doing and she said, 'Yeah, this is like old home week for me.' It was easy for her to dance on this stage because the first time she had performed as a professional, her mother had literally kicked her on stage as a Meglin Kiddie—they were a troupe of little tap-dancing children. She said she'd heard great things about what I was doing, that Cukor thought I was terrific. She said, 'Listen, honey, I've got my money in this thing. If George says you're doing something to help the picture, I'm all for you—you're all right in my book,' so she wished me good luck and went her way and I found a smock and went mine. But that was something . . . it was an emotional blanket that started me off with that lady."

After all these early scenes had been filmed, Cukor and the company spent the next two days filming the ending scenes, which brought the story full circle. Esther, now Vicki Lester, the biggest star in the movies, attends a benefit show at the Shrine Auditorium shortly after Norman's suicide, where she goes onstage and introduces herself as Mrs. Norman Maine. The scene was photographed with two cameras: one in the first row of the first balcony, which gave a good close shot of Vicki on the stage, and one in the last row of the second balcony, which offered a stunning shot of the eye-filling Shrine proscenium arch and drop curtain. Cukor had wanted to move from a close shot of Garland to the extreme long shot from the second balcony in one continuous pull-back, but there was no way of accomplishing this in one unbroken shot. So Leavitt, using a zoom lens on the camera, pulled back as far as he could from the first balcony; and the camera in the second balcony, also equipped with a zoom lens, picked up from there. It was decided that the two separate shots would be combined in a dissolve by the laboratory, which meant that the pull-back speeds would have to be carefully synchronized, so the movement would cut together smoothly.

Again with this ending scene, Hoyningen-Huene had a very specific idea about the color mood: "In contrast with the bright opening sequence, the final sequence is dominated by a deep sky-blue mood, not gay. Miss Garland, now riding the crest of film success, is dressed in gold. But her appearance has *Pagliacci* overtones and the crowd knows it. The sky-blue color contributes a serene quality."

Immediately after finishing this last scene, Cukor had Allen revamp a section of one of the Shrine's balconies and used it as the movie theater where Norman and Esther watch the sneak preview of her first starring film. The final two days at the Shrine involved close-in work of the arriving stars and celebrities being interviewed in the lobby by a typical Hollywood interviewer. For this, Cukor cast the real thing: a local announcer named George Fischer, a long-time emcee at premieres. As his female counterpart, Joan Shawlee, a little-known young character actress, gave a hilarious impersonation of a gushing radio columnist describing "lovely Lola Lavery" from her wardrobe ("She's wearing a black sheath and a blue fox—isn't it marvelous? And the diamonds in the hair!!") to her character ("We've just had the pleasure of talking with Lola Lavery. . . . Have you ever seen anyone so sweet, so unspoiled and down to earth? She's a darling girl"). All of this was filmed with very little difficulty and very little excess footage, and work at the Shrine finished on budget and on schedule on January 8.

· · ·

Back at the studio, work progressed quickly and smoothly on scenes involving the housewarming party of Norman and Esther, which had been postponed because of Garland's dissatisfaction with her costume; this was
completed in two days. Then the "New York street" on the Warners back
lot was dressed up with neon signs, puddles of water, and 112 extras to
create a believable facsimile of a busy street in a small Southern California
town, where Norman and Esther arrive for the preview of her first starring
film. Following these relatively simple scenes, Cukor shot the sequences of
Norman being bailed out of the drunk tank by Vicki and Oliver Niles on
Christmas Eve. These exterior shots were done on location at the Lincoln
Heights jail in downtown Los Angeles; the interiors would be done later
at the studio.

"Cukor had told us that he wanted rain when we did the scene of
Maine's funeral," Russ Llewellyn relates. "So we waited and waited and
finally we got lucky. We got a bad forecast and we rushed right through
and made it. It was a hell of a day's work. We had four hundred extras and
we ruined the lawn at the church." The scene was staged at the Church
of the Good Shepherd in Beverly Hills, irreverently known locally as "Our
Lady of the Cadillacs." It was a difficult sequence to shoot, since the church
hierarchy would not allow lights in the church itself, making it almost
impossible to photograph Garland, Bickford, and Noonan as they came out
of the darkness of the church vestibule. Compounding the problem was the
fact that Garland was wearing a heavy veil and both Noonan and Bickford
were in dark suits; Leavitt could not get enough exposure to separate the
characters from the darkness of the church. The solution that he worked
out was to use a side door of the church for their exit, as it was backdropped
with a stained glass window in the wall behind the door, which gave enough
backlight so that the three figures could be seen. The edict against flood-
lights in the church was circumvented by having photographers' flashbulbs
go off as soon as the doors were opened, which lit the faces and figures of
the principals in a dramatic, staccato fashion. Interspersed with this was the
frenzy of the fans, hysterically pushing and shoving in their efforts to see
Vicki; all this gave the scene a raw, cold semidocumentary look that added
greatly to the dramatic impact of Vicki's screaming, wailing collapse as her
veil is ripped off by her adoring fans with their ghoulish demand to "give
us just one good look!"

                              •   •   •

Next, Cukor returned to the scenes in the Malibu beach house where Esther, after getting Norman out of jail, tells Niles that she is giving up her career to care for her husband, who overhears all this and, devastated, decides to commit suicide. These were crucial scenes in the story, melodramatic and almost unbelievable. Hart had lifted them almost intact from the original, with virtually no rewriting, relying instead on their highly charged dramatic intensity and Cukor's subtlety to make them come alive.

To do this, Cukor depended more than usually on mood. The setting was supposedly an exterior, a modern glass-walled house with a terrace overlooking the ocean. The time was a late winter afternoon, which deepened into twilight as the scene progressed, giving the scene the necessary feeling of coldness and melancholy. For Sam Leavitt, the sequence was another in the long series of problems that had to be solved in a practical, realistic manner. "Cukor wanted it to be late afternoon," he recalled. "The sun goes down, down . . . the shadows get blacker and longer. You have to think what to do: how's it going to look? So I had to put some color lights over the lights, the kind that would make it look like late afternoon. You have to make it look beautiful as well—make Judy look good, and Mason, and when they're both together, you have to make them *both* look good. You can't make them look flat; you have to get a molded look, with lights and shadows that are dramatic and add something to the scene." Leavitt's lighting and photography problems were complicated by a subtle bit of symbolism that Cukor had used throughout the film to try to hint at Maine's fate. In an early scene in Maine's bedroom, he had shown a close-up of the actor's tuxedo shirt on the floor, its arms outstretched as if it were floating in the dark. In the scenes of Maine on location, the first shot of the actor was of him unconscious, floating on his back in the water before being pulled to safety; and in the shots of him alone in the beach house, putting golf balls, he is backdropped by waves breaking on the shore as seen through the windows of the living room. For this presuicide sequence, Cukor wanted to have Maine behind the sliding glass doors, surrounded by the reflection of the breaking surf and the ocean. It seemed impossible to do this in the manner Cukor wanted without going on location, but Leavitt and the special effects crew came up with an ingenious solution to the problem, which Cukor explained: "All we had was the interior set and a little exterior set of the terrace right outside the house, so we had to suggest the location by a process shot of the reflection of the ocean." This involved erecting a large "process screen" opposite the beach house set, then projecting onto it from behind footage of the ocean and the surf, whose reflection would be picked up by the glass doors and windows. Thus, when Mason stood inside the sliding glass doors of the set, the reflection of the water seemed to surround him and wash over him. And Cukor attempted to give the scene a further air of reality: "I don't like doing exteriors on an interior set, but if you can get a sense of movement in the air, you can keep the scene alive. Judy Garland wore a very light chiffon scarf, and the air moved it. It was tricky, because if we'd had a regular fan, it would have made so much noise, we would have had to postsync the dialogue. So we had wind tunnels, where the fan is placed outside the stage and the air is brought in through a big canvas tunnel that kills the sound of the fan. So you got the illusion of being at the ocean, and we were able to keep the exterior alive."

After these problems had been solved to everyone's satisfaction, Cukor turned to the difficult scene showing Norman overhearing the conversation between Esther and Niles and his agony at the knowledge that once again he has "destroyed everything I touch." There was no dialogue; it was an entirely silent bit and needed all of Mason's gifts as an actor to get the points across in a believable and affecting fashion. Mason related: "The great thing about a relationship between a director and an actor is that it is a cooperation. An actor should help the director—he should try to figure out what particular talents this director has and how he could help serve him and cooperate with him. One of my best experiences was working with George. He is at the top of the list of the few really gifted directors I've worked with."

Cukor elaborated on Mason's comments: "I never rehearse the emotions of a scene, only the mechanics. The scene didn't require anything special . . . it all happened so naturally. It was very moving, mainly because of James Mason. He is a complete actor. He is a man who has the greatest discretion . . . rather reserved by nature . . . a mysterious, enigmatic creature. . . . I knew that this scene would be a case of letting him find things out for himself. To see that man break down was very moving. All the credit for that goes to James. He did it all himself. What I did was to let him do it and let it go on and on, let the camera stay on him for an eternity. All his feelings came out . . . he became so involved, in fact, that he could hardly stop, and I just let him do what he felt."

If Mason's scene "didn't require anything special," it was because of his abilities as a dramatic actor, his experience at his craft, and his willingness to explore his own hidden emotional world. Garland, however, was a different matter. "Until *A Star Is Born,*" related Cukor, "Judy Garland had only played musical comedy. A lot of people in musical comedy are like mimics or impersonators, which is not real acting. They promise more than they deliver. You think, 'if only they could play out a scene, how good they'd be,' and very often you're wrong." Cukor was now to find out whether he had been wrong in his early impression that Garland "possessed the emotional ability . . . to be a great dramatic actress." Up to now in the filming, Garland had been giving a performance that was near her old MGM standard: warm, amusing, and with flashes of a deeper emotional sensitivity; but nothing in the script had challenged her to go beyond the smooth, easy style of "personality" acting that she had been trained in. Now, however, Hart's screenplay required her to probe into areas that were foreign to her as an actress.

The first of such scenes now scheduled to be filmed took place after Norman's funeral. Esther has cut herself off from all contact with everyone and everything and stays at home, isolated and brooding. Danny McGuire comes to pick her up for a guest appearance she has promised to make at a benefit—ironically, at the Shrine Auditorium. When she demurs, he tries to persuade her and she turns on him, near hysteria, whereupon he lambastes her as being "a great monument to Norman Maine . . . he was a drunk and he wasted his life, but he loved you . . . and took great pride in the one thing in his life that wasn't a waste—you. . . . Now you're doing the one thing he was terrified of—you're tossing aside the one thing he had left. . . . You're the only thing that remains of him now . . . and if you just kick it away, it's like he never existed. Like there was never a Norman Maine at all."

According to Cukor, "Judy . . . was a very original and resourceful actress. We'd talked about the scene only a little, but we both had a general idea of what it should be. The basic idea was her melancholia, her state of total depression. While we lined it up she just sat there, very preoccupied. Just before the take I said to her very quietly, 'You know what this is about. You really know this.' She gave me a look and I knew she was thinking, 'He wants me to dig into myself, because I know all about this in my own life.' That was all. Then we did a take."

If the scene was trying for Garland, it was nerve-wracking for Tom Noonan, who was playing Danny McGuire. His entrance had to be shot seven times due to his nervousness. When this had been done to Cukor's

satisfaction, they moved to the core of the scene, which was Vicki's hysterical reaction to Danny's insistence that she come to the benefit. Garland's
playing of this was evidently so fierce that it completely threw Noonan, for,
as Earl Bellamy recalls, "Tommy was not new [to acting], but he hadn't
done anything as big as this, and it was intimidating the way Judy came
on. He was very taken aback. It was very rough for him, and we finally had
to stop, and Cukor took him aside and said, 'Now listen, come on . . .' and
so we started it over." Cukor remembered that "[in the scene] she has
trouble articulating anything, she seems exhausted and dead. [He] . . .
chides her about not giving in to herself . . . and she loses her head. When
. . . Garland did this, it was one of the most tremendous outbursts of
emotion I'd ever seen. It was *absolutely* terrifying. She [got] up and
screamed like someone out of control, maniacal. . . . She had no concern
with what she looked like, she went much further than I'd expected.
. . . I was sitting right there with the camera next to me but I felt that I
was watching some awful cataclysm of nature. . . . I was . . . scared that
[Noonan] might be thrown . . . [but this time] he stayed right with her,
at one moment he even grabbed her and she tried to get away. (You have
to be careful about moments like that, they musn't be too rehearsed or slick,
and they musn't be too goddamned much. But this was exactly right, an
ugly, awkward, desperate scuffle.) So he grabbed her and held her and spoke
his next lines with great force and energy. The lines were meant to shame
her—and her reaction was unforgettable. She turned around and you saw
that all the anger and madness and fear had disappeared. Her face looked
very vulnerable and tender, there were tears in her eyes. So I said 'Cut!'
and then, 'Quick, let's do it once more!' and they dried Judy off to get her
ready again. One of the hazards of picture-making . . . is that you get a scene
which turns out wonderfully, but next morning they tell you the sound was
no good or there was a scratch on the film. That's why I wanted to do it
again immediately. So Judy did it again—differently, but just as stunningly.
Scenes can never be reproduced exactly, and you shouldn't try. . . . When
it was over I said to Judy, 'You really scared the hell out of me.' She was
very pleased, she didn't realize what an effect she'd made. And then—she
was always funny, she had this great humor—she said, 'Oh, that's nothing.
Come over to my house any afternoon. I do it every afternoon.' Then she
gave me a look and added, 'But I only do it *once* at home.'"

· · ·

It was at this juncture in the filming that Moss Hart arrived in Los Angeles to, as he had written Cukor, "take a look at the picture and see if you need any rewriting, before whatever retakes are necessary." The picture was in rough form; there were scenes that had not yet been photographed, three of the musical numbers hadn't been done, and there were alternate versions of some scenes included in the rough assembly, as Cukor had not yet decided which portions of each he wanted to use. Hart spent the better part of four days in mid-January looking at the picture and conferring with Luft and Cukor about what he felt to be the strengths and weaknesses of the work that had been done. In an interview with Ed Sullivan shortly after this, Hart commented on what he considered to be a new maturity in Garland as an actress: "It has nothing to do with technique," he said. "It is a curious instinct that she possesses. Give her a scene and instinctively she'll play it right. Watching her, you get the almost weird impression that she's—I don't know quite how to explain it—but it's something like a great musician plucking the strings of a harp."

His observations and suggestions about the picture overall were relayed in a five-page memo to Jack Warner, Luft, and Cukor; most of them concerned cuts that he felt could be made in many scenes. His most drastic suggestion for a revision was completely refilming all of the scenes at the Downbeat Club, the after-hours musicians' hangout where Norman first hears Esther sing:

I've revised and re-written this scene as of today, and I suggest cutting the action at the very beginning of this scene, that part that has Esther handing out coffee to the band. The whole start of this scene is not right, and I suggest you devise a new first part for this. . . . in the Academy Awards sequence, the television screen is extremely distracting to everything played and completely bewildering. I feel the scene is immeasurably hurt by the presence of the TV screen.* The night club terrace scene should be retaken, as should the sanitarium scene. As you will note, this calls for only three re-takes . . . the rest are cuts . . . and I must say in terms of a picture as big as this, it seems very small to me.

Moss

*When Hart saw the rough cut, the TV screen was blank, as the special effects department had not yet added the footage shot for this purpose.

Hart then left for New York, where he was to direct a new play, *Anniversary Waltz*. On his flight back east he elaborated on his thoughts about *A Star Is Born* in a letter to Jack Warner:

> It was my idea to come out there and spend a week just looking at what had been done because I take a personal interest in every picture I write. This one, in particular. You already know what I like and didn't like about the picture. . . . I think it emerges as a major picture and should be a very successful commercial one, which I, like yourself, am always interested in. . . . One of the major jobs of the picture from now on will be the editing and the cutting. One of the dangers of a picture which has run as long in the shooting as this one has, is that by the end of it everyone is understandably weary, and as far as I am concerned . . . I do feel this picture . . . will be helped by a creative job in the editing of it. . . . And I wonder if it [is] possible, since I shall be in rehearsal with a new play, when the final editing, or even a semi-final editing is done and a rough cut is available, if a print could not be sent on to me in New York, since I cannot come out again. I would look at it and suggest some cuts. I hope you or whoever is concerned with the final editing will not do a rush or a quick job on it. . . . I urge . . . at the risk of repeating myself, that the cutting and editing be done as carefully and creatively as the script and the shooting was done. I think you are going to have a very successful picture, Jack. Not a little of which is due to your courage and belief in seeing it through, in spite of all the difficulties I know you have had. . . .
>
> > As always,
> > Moss

Warner's reply was reassuring:

> Dear Moss:
> Thanks for your lovely letter . . . Your concern with editing of this picture strikes a sympathetic note with me, as I share your feeling and will make certain the editing is done with sensitive care and taste. . . . All the best to you and Kitty,
>
> > Jack

Hart's memo and his letter to Warner prompted an extensive re-examination of the work that had been done on the film and the work still to come. Warner, after lengthy conferences with Luft and Cukor, gave permission to redo not only the sequences that Hart had suggested but also twelve other scenes in the film that he and Cukor felt either had been rushed or were otherwise not up to the quality of the rest of the picture. To do this would add at least another ten days to the shooting schedule and increase the budget by another $250,000, boosting the cost of the film to almost $4 million, making it the most expensive picture Warners had ever made.

This fact was soon known throughout the industry and was gleefully seized upon by David Selznick. He and his executives were still trying to devise a suitable strategy that would force Warners to turn over to them the negative of the 1937 original; so far, all their demands and legal threats had proven ineffective. Selznick now decided to confront the matter head-on with a personal appeal to Jack Warner before his attorneys went ahead with formal legal action. As he remarked to them in a memo:

> I hear from everybody . . . that *A Star Is Born* is going on and on like a river . . . and it is apparent that [it] is going to be the most expensive picture [Warners] have ever made, perhaps the most costly anyone in the industry has ever made, and that they need the entire world market, without complications, if they hope to get their costs back, not to speak of a profit. I think we ought to discuss . . . what, if anything, to do about . . . bringing the facts before Luft and Miss Garland, for among other things . . . I am eager for [everyone] to know that this is nothing that has come up lately . . . but something on which we put Warner on notice long before they started production. Otherwise, this matter may boomerang on us badly in terms of trade relations . . . especially in view of the trade's adoration of Miss Garland and the fact that they are rooting for her great success.

The result of this memo and a series of conferences with his attorneys and other advisors was a four-page, single-spaced letter to Jack Warner, largely written by Selznick himself:

> Dear Jack:
>   We have known each other for so many years and so well that I feel obliged to call to your personal attention the facts on *A Star Is Born* before it is too late.
>   I hope you will forgive me if I point out that you are pouring millions into a remake of my picture without having bothered to clear the foreign rights. I . . . call your attention to the fact that I was the creator of this subject.

I was not only its producer, the very idea was my own, and so much of its writing did I do that when Bill Wellman received a writing "Oscar" for it, he frankly stated in his remarks of acceptance that it should have been given to me. . . .

Now I am not seeking anything philanthropic from you, Jack. On the contrary, I feel that it is I who am doing you the favor in putting you on notice before it is too late. Also, I feel bad about Judy, who I understand owns a substantial piece of your film. . . . I do not want to be responsible for causing you tremendous headaches, or to be improperly charged by you with never having brought the matter to your personal attention. . . .

It may be, Jack, that your lawyers will tell you that you are absolutely in the clear, and that you have nothing to worry about. . . . Perhaps this is what they have already told you. . . . I, of course, intend to follow the guidance of my own lawyers. . . .

In the absence of any immediate constructive approach by your company to this problem, you may expect legal actions to be taken by us in every single territory of the world where we own the film. If I don't receive a prompt reply to this letter, I shall regrettably be forced to assume that there is no change in your attitude, and to act accordingly.

> With kindest regards,
> David

Jack Warner's reply to this broadside was brief and to the point:

Dear David:

This is to acknowledge receipt of your rather voluminous letter . . . regarding *A Star Is Born*. Please know that I appreciate the spirit in which you have sent this letter to me. However, inasmuch as the contents of your letter raise many points with which I am sure our Legal Department is familiar, I naturally will have to be apprised of the department's views before any reply can be made. As soon as I have all of the facts before me, either I or one of our executives here at the studio or at our New York office will get in touch with you or your New York office. Of course, David, my failure in this letter to treat in detail upon any of the points raised in your letter is in no way to be construed that any of them are recognized or conceded by me.

> Kindest personal regards,
> Sincerely,
> Jack

Selznick's bringing this matter to Warner's attention must have caused quite a stir at the studio, since this was the first time that Jack Warner realized that he was doing exactly what Selznick had described: "pouring millions into a remake without having bothered to clear the foreign rights." While Selznick's attorneys had indeed notified Warner's attorneys of this, legal matters were seldom brought to Jack's attention unless they involved contractual negotiations. In this case, Selznick's claims were just that— claims. Now that Warner was aware of it, it must have infuriated him, especially in conjunction with another matter regarding *A Star Is Born* that had been brought to Warner's attention, which prompted this memo to Alperson:

> Dear Eddie:
> People have advised me that they have seen *A Star Is Born* on television within the last three months. You told me this picture had been removed for an indefinite time and that it only had appeared on television a few times. Have you a print of this picture running on television? If so, I am very, very much disappointed. Would appreciate your writing or phoning me about this immediately.
>
> Regards,
> Jack

Another factor irritating Warner was the fact that both Alperson and Luft were convinced that they were in possession of all rights, including foreign, and that they had signed a contract stating so. To discover now that this invaluable component was, in fact, not part of the deal meant that the project could turn into a major problem for Warner. On the one hand, what he was seeing in the rushes made him confident that he had the makings of a great picture. On the other hand, the cost projections, the number of days the film was behind schedule, Luft's inexperience, and Garland's erratic absences probably made him regret, at this point, that he'd ever heard of *A Star Is Born,* Ed Alperson, Sid Luft, or Judy Garland.

While Selznick and the Warner Bros. attorneys played tug-of-war with the 1937 negative, Cukor was moving the production forward as quickly as possible. In addition to the three musical numbers that had yet to be filmed, there were also the retakes of work already done and a considerable number of dramatic scenes that hadn't been filmed at all. One of the most crucial of these took place in Vicki's dressing room at the Niles studio. In the original, this had served as little more than a bridge to the scene between Niles and Maine in the sanitorium; it had been brief and made the plot points that Niles was noble and caring, that Norman was trying to stop drinking, and that Vicki was distraught. Unfortunately, as written and staged by Wellman, it dealt with the drama of her concern and anguish not at all. Hart's rewrite of this scene seized upon the possibilities inherent in the pressure on Vicki. She is first seen filming a very upbeat, cheerful musical number; during a break, she is visited in her dressing room by Niles. When he asks Vicki about Norman, he is met with silence; then she breaks down:

> He's trying awfully hard to stop drinking . . . he really wants to . . . but what is it? Why does he try to destroy himself? . . . I've got to find the answer . . . I can't live this way! You don't know what it's like to see someone you love crumbling away before your eyes, day by day, bit by bit . . . and to stand there helpless. Love isn't enough . . . I thought I was the answer for Norman . . . but love isn't enough. And now I'm afraid of what I feel in myself . . . because . . . I hate his promises to stop—and the watching and the waiting to see it begin again. I hate to go home to him at night—and listen to his lies. . . . But my heart goes out to him, because he *does* try . . . but I hate him for failing! . . . and I hate me because I've failed too. I don't know what's going to happen to us, Oliver! No matter how much you love someone—how do you live out the days? How?

The intensity of the emotion, the honesty of the character in admitting to hatred, fear, and despair, and the picture that the dialogue painted of the disintegration of a person and a relationship marked a major advance in the treatment of character and subject in the ultimate Hollywood escapist fantasy: the musical. Hart added a coda in which Vicki, after Oliver promises to put Norman back to work, goes back out to the sound stage and finishes her song. His construction of the scene—bracketing it with the song—gave an added poignancy and depth to Vicki's breakdown.

The musical number, called "Lose That Long Face," was still being worked out by Barstow, but it had been decided that Vicki would be costumed as a waif, selling newspapers. There had been some talk of having her do the number in blackface, but a makeup test convinced everyone it would be unwise. For her costume in this scene, Cukor had brought in some Jacob Riis photos of turn-of-the-century tenement children, and the wardrobe department had outfitted Garland as a ragamuffin, complete with straw hat and freckles.

Cukor had decided to film the Niles/Vicki scene in one uninterrupted take. The CinemaScope camera was set up so that Garland and Bickford were at opposite ends of the wide screen; the lights surrounding the dressing room mirror and the reflection of the overhead lights in the mirror gave the scene a harsh, clinical quality, which emphasized the intensity of Vicki's feelings, her anger and her sorrow.

As Del Armstrong recalls, "Cukor knew how to get the most out of actresses. Because of his particular lifestyle, he knew how to hurt a woman, and he used it several times to get them into a mood for a crying scene. Usually it's in the quietude of their little rehearsals—he says 'I want the set now' and everybody goes away, and what he says to her and she says to him, usually nobody can hear it. Different directors have different ways of getting an emotion going, because maybe she comes in in the morning bright and gay and full of laughter, then all of a sudden she has to drop for a scene, and he has to abuse her a little bit, in order to bring her down.

"[In this scene] I had great admiration for Judy, being able to get up to those highs. I don't know how she managed to do it within herself, especially with Cukor. He was notorious for dozens of takes—well, any emotion will drain doing it that many times. So towards the end of the last takes, I'd have to come in and furnish the tears for her, and maybe help her get up to the point where she was in the last take. She always surprised me in her ability to do this—I would come out of her dressing room with her and maybe we were joking about something and she'd go right into a scene and then snap, she'd change like that, which usually surprised me a bit. But she had that talent, even though she needed constant reassurance. . . . She was never confident in her own ability as a dramatic actress.

"I remember we worked on that scene all day; we finished at nine o'clock at night or something. Now, my relationship with her was always kind of separate and apart from the movie; it was . . . on a little more personal basis. And on this day, she was so wrought up after the day's work, so I took her home because she was near hysterical . . . and we had to stop right outside of Hollywood High School and give her a chance to throw up. It was just emotions—it wasn't from drinking—it was just an upheaval, a nervous disorder, like ulcers or something. I don't think she came to work the next day, either."

Regarding Garland's absences, Cukor remarked that "she works intensely and can only sustain the pace for short periods, but it's well worth it, for she is a revelation in her emotional scenes. She manages to get the same thrilling quality in them that she does when she's singing a song—at her best. She makes them heartrending, real and electrifying."

Garland recovered and was back at work after her day's absence to film the interior scenes of Esther and Niles bailing Norman out of the night court. Bellamy remembers an amusing quirk of Cukor's: "When he'd come in in the morning I would always pull out of the script the scenes that we were going to do, just those pages, and he always worked with them. And then at lunch time I would have to give him a new set of pages, because by then the ones that I had given him in the morning were such a mess—all crumpled up so that he couldn't read them. And then by evening when we finished, the new pages were just as crumpled, because he would hold them real tight in his hands or stick them in his pockets, or sometimes chew on them. But that was his way of working."

By the end of January the production was twenty-nine days behind schedule, and other commitments began looming for the actors and for Cukor. Walt Disney had signed Mason to star as Captain Nemo in his live-action feature of Jules Verne's *20,000 Leagues Under the Sea*, and the actor was due to start work in April. MGM wanted Cukor for preproduction work on his next film for them, an adaptation of John Masters's bestselling novel *Bhowani Junction*, to be filmed on location in India in the fall. And Columbia wanted Earl Bellamy back. "In January," he recalled, "I'd been with the picture from June or July, loaned out, and Columbia said, 'That's it, Earl, you have to come back.' " Just before he left, he experienced his one and only case of Garland temperament. "One morning, she came into makeup and I went up the stairs into the makeup room where she was and walked in and said, 'Morning, Judy, how are you?' And she lit into me like . . . it blew me right out of the water. All I said was 'Good morning,' and she had some problem and she ripped into me and it made me mad, so I went out of the makeup room and I slammed that door—it's a wonder it still stayed on the hinges. Later on I went and called her and said, 'Judy, we're ready for you,' and she came on the set, she walked to the center of the set and she said,

'Hold it, everybody—hold it, quiet.' She said, 'I did something today to a fellow I like very much and I want to apologize to him,' and she turned and said, 'I'm very sorry about this morning, Earl.' That was it. And to this day, I don't know what her problem was. I don't care—I thought it was very wonderful of her to do such a thing."

Tension, Problems, and Crises

With Bellamy gone, the burden of the production now fell on Russ Llewellyn's shoulders, and the first major problem he had to deal with was Cukor's growing irritation at what he considered Sid Luft's unwarranted interference in matters Cukor felt were best left to himself and Hart. The company was shooting a scene in Laguna, showing Norman and Esther surveying the property for their beach house and having an impromptu picnic with Esther singing "It's a New World" as the two have a tender love interlude. "We're going down to Laguna in the car," relates Llewellyn. "We'd sent Judy down the night before so she could be with the makeup and wardrobe crews first thing in the morning—we had to finish in one day. Cukor pulls out these papers and looks at them. He says, 'Mr. Luft sent these to me last night . . . ,' then in the car he blows his cork—he's mad and he tells the driver, 'I want to stop at a telephone booth.' So he gets out of the car and calls Moss Hart in New York—you know, you couldn't change a sequence of any kind without Hart's okay. And he came back to the car and he says, 'You know what Hart said to me? He said, "You mean to tell me you're on Pacific Coast Highway at seven o'clock in the morning, calling me from a pay phone?" ' He said, 'Yeah' and Hart died laughing. So we went down and finished the scene and I thought that was the end of that."

But it wasn't. What had infuriated Cukor was that Luft had evidently taken it upon himself to get another writer to shorten the scene between Norman and Esther at the Downbeat Club after he has heard her sing. It was four pages, primarily dialogue, and was due to be retaken on February 18. Luft recalls that, in the early part of the month, "I called Moss and said, 'Moss, Judy and Mason are in the goddamn banquette talking and talking, and I'm starting to yawn.' Moss says, 'Cut the goddamn thing, it's too long.' I said, 'George won't cut it,' and Moss says, 'You cut it.' 'I can't cut it—I'm not a writer.' He says, 'There's a guy on the lot—he's capable, get *him* to cut it.' George wouldn't let anybody cut it, but we finally had to do it because it was static and went on and on. But listen, I was the producer, I *had* to do it. So that was the run-in I had with George. He didn't want to step on Moss's toes; he thought that everything that Moss wrote was a jewel, and indeed it was. But George was hotheaded, you know, and he didn't want Hart maybe saying someday, 'You cut my scene,' so he wanted protocol to be his guide, to have Moss cut it. But he couldn't."

Whoever did the cutting did indeed nearly ruin one of the most crucial scenes in the early part of the story. Cukor had read the newly shortened version to Hart over the telephone in Laguna, and this prompted a telegram from the infuriated writer to Warner, Luft, and Cukor:

> I want to protest as strongly as I can at the way this scene has been cut. It is their big scene together, the scene that kicks off their relationship and the scene that establishes Norman Maine as the kind of person he really is. I wrote it that way and it should stay that way. Whoever cut it has calmly proceeded to take all the character and juice out, leaving it as dull and cliche as possible, and that is exactly the way it will play if you don't restore the cuts. Further it seems to me that since you ask me constantly to rewrite and since I have the interest and courtesy to come out on my own to help in whatever way I could, you might return the courtesy by letting me know when this kind of grotesque and harmful cutting is being done. I hardly think I deserve this kind of dismissal.

Warner, upon receiving Hart's telegram, looked at both versions of the scene and telegraphed Hart: "When I received your three-way telegram, I knew exactly who the culprit was and I knew you did too. Since then I have had the scene re-written just as you wrote it. As a matter of fact the re-takes start . . . Friday. It is too bad that Luft did not talk this over at least with Cukor before he put through the [revisions]." Luft had, as has been noted, told both Cukor and Hart about his unhappiness with this scene; evidently, neither of them paid the slightest attention.

In the end, Luft did achieve his ends, for the scene was considerably improved by the rethinking of it. As Cukor wrote to Hart:

> Since I did the big scene from *Troilus and Cressida* when Sid Luft tried to re-write your deathless prose, I think . . . it would be a good idea if you could . . . divide up this scene. . . . In light of the unceremonious way [Norman]

treated [Esther] on the Shrine stage, and all the hurly burly that went on between them, the scene at the Downbeat Club now could be pitched much higher, as it were, played more boldly. Their relationship has progressed further [than it is] in the present scene. I should think the rather genteel way that James now plays it would seem wishy-washy. He will be more bossy, imperious, and she is obviously swept in with him. I love me telling you the plot of the picture. We expect to shoot this scene later this week, so the sooner we get the new lines, the better. This, of course, is contrary to the Luft school of dramaturgy, which feels that a scene is all the better if it is transmitted by telephone to a phone booth at a gas station, preferably in Laguna. All has been quiet on the Potomac. Let's hope it stays that way from now on till the end.

Evidently it did, for on February 25, Warner wired Hart: "All re-takes have been made on Downbeat Club dialogue and really are wonderful. What amazing improvement by breaking up scene from Club to parking lot to process in car. All dialogue remains exactly as you wrote it. Know you will be happy to hear this. Very best . . . Jack Warner." Cukor elaborated on these retakes in his own letter to Hart:

We have redone the terrace of the Mocambo [nightclub], and I must say, it seems mighty nice. I think we have generated a lot of sex. She looks attractive and the whole thing is a great improvement over the original. We've already done the Downbeat Club and the parking lot, and it comes off with a lot of zip and pep. She looks perfectly charming in a new Jean Louis dress, and I know that this too is an enormous improvement over the way we first did it—it has fun and spirit. It's been like pulling teeth because Judy has really been under the weather. Walt Disney is breathing down James' neck so we have to get on with it. As for me, I think I'll be doing *The Shanghai Gesture* in the summer theatres this year, with me in the Mrs. Leslie Carter–Florence Reed part, because who better than I can read the famous speech "I have survived"? I hope all is going well with both of you.

George

What Cukor was actually planning for the summer was his annual vacation in Europe. With the production nearing completion, he made plans to leave in late March, leaving postproduction in the hands of the professionals at the studio but making certain that he would return in plenty of time to oversee the last-minute details of the film before it was sent to the labs for final printing, which was now tentatively scheduled for midsummer. However, there were still more retakes to be done, plus the three remaining musical sequences, including the big production number for the film-within-a-film, which would transform band singer Esther Blodgett into movie star Vicki Lester. There was still some uncertainty as to which of the three numbers written for this spot would be used. Also still to be done was the final dramatic musical number, "Someone at Last"—dramatic in the sense that it was a song arising from a plot situation instead of being strictly a production number as were "Gotta Have Me Go With You" and "Lose That Long Face" (the latter, too, had yet to be filmed). The script called for Esther to perform this number in the Malibu house in an effort to cheer up a despondent Norman after he has been fired by Niles. Hart had lifted the scene intact from the original: Esther rushes home from the studio to be with a lonely Norman, who, since it is the servant's night out, has "prepared a little snack with my own lily white hands"—huge sandwiches, a massive salad, and glasses of milk; they have a love scene. Then, Hart wrote in a new scene:

Norman: "We're forgetting we're hungry." (picking up a glass of milk) "Cheers! What went on at the studio today? The old alma mater!" Esther forces a bright laugh and brings a smile to her face: "We started shooting the big production number today—and it's the production number to end all big production numbers! It's an American in Paris, Brazil, the Alps, and the Burma Road! It's got sex, schmaltz, patriotism, and more things coming up through the floor and down from the ceiling than you ever saw in your life." She launches into the production number, taking all the parts herself—the ballet, the chorus boys, the show girls, the director, the leading man, a burlesque of herself, singing the main song, using anything she can lay her hands on in the room for props. She leaps on and off sofas, turns over chairs—it is a tour de force designed solely to make Norman forget himself and laugh. And finally he does—wholeheartedly. She falls into his arms, exhausted. Her own laughter joining happily in his.

For this, Arlen and Gershwin had written a sixteen-bar refrain called "Someone At Last". Even though the song was intended to be a parody of musical production numbers, Gershwin's lyric very subtly set the undertext of Esther's emotional longing. Gershwin's genius for using lyrics to illuminate character and comment on situations is one of the most underrated aspects of his work on A STAR IS BORN. As pointed out earlier, the titles of the songs not only indicate the progression of the story but are also reflective of the emotional and mental state of Esther/Vicki. The lyrics express the unconscious love and longing that she cannot articulate to Norman until it becomes apparent that she might lose him. Gershwin's lyrics for the first three songs speak of Esther's pent-up emotion ("You want a love that's truly true, gotta have me go with you"), her fear of loneliness ("the winds grow colder, and suddenly you're older") and her sense of time wasted ("All the years that I wandered and pondered were squandered"). "Someone At Last" speaks colloquially of the near fulfillment of a dream and of Esther's need for a sense of self-worth ("With my someone, I'll be someone at last.") This subtext is consistent with all of Gershwin's lyrics for the film and is remarkable in view of the fact that the song, as positioned in the script by Hart, is performed by Esther in an effort to cheer up a despondent Norman.

Garland had previously recorded this sixteen-bar verse and refrain, but now a routine, incorporating all of Hart's descriptions, had to be devised—a veritable tour de force. The problem in achieving this with the song as written lay in the difficulty posed for the choreographer, Richard Barstow. He had been struggling for some time trying to find an approach to the song that would manage to incorporate all the elements that Hart had indicated in his stage directions; but weeks before the number was to be staged, he still had not come up with a concept that would enable Garland to display the full range of her versatility and especially her considerable comedic skills. Luft and Garland, knowing of Barstow's block, surreptitiously turned to the man who more than any other had been responsible for her early successes at MGM. Roger Edens was a composer-arranger at that studio in 1934, when the thirteen-year-old Garland had been signed to a contract; a former pianist for Red Nichols's orchestra, he had played in the pit bands for several Broadway shows and eventually had become accompanist/arranger for Ethel Merman in the early stages of her career. When Garland was put under contract, it was Edens who coached her, worked with her, and became her unofficial advisor and protector. It was he who had written the variation on "You Made Me Love You," entitled "Dear Mr. Gable," which gave the youngster her first taste of fame and public acceptance when she sang it in *Broadway Melody of 1938.* Over the years, she and Edens had stayed close, personally and professionally; he had even written her show for the Palace Theater, albeit uncredited.

Now, she and Luft turned to him for advice on what to do with "Someone at Last." In early January, Garland and Edens began working on ideas at her home in the evenings, the only time the two could work, as he was still under contract to MGM and she was laboring during the day on the film. Edens picked up on Hart's idea of lampooning a big production number by setting the song in different parts of the world, arranging the song so as to parody Hollywood's presentation of various cultures: Garland would play it as a French torch singer à la Edith Piaf, a Chinese sing-song girl, a big-game hunter in Africa, and a Brazilian samba dancer, with a side excursion into what they both called "early Judy Garland." Edens's manic inventiveness struck sparks off Garland, and the two of them recorded a twelve-minute audition record of the piece as they envisioned it for Cukor and Barstow. The latter thankfully seized on the zany ideas and bits in the skit, while Cukor, liking the basic approach, sent the record off to Moss Hart, who edited the scene down considerably and rewrote the dialogue and ad libs that Garland and Edens had improvised during their wild and woolly late-evening sessions. This new material was then orchestrated by Heindorf, using the Edens/Garland record as a guide, and Garland recorded this new section. Meanwhile, Barstow worked out the routine, using the furnishings of the Malibu home as props. His staging was done with very little help from Cukor, who remarked candidly, "I am not a musical comedy director. I just don't have the experience . . . or the assurance of Donen or Minnelli. . . . I am not very skillful about putting songs in. . . . It has to be natural . . . the screen is terribly logical." The beauty of this number, as far as Cukor was concerned, was that it *was* so logical. Everything in it stemmed from the reality of the situation: Vicki ostensibly singing to a playback, using only furnishings and other household items to represent a movie camera, a concertina, a harp, maracas, and a tiger.

Garland and Barstow rehearsed the number very carefully over a period of weeks; then Cukor came in to set up the manner in which it would be photographed. "It was carefully rehearsed," recalls Cukor, "very carefully rehearsed to give it the effect of improvisation, of spontaneity."

Even with the careful rehearsals, it was still a complex number to stage and photograph, due to its length, the many tempo changes, and the challenge of matching the action to the playback. Cukor began filming on February 4, and according to the production log: "Camera and set ready at 10:00 a.m., Judy Garland worked from 11:00 to 7:00. First shot at 2:15. Six takes of start of number, bars 1–16. Adjust lights for added business and light changes. Took bars 17–36 from 4:25 to 5:30. Five takes. Shot bars

37–52 from 6:20 to 7:00. Five takes." The work continued at this pace over the next three work days; then Garland called in sick, leaving Cukor with nothing to do but shoot close-ups of Mason's reactions. Recalled Mason: "I personally could have done without [this number]. It was quite a long one and all [I] had to do was to laugh, smile, and chuckle for about five minutes."

That was true, but the scene immediately following the song was entirely Mason's. After Vicki has cheered Norman up, they start to make love and are interrupted by the doorbell. A deliveryman has a package for Vicki Lester; when Norman says he is her husband, he is instructed to "sign right here, Mr. Lester." When Norman closes the door, Cukor lets the camera stay on Mason's back, and the actor eloquently manages to convey Norman's sense of futility, frustration, and defeat with a slight sagging of his body and a droop to his shoulders. When he turns, the humiliation and dejection in his face are revealed. Going back into the living room, he brushes off Vicki's quip "Now that the supper show is over, let's have supper" and instead makes for the liquor bottle.

"Someone at Last" was definitely a tour de force, but it was also a grueling test of the actress's stamina, as it was one of the most physically demanding of all the sequences in the film. Veteran actress Ina Claire, a close friend of Cukor's, visited the set one afternoon and watched Garland do several takes, after which she commented: "That girl should work for two hours and then take an ambulance home." To capture Garland's performance and her energy with no chance of mishaps, Cukor resorted to an unusual (for him) technique: "I . . . set up two cameras for this musical number," he related. "We did it with an 'A' camera, and we used a supplementary one, just to see what would happen. When it was all over, we found that the 'B' camera, the one we had there for fun, [was sometimes] the really interesting one. It wasn't always in perfect focus, the composition was not perfect, but it was very exciting, very dynamic."

By the time work had finished on "Someone at Last," *A Star Is Born* had been in production for four months, prompting lyricist Ira Gershwin to write to a friend, "We finished our work on it almost a year ago . . . and the picture should be finished shooting by the end of this month. Almost like the von Stroheim days—twenty or so weeks." In the interim, he and Arlen had composed four songs for Paramount's film version of Clifford Odets's play *The Country Girl,* starring Bing Crosby, William Holden, and

Grace Kelly, which had been shot and edited and was almost ready for release while *A Star Is Born* was still in production.

Gershwin's prediction that *A Star Is Born* would be finished by late February proved overly optimistic, for with the two additional musical numbers and the retakes still to be done, the production looked to have another four weeks of filming before completion. However, as far as Cukor was concerned, as he revealed in a letter to a friend written on February 26,

at long last, the picture's finished—much to everybody's surprise. . . . All that's left now are two musical numbers and some re-takes, and goodness knows when we'll manage to get those. Up until the last few weeks everything went quite well, with just a certain amount of delay. After that, I'm afraid that Judy slipped right back into her Metro pattern—illness, lateness—all very mysterious and disquieting. It has been expensive for the studio, and trying for all concerned. However, there's unbounded enthusiasm around the studio for the results of our work. When the rough cut of the picture has been shown to the usual "tough eggs," the Sales Department, Publicity Department, etc., they leave the projection room, sobbing and carrying on. Usually I have misgivings about this kind of studio enthusiasm, but in this case I have a hunch myself that it's all pretty good. Even though concentrating for such a length of time on one picture is a strain, I find that my interest and excitement has never abated. I don't remember being this het up by anything in years.

Cukor maintained his enthusiasm during the period devoted to the retakes despite the tension and fatigue that began to affect the production and everyone concerned with it. Lucy Marlow remembers vividly one particular incident: "We were redoing the scene between Lola and Norman in Maine's home. He was lying on the sofa watching television and I was supposed to come running in in a wet bathing suit. They had put a hose over my head and got me all wet; so I ran in and my slippers were soaking wet and the parquet floor was very slick, and when I ran in I slipped and fell flat on my back with the cameras rolling. The wind was knocked out of me and I couldn't speak. Mr. Cukor yelled 'Cut!' and everybody came running over to me . . . and I heard this laughter. It just rippled up and down the scales—it was so distinctively Garland. And she came over and actually cradled my head in her arms. I was trying to talk, and I was struggling around trying to stand up, so they knew I was all right, but she said, 'Honey, lay there, just lay there, and we'll sue the S.O.B.' She was talking about Jack Warner . . . evidently they were having real conflicts."

Several days after this, Garland was back on the recording stage, working with Ray Heindorf on the next-to-last song needed for the film, "Lose That Long Face." This was the number that would bracket her dressing-room confession scene with Niles. As Gene Allen recalls: "Mr. Cukor wasn't very excited about that number. He felt that the picture could do without it. I believe he tried to talk them out of doing it, but evidently he couldn't, because we got word to get a set ready. So we took an old standing set from *A Streetcar Named Desire* and we painted it all white, and we did the number on it. It was one way to save money."

With the prerecording done, the set ready, and the thirty dancers rehearsed, all that remained was for Garland to finish rehearsing with her "dance-in" and then to go before the cameras for a week's filming. This was scheduled to begin on March 2, but, unbeknownst to Garland, Cukor would not be directing the number. Instead, a Warner contract director named Jack Donohue would be in charge.

Forty-five-year-old Jack Donohue had started his show-business career as a child dancer with the Ziegfeld Follies of 1920 and had risen to become dance director for numerous Broadway and London stage shows. He'd moved to Hollywood in the 1930s and jumped back and forth between the stage and films in the intervening years. In 1952 he staged the musical numbers for the Broadway revival of Gershwin's *Of Thee I Sing,* and the same year he became the resident dance expert at Warner Bros., staging the numbers for the Doris Day vehicles *Calamity Jane* and *Lucky Me*—the latter was being shot in CinemaScope almost simultaneously with *A Star Is Born.* He was an old-time hoofer, and his dance direction reflected this, being fast and unimaginative. As a director, he was also fast and unimaginative, notorious for single takes and fast shooting. He was assigned to "Lose That Long Face" (which Barstow had choreographed) because Warner wanted to avoid Cukor's meticulous approach to what was, after all, a fairly routine production number—and Cukor, as Allen noted, had very little interest in the number or in its staging.

Russ Llewellyn recalls that on the day shooting was to start, "Garland doesn't know that Cukor's not going to direct. We got her into makeup, got her into wardrobe. The set's lit, we got the dancers in there, and she comes on the set. Donohue says, 'All ready, roll the camera.' And we roll it, we do a take, and he says, 'Cut. Next setup over here, boys—give me another angle right here.' Now Garland is used to twenty-five, thirty takes with Cukor. And this guy is printing take one. She says, 'Where's Mr. Cukor?' We tell her, 'Mr. Cukor won't be on this.' That poor girl went out of her mind. You've never seen such tears; she shouted, she just went crazy. I never felt so sorry for anybody. She ran to the phone, got hold of Warner, and screams, 'I want to talk to Mr. Cukor!' But he's nowhere. Finally she just slams down the phone, goes out, gets into her limousine. The driver told me that she had a bottle of vodka and she drank it all the way home. And we never heard from her. Now, the studio is going crazy trying to get hold of Cukor, but he wouldn't talk to anybody. So something had to be done. They talked Cukor into coming in and standing behind the camera while Donohue directed, and Cukor would tell her if it was any good or not. So they finally worked it out that way and got it finished. But that poor girl went crazy."

The production log bears out certain aspects of Llewellyn's version: Garland did work for one hour on the first day, then went home "ill" and stayed that way for the next four days. However, according to the studio records, her "dance-in," Gloria DeWerd, went to Garland's home on those four days to rehearse the actress in the dance every evening from eight to ten. Cukor related his own account of these events in a letter written near the end of production:

I don't know when I will be "sprung" from this particular assignment. I am now working with the cutter, but there are still some loose ends to be done. When we will get at these I don't know. In fact, it's not at all certain that anything else can or will be shot. After an auspicious start, and a very exciting time during most of the shooting, I'm sorry to say that it all ended in a kind of shambles. All that was left to be done was a simple dance, which had been rehearsed and set, and an elaborate production number, on which no work had been done at all. . . . About three weeks ago, strange, sinister and sad things began happening to Judy. I suspect there's a crisis in her domestic situation. . . . It's all very odd. Her behavior about the number with the dance director was in her best MGM tradition. The number should have taken a week to rehearse and about three days to shoot. It came to a stop last week after the dancers had been paid for six weeks, and Judy never completed the number. The studio finished it as best it could with a double. Judy had said she wanted a week's rest before she started the number, and the studio could do nothing but accede to her demands. I have observed that after her so-called rests, she always comes back in much worse shape than when she left. I think there's much more drinking than resting. When she came back this time her behavior was really unconscionable. Sometimes she'd come in for an hour and then leave, because she was absolutely exhausted, then go straight to the races. Or, she'd be too sick to appear at the studio at all, and the next day one would read in Louella Parsons's column about how "cute Judy was when she got up on the floor of the Mocambo last night and sang a couple of numbers." She abandoned all pretense of reporting for work on time. Finally the studio got fed up with having the cast and crew sitting around twiddling their thumbs—all being paid, mark you—so they worked out a system whereby they would call Judy at eight-thirty in the morning. She would tell them if she was coming in and they would make their calls [to the cast and crew]. This went on for a few days, with everybody jumping through hoops when she gave the signal. Then it got so they couldn't get her on the telephone. In fact, no one would answer the telephone at her house. This is the behavior of someone unhinged, but there is an arrogance and a ruthless selfishness that eventually alienates one's sympathy. She's always saying that the trouble with her is that she's so honest and direct, and that everyone lies to her. The fact is that when she's in this state the truth isn't in her, she's devious and untrustworthy. I found that she not only had no regard for anyone, but very little loyalty. I suppose it's wrong to judge her by sane standards, but if you're forced by your work to be at the mercy of such erratic carryings-on, you find yourself responding to it in an all-too-human way. What will happen next I don't know. The studio frankly is at a loss because these numbers are necessary to the plot of the picture. She may snap out of it in a week or so. During the picture there were some minor crises and she pulled herself together and was fine for quite a long spell. When I finish cutting, I'm not going to hang around. Warners aren't prepared to pay me a salary for just sitting and waiting; Metro doesn't see any reason why they should (I agree with them); and I don't see why I should make any sacrifices, so there you are.

What happened next was a demonstration of Jack Warner's nerve and his proclivity for high-stakes gambling. He waited until Garland, in Cukor's words, "pulled herself together." She had worked sporadically on "Lose That Long Face," as the production log indicates, but the number was finished with Gloria DeWerd doubling for Garland. Unfortunately the difference in performance was so obvious as to make the footage unusable, so Warner, gambler that he was, looking at the pile of chips he had riding on the production, upped the ante, giving Luft approval to keep the cast and much of the crew on salary while waiting for his star to return to normal.

During the time it took for this to happen, the company was not completely idle. James Mason recalled this period: "Judy was not always reliable. . . . There were quite a lot of days . . . when to give Jack Warner and the others the impression that we were hard at work, I would be required to do an inordinate number of 'driving' shots. I mean simple shots of me driving the Mercedes or the Mercury in or out of the studio, in or out of the grounds of the house supposedly occupied by the Maines, among the Hollywood Hills, in downtown L.A., along the Pacific Coast Highway, etc.

"The higher-ups tended to forget that they had undertaken this operation knowing full well that Judy did not have a reputation for reliability; they forgot that prizes are not won nor audiences bewitched by an exercise in reliability . . . To get something as unique as Judy's talent, some patience and sacrifices were needed. If the film went over budget only a very small fraction of the overage was due to Judy's erratic time table. When I think of it, my God, they were well off! Judy was by no means a temperamental star. 'Temperamental star' is usually a euphemism for selfish and bad-tempered, and a temperamental star of this sort can be a *real* time waster. I know. I have worked with some . . . But this was not Judy."

What caused Garland's erratic behavior has been the subject of much conjecture over the years. Probably the most accurate assessment of her situation was given by Gerold Frank in his biography of the actress:

There were . . . times when nothing stimulated and all depressed her, when, no matter how hard she fought, she had to turn to pills, to liquor, to chemical help. Her dilemma was intensified by lack of food; she would go through periods like an alcoholic, but with medication rather than whiskey; she would become toxic; she would be unable to eat . . . food would at least help absorb and dilute the drugs. . . . Judy had never grown up emotionally. This had nothing to do with her mentality, or sharpness, or cunning—intellectually and physically she was a grown woman; emotionally, she was still Baby Gumm. . . . Any stress could precipitate the problem. She couldn't describe what it was because she couldn't describe it to herself. It wasn't actually a pain; it was crankiness, irritability, depression. When she took pills to knock out the depression—she wanted to be gay, entertaining, that was what she had been brought up to be, that brought her all rewards, her very identity—

then the pills, and lack of food, did lead to acute physical pain—to migraine, to drilling lights in her eyes . . . which in turn led her to take more pills to knock out the pain. Then, when the pain vanished, there was a great lassitude, a feeling of intense malaise, and an overwhelming fear that she'd get out there and be unable to sing, unable to act.

In his autobiography, *I Remember It Well,* Vincente Minnelli related that

it took me some time to find out that . . . her screams of pain and shortness of breath—were due to [the fact that] she was suffering the agonies of withdrawal, and sadly she didn't tell me . . . Judy probably didn't know herself. I had taken her tangible demons for mental phantoms. She would come through the ordeal with the help of a combination sedative and analgesic administered by a physician who came to our house. Judy would awake from the siege, renewed, and with invigoration and anticipation. Life for her was beautiful on those mornings when she awoke from the nightmares of the previous evening.

And so it was on *A Star Is Born.* With Luft's help and a two-week rest-and-withdrawal period, Garland returned to Warner Bros. on April 10, ready to finish what she would later refer to as "the most important picture of my career." During her extended absence, Cukor and editor Folmar Blangsted had assembled a rough cut of the film, and on March 25 it had been screened for Luft, Garland, Warner, and several of the other top executives of the company. Concerning this showing, Cukor wrote to Moss Hart later in the week:

My reaction to the picture was clouded. I was so distracted by scene after scene not coming off, especially since I remembered the rushes as being completely successful. I'd never seen the picture assembled before this running. Some of the cutting took me aback to say the least . . . James did seem to go on with his drunken meanderings backstage; the proposal scene on the recording stage was a mish mash, with the wrong reaction in the wrong places. Mrs. Fiske's phrase "The firm, firm touch on the wrong, wrong note" was sure applicable here. But we're getting on just dandy with the re-cutting. The first reel, the exterior of the Shrine, is finished. It's a real humdinger. We're well into the backstage of the Shrine, and that's going to be mighty exciting too. We're working meticulously and carefully. I'm not letting them give me the bum's rush. They tried, mind you. . . . But when it's all straightened out, production numbers added, etc., we'll have an honest, exciting, impressive and moving film. Far wiser heads than mine (Sid Luft, Alperson, Jack Warner . . .) were delighted. They stated unequivocally that we all had a winnah.

It was after this screening that Warner evidently decided that they indeed "had a winnah"—almost. The picture, even in its rough, unfinished state, was so obviously exciting and moving that he was convinced that with just a little more time, effort, and money, it could be one of the finest pictures ever made by Warner Bros. Accordingly, he told Luft and Cukor to reshoot not only the unfinished "Lose That Long Face" but also five dramatic scenes that Warner felt did not show Garland off at her best, either photographically or dramatically.

Work on these reshoots began on Tuesday night, April 13, back at Robert's Drive-In at Sunset and Cahuenga; and for the next five days, Cukor moved the company through the retakes quickly and effortlessly. Garland, rested and enthusiastic, worked tirelessly and energetically. Ironically, the last dramatic scene taken was a redo of the first day's shooting from way back in October: Garland as Esther Blodgett, stand-in for a star, hiding her face and waving from a train window. After that, Cukor even stayed on the stages to watch while Richard Barstow began redirecting and reshooting "Lose That Long Face."

Having made all his cuts and corrections on the film with editor Blangsted, Cukor left Hollywood on April 28 for New York, where he would do several interviews about the film before sailing for Europe and an extended vacation. When queried by Hy Hollinger of *Variety* as to why the film took so long to shoot, Cukor, ever the gentleman, replied, "I really don't know; maybe it's because I'm a slow director." He was so delighted and relieved to be finished with filming that he even forgave Garland her previous antics, commenting later that "all through the shooting . . . I remember going up to Judy after each take and whispering, 'Not as good as Kay Fwancis.' It was a bit of a running joke and it helped both of us through the long shooting schedule without endless discussions about what this or that scene meant or constant psychological investigation about the significance of the whole thing. . . . I remember on the last day, the very last take with Judy, I went up afterwards and in confidential tones told her, 'That was better than Kay Fwancis.'"

While Cukor was on his way to Europe, James Mason checked in at the Disney Studios in Burbank, to begin work on *20,000 Leagues Under the Sea;* but at Warner Bros. there remained much more work to be done on the unfinished *A Star Is Born.* Aside from the cutting, special effects, scoring, dubbing, and myriad other postproduction details, one more musical number was still needed. Ira Gershwin, who had been at the March 25 screening, commented:

> Everything about the picture looks and sounds great. There's only one problem: what to do about a production number that's to wind up the first half (the showing is to have an intermission—the picture runs about three hours so far). The situation in the film is the sneak previewing of Vicki Lester's first movie—a showing which makes her a star overnight. All that's necessary is to put Vicki in a good number for four or five minutes, then show the audience's enthusiastic acceptance of a new star, as they fill out the preview cards in the lobby. Arlen and I wrote three songs for this spot: "Green Light Ahead," "I'm Off the Downbeat," and "Dancing Partner," all good by anyone's standards, but it seems that the choreographer couldn't get any production ideas. Could be that they may even interpolate an outside number which would be a shame.

Everyone agreed that a song was needed at this point; what no one could agree on was just what *kind.* According to Sid Luft: "The three songs [that Arlen and Gershwin had written] were bad songs. Jack Warner said, 'We need a . . . big musical number here; we gotta show what makes her a big star.' "

Luft had anticipated this, and early in April he had, unbeknownst to Gershwin or Warner, again contacted Roger Edens. "I called him," recalls Luft, "and he came over to the house, and I said, 'Roger, could you do something for me? We need a four-or-five-minute production number— something expansive.' " Edens evidently discussed Luft's request with a young songwriter named Leonard Gershe, and together the two devised the idea of song recounting the supposed "overnight" success of a singer. In it's original form, it was simple, humorous and touching in depicting the struggles of an unknown from Pocatello, Idaho to climb to the top of the show business ladder. They gave it the title "Born In A Trunk," after the famous theatrical phrase. When Edens told Luft and Garland about it, Luft recalled: "Judy and I thought it was such a great idea—the theme of it, that it doesn't happen overnight, that it's all hard work. It was a great idea and the timing was right."

It appealed to Garland for another reason. For the first act finale of her act at the Palace, she had sat on the edge of the stage and done a medley of songs that were identified with the famous performers who had played the legendary house. It had always been an audience pleaser, with standing ovations, and she considered it a good-luck piece. Garland asked Edens (who had come up with the idea for the Palace) if "Born In A Trunk" could be re-written to incorporate a medley of some of her favorite songs. "[The piece] was written as favor to me and Judy", related Luft. "[Roger] was under contract to Metro, and he couldn't be caught doing something for Warner Bros., so he moonlighted and Lenny Gershe received solo credit."

The two men were fast and facile professionals; using the structure and format Edens had devised in 1952 for "The Broadway Ballet" in MGM's *Singin' in the Rain*, they completed the entire number within two weeks and Luft and Garland were able to present the entire number to Jack Warner and Cukor in late April. They were counting on Warner's well-known love of music, especially big song-and-dance spectacles, a holdover from his own youthful days as a boy singer. Warner, remembering the impact of the same type of number in Garland's stage show, and still concerned that there were too few songs in the film, was very excited by the idea, feeling that it would wind up the first half of the film in a rousing and showmanlike manner. Cukor, however, felt that the film was already too long, and that "Born in a Trunk," at least as outlined by Luft and Garland, would add considerably to the running time without adding to the dramatic impact of the story. But he was only the director, and in those days directors could easily be overruled by producers and heads of studios, which is exactly what happened. As Ira Gershwin perceptively remarked: "This sequence was . . . excellent for its original purpose—vaudeville and nightclubs. . . . But it added fifteen minutes to [the] film, held up the show, and cost $300,000. Big mistake (but all none of my business)."

Gershwin was right about everything except the cost; the budget okayed by Warner was $250,000 for a rehearsal and shooting schedule that would last from June 7 through July 28. Edens and Gershe had literally written a short subject, a major production that opened with Vicki/Esther seen doing a rousing version of "Swanee" as the finale of the show she is in. As the audience cheers and applauds, she sits down on the stage apron and recites and sings the story of her life as a trouper, from the day she was "born in a trunk in the Princess Theatre in Pocatello, Idaho," through her first appearance on a stage as a tot running on to take part in her parents' bows. She is seen next as a teenager, making her solo debut, singing "I'll Get By"; then the "show must go on" tradition finds her performing "When My Sugar Walks Down the Street" with her father after her mother's death; her efforts at finding herself an agent are covered in accelerating versions of "You Took Advantage of Me"; while her days as a chorus girl are highlighted by "The Black Bottom." Visions of herself as a chanteuse are humorously depicted in "The Peanut Vendor"; then she finally makes it into a smart Manhattan supper club, singing "My Melancholy Baby," where she is discovered by a Broadway producer, who gives her a chance for stardom, singing and dancing to "Swanee." Coming full circle, she ends her account with a powerful, full-throated, anthemlike finale about having been "born in a trunk in the Princess Theatre in Pocatello, Idaho."

Warner's enthusiasm for the number was such that he evidently took upon himself the responsibilities of producer, telling Luft in a May 15 memo:

> Now that Huene is back and everyone is on salary, let's see if we can get this into rehearsal as quickly as possible. . . . My impression is that the number should be in front of the cameras by the first week in June, or before, if possible. If everything is well organized and the sets are ready, I am sure Judy can get up on the number in quick time. Just hearing her doing it a few times at home, I am sure she can. The important thing is to prepare the costumes, the sets, and Barstow's work so that we can get the rehearsals going. I may be repeating myself, but it is so important that I must do so, as time is the thing that really counts. Whenever you are ready for a run-through, I will appreciate your getting in touch with me as I would like to go on the set with you to watch the number and note how long it runs.

Warner, probably at Garland's suggestion, had hired the prestigious Irene Sharaff to design the costumes and sets for the sequence, hoping that she would be able to achieve the same results that she had on *An American in Paris*. For Gene Allen and Hoyningen-Huene, this was a ticklish situation: "She designed none of the sets," states Allen. "She did the costumes, and they were sensational. Her agent was Irving Lazar, so somewhere, that's how all that language [about sets] got in there. We worked very well together. Cukor had left, but he had asked me to stay on, to protect his interests. He did say he would like to keep it in the same style that we'd done. So *I* designed all the sets; I did some sketches, and Sharaff thought they were terrific and Huene thought they were terrific . . . they were all the sketches for all those numbers. I did them all in probably two days, including the big red scene I did for 'Swanee.' I just did rough little sketches, but the great thing was when you're working with a team like Irene Sharaff and Huene, to be the creative person who has this kind of idea and they say 'That's terrific, we like it—do it.' And Dick [Barstow] went along with it. [The scenes in the agent's offices] were all [based on] Mondrian—at least the last one was. For 'The Peanut Vendor,' where they're playing the rhumba, George Huene took my sketch of the bar and followed it through. I had done rough little sketches and I had given everything a greenish cast, and Huene took it and said, 'This is what it is—this is the color,' and so they did it just that way, with the people in green makeup. Some of it's almost too stylized, but it works. For that stage curtain, when [the girl and her family are performing in the beginning of the number], Irene Sharaff had Lenny Gershe do all the ads that are painted on the curtain—like the one for the spiritualist, 'Chummy chats with far off friends,' that sort of thing. He just made them up and they were perfect."

While sets were being sketched and costumes designed, Ray Heindorf and his staff were hard at work arranging and orchestrating the number; and on Thursday, May 28, Garland began recording the songs and narration. Earlier, on May 17, Sid Luft had scheduled a screening of the incomplete film for several of his friends. Hearing of this, Warner "decided to ask a few people working at our studio to whom I had promised to show the picture." These "few people" included Mervyn LeRoy, Raoul Walsh, Billy Wilder, Elia Kazan, George Stevens, and John Farrow. Warner was proud of the film, but he also wanted the opinion of other professionals as to what they liked or didn't like about it. The only person who responded in writing, evidently, was Kazan, who was preparing an adaptation of John Steinbeck's best-seller *East of Eden,* which Warner was trying to persuade him to film in CinemaScope. Kazan's memo to Warner is interesting in its insights about the process and the film:

Re: *A Star Is Born.* I think you were right in using CinemaScope there . . . it gains immensely from the wide screen treatment. I am still against it for "Eden." We are going to have to depend entirely for our effect upon how much human drama and emotion we can get on the screen. This to me means only one thing: Close-ups. . . . Cukor, even in the dressing room scene, which is beautifully played, had to rely upon a close two shot. I feel he directed the scene, and Garland played it, beautifully. But I felt still that photographically the old way offers much greater opportunity to get the very most in effect out of human drama. . . . In *A Star Is Born,* it was worth giving up a little here and there in the human scenes for what you got in the colorful mass scenes and numbers. We have no numbers . . . our drama is one of interplay between characters.

Kazan wrote a much more honest (and critical) review of the film to his old friend Moss Hart, in the hospital with a bad back:

I saw *Star Is Born,* and I thought Cukor had directed it without a sense of proportion. Everything had been blown up or glamorized. Numbers which were supposed to be the essence of informality were informal on such a huge scale! I also thought he had put too much self-pity into the feelings of the two leads. On the other hand, there is some magnificent work in it and Judy has superb moments. I think it is a little swamped in its "show" aspects . . . [but] it is a most colorful and lively show, with some especially good scenes.

Hart evidently heard from several people about this screening, for he wrote to Warner on May 25:

Dear Jack:
I have had a goodly number of reports from people to whom you have shown the picture—all completely laudatory—but all complaining about the length—particularly the beginning . . . harmful and unnecessary length. So much so that I am apprehensive that what appears to be a fine picture might be jeopardized by an . . . unwillingness to relinquish some parts for the good of the whole. Therefore, I wonder if I might offer my services to the extent of suggesting some cuts. It would have the virtue of me seeing everything with a completely fresh eye, for certainly you must all have viewed the picture so many times. . . . It would be too bad if all our efforts were to be harmed by . . . an unwillingness . . . to make . . . some necessary deletions for the good of what appears to be from all the reports a quite wonderful picture. You once promised me—I think it was a promise—that you would send me on a print of the finished picture and let me make some suggestions

for cuts. Isn't this now possible? . . . If this is a presumption on my part, please put it down to my continuing and abiding interest.

Warner, in a reply dated May 28, quickly tried to allay Hart's fears (and turn aside his offer, albeit politely):

Dear Moss:

. . . The real lowdown on the showing of A Star Is Born is . . . the picture was way overlength and since this running, I personally cut out about 1500 feet. This should have been done before but I thought we should leave everything in for this [showing]. However, after seeing the results of this particular screening, I made the proper trims. In no way did they interfere with the quality of the telling of the story. . . . Before the new number is completed I can see at least five weeks' work. It is being put together with intelligence and with an eye to quality as well as entertainment. When everything is in the film, I will be more than happy to enlist your aid, but if we take the film away from the Sound and Music Departments and send it to you, it will be delayed [that much longer]. However, once we get the picture finished and previewed and find anything wrong on which I think you can be helpful, I will telephone you. . . . Between you and me, Moss, there will be very little to cut in this picture once we get into the story. The writing, direction and performances of the people themselves are so good that there is nothing that really can be cut. . . . I am taking the responsibility for editing . . . following the very intelligent manner in which George assembled the film with the editor. . . . When the picture is finally put together I think it will run three hours and from ten to fifteen minutes. . . . I cannot tell you in words how I feel about your kind interest in the entire film. I know all of us will be proud of the outcome and will be repaid many times over for all the hard work, headaches, heartaches and all the other aches that go into the making of a film of this size.

"Born in a Trunk" went before the cameras as scheduled on June 30, 1954. Sam Leavitt had moved to 20th Century–Fox to photograph Carmen Jones for Otto Preminger, so the new cameraman was Harold Rossen from MGM, who had photographed The Wizard of Oz, On the Town, Singin' in the Rain, and numerous other Technicolor extravaganzas. The first number filmed was the opening section of "Swanee," for which set decorator George Hopkins came up with the idea of banks and banks of roses behind Garland, as she accepts the plaudits of the audience. They worked from eight a.m. until six p.m. and continued at this pace for the next week, filming the songs "Born in a Trunk" and "Black Bottom."

Garland was very candid about her approach to these numbers in an interview she did at the time of the filming:

> It's difficult to be objective about one's performance. You simply cannot . . . see yourself as others see you . . . especially in making a movie. There's no audience to play to, only a large crowd of technicians behind a . . . camera. But . . . they are a surer guide to achievement than any other. After all, this is a group that is paid to do a job. They are not there primarily to be entertained. So, when, after I sang a song on the set . . . some of these veterans applauded, I knew that it was a spontaneous reaction. I would try to make the electricians and the cameramen and the others react to the song. If it was a humorous number, I would try to make them laugh. If it was the blues, I would try to make them feel in the spirit of the song. Only when they had shown the emotion the particular song was supposed to evoke did I feel that I had reached them. . . . In singing the songs from the picture, I tried to make each of them an emotional experience.

By the time the first week's work had been finished, it was obvious that there were not enough hours in the day to accomplish everything that needed to be done. The costumes that Sharaff had designed for Garland were being constructed at Western Costume in Hollywood; she had to be there at least two hours a day for fittings. Barstow was rehearsing the dancers at night and shooting during the day. Garland was not in performance shape until early afternoon; she was a night person, and her energy was at its highest level in the evenings. Moreover, Los Angeles was having one of its periodic heat waves, and temperatures on the non-air-conditioned Burbank stages sometimes reached into the nineties. So Luft went to Warner with the idea that the filming on "Born in a Trunk" be done at night, leaving the days free for Barstow's work with the dancers, Garland's fittings, recordings, and other chores connected with the picture, and thus relieving some of the intense stress that the actress was under. Already she had called in sick on the 10th; she was back the next day, but Warner, fearful of another repetition of the "Lose That Long Face" experience, readily assented to Luft's novel idea, even though it added considerably to the cost of the number, what with overtime, double time, and golden time for everyone involved.

So, beginning on July 15, *A Star Is Born* entered the final phase of its production, with filming, under Barstow's direction, continuing until well after midnight for the next two weeks. Luft, contrary to his previous custom, was on the sets constantly, supervising Garland, moving things ahead, and generally seeing to it that the number started on schedule and that Garland remained happy, even though exhausted. The final night of shooting, July 28, was given over to retakes of the "Peanut Vendor" segment; the last of five takes was completed at 2:55 a.m., after which cast, crew, and a bleary-eyed contingent of invited guests ate cake, drank champagne, and celebrated the end of one of the longest shooting schedules in modern Hollywood history.

The next day a memo went from Warner to Bill Mueller, head of the editorial department: "Have your department work overtime Saturday and Sunday, if necessary, in order to get *A Star Is Born* dubbed in time for the preview on Monday."

Cukor had returned from his European vacation and was eager to see the finished picture with a nonprofessional audience. The first preview was held in the Los Angeles suburb of Huntington Park on August 2; Cukor, full of trepidation, wrote to Hart: "I wish the picture were a little shorter. Neither the human mind nor the human ass can stand three and a half hours of concentration." But his fears were somewhat put to rest by the audience reaction, which was frenetic and hysterical. Warner himself, after the second preview, at one-thirty in the morning, telegraphed Hart (still in the hospital):

Dear Moss:
   Did not wire you last night after first preview at Huntington Park which was fabulous as wanted to wait until the second preview tonight at Encino Theatre on Ventura Blvd. to verify the tremendous audience reactions. Just impossible to find words to tell you how picture went over in both previews. A star was really born again. With deep affection for the wonderful things you did beyond the line of duty. My love to Kitty and yourself.

Cukor, in a long letter to Hart, wrote:

The previews . . . were extraordinary occasions. Judy generates a kind of hysteria from an audience. This was especially noticeable at the first preview in Huntington Park. They yipped and screamed and carried on about the musical numbers; they applauded the dressing room scene with Bickford, well into the number. I was worried that this response was excessive. However, the next night the picture had the same impact on the audience without the racket. It was at the previews that I saw for the first time the cuts that Jack Warner had wrought . . . I won't go into detail about how heavy a hand he used—how inept and insensitive—because you might rupture another disc. He snipped here and there, seemingly without reason. He succeeded in muddying things up, making scenes pointless and incomprehensible—all this without losing any footage to speak of. He cut out completely the scene in the car from the Downbeat Club to Esther's motel. The meaning of her shampooing her hair and of his hitting golf balls was lost. More serious was the audience knowing nothing about Esther's background and struggles. This gave the effect of Norman just being on the make. He succeeded in making the first reel—which everybody agreed had been very exciting—tame and conventional. These are just examples of what went on all through the picture. Afterwards, there were a series of not-too-pleasant encounters. I must congratulate myself on being very firm with him. Sid and Alperson were most intelligent and cooperative about this. I refused to be put through all the effort and strain of re-cutting the picture, and have all that work go for nothing, because "J.L." considers himself a great cutter. Apparently he doesn't think it enough that he's a great showman, very rich, a wonderful guy besides, and a million laughs. He demands that it be acknowledged that he knows more about the cutting and dubbing than anybody in Burbank. Actually, I have a high regard for his opinions and reactions as a showman, if not always for his taste. I pointed out to him that I knew *this* material better than he did . . . after a lot of wrangling, I won my point. I don't think I convinced him, but the picture is being cut the way I think it should be. . . . As I dictate this, I seem to emerge as quite a boy—talented, courageous, a two-fisted fighter. I'm not suggesting that all of my original cutting was perfect. Seeing the picture with an audience revealed certain things to me. . . . The audience indicated several places where the picture could be sped up here and there, and delicate adjustments made, without being ruthless or heavy-handed. What made my job of persuasion a wee bit more difficult was everybody saying to Sid and Judy, "Don't cut a single inch of it." This was absolute nonsense. As of yesterday, we managed to cut out about 12 minutes without in any way hurting the quality of the picture. I had an idea for a further cut—the proposal scene on the recording stage. Charming and original as it is, it seems to me now, after the passionate love scene on the terrace of the nightclub—to be anticlimactic, backtreading, as it were. I suggested that this scene might be cut but Jack Warner was adamant. To

sum it all up, all the errors that we can catch are being corrected. So much
for the Bellyaching Department. . . . My love to you and Kitty,

George

To get the film down to a three-hour-and-two-minute running time,
Cukor and editor Folmar Blangsted, in addition to shortening and tighten-
ing much of the footage, deleted the scenes of Maine searching for his keys
after his manservant has hidden them in the glass containing the servant's
false teeth, and of Norman going back to the Shrine Auditorium to try to
find the identity of the girl and finding the name of the orchestra in a
souvenir program. Also removed were scenes of Esther packing up and
leaving the Oleander Arms while being lectured by the landlady; of Esther
auditioning for a job in a seedy downtown Los Angeles bar; and of her
washing her hair and cooking on a hot plate in her rooming house just
before Maine arrives to look for her. "Born in a Trunk" was shortened
slightly by removing the sequence showing the mother's death and the song
"When My Sugar Walks Down the Street." Also cut were the scene on
the beach at Malibu when Norman and Esther plan their home and have
a picnic, with her singing a tender version of "It's a New World," and
Norman's scene with Oliver on the set of the Chinese junk, with Norman
as a swashbuckling pirate. The beginning of the Academy Awards ceremony was shortened considerably, thereby eliminating nearly all of Amanda
Blake's footage. (But not her credit in the main titles—an oversight that
no one thought to catch in the rush to get the film finished for the premiere.
All that's left of Blake are two quick shots, one as she walks off stage, and
another of her seated at the table just behind Garland.)

Once the film had been shortened to Cukor's satisfaction, it was turned
over to the music and sound departments for the last of its vital components, the musical underscoring and the mixing of dialogue, music, and
sound effects. "A Star Is Born was such a beautiful picture to work on,"
recalls Ray Heindorf. "It was very dramatic and moody, and it was the kind
of film that if it wasn't a musical, probably would have had a background
score by Steiner or Korngold. . . . With songs that are written for a picture,
you can't sing them fifty times, but you can play them throughout. A hit
is not made by singing a song once, a hit is made by letting the people hear
it—throw it at them, just keep plugging that one song. So I themed 'The
Man That Got Away' throughout." Actually, Heindorf used the song in
fifteen different variations throughout the film, starting with the main title,

where he orchestrated the opening measures of the song for the full sixty-piece Warner Bros. orchestra; this was followed by a mini-overture of "It's a New World" and "Lose That Long Face," returning to a brassy, syncopated version of "The Man That Got Away" as the credits ended. The usual studio practice was to have a staff orchestrator do the arrangements, but as Heindorf confessed: "I always wanted to do my own work. I enjoy orchestrating, especially on the main title—that [is] the most important part of a picture. A good main title will make an audience receptive to what's coming, so we always spent a little more time on the beginning of the picture."

Warner's dictum that he wanted music to "start where it says 'Warner Bros. Presents' and . . . end where it says 'The End' " was the guideline Heindorf (and all the other Warners staff composers) used when "spotting" music in a film. "The first thing you have to do," explained Heindorf, "is to see the picture. You seldom saw it complete when you started to write for it; there were always a lot of things missing. So you didn't just see it once, you saw it many times. After a while the spotting of the music wasn't that difficult, because . . . when they didn't talk, we played."

Heindorf's sensitivity to the needs of a scene was subtly demonstrated in his scoring for Maine waking in his bedroom in the middle of the night, trying to remember, through his alcoholic haze, the name of the girl he's promised to take to supper. As he is sprawled out in his bed with the curtains blowing in the breeze, the orchestra quietly plays a muted string arrangement of the "hey, you fool you" phrase from "Gotta Have Me Go With You." As the camera dollies forward, Maine sits up suddenly and unsteadily while the orchestra mimics his motion. As he tries to clear his head and think, the brass jogs his memory by playing the first eight bars of the song, which is then repeated in a minor key by the strings and percussion as the scene segues into the Cocoanut Grove ballroom. The music serves a dual purpose: by seemingly waking Maine with the ghostly echo of the song, it eliminates the necessity for Hart's spoken aside ("Promised to take a girl to dinner . . ."), then serves as a bridge into the next scene.

One of Heindorf's most expansive uses of "The Man That Got Away" occurs after Maine calls Niles at four a.m. to tell him about Esther. As Norman hangs up the phone, he absently hums the opening bars of the song; then he stops and begins to think about Esther, and the cello picks up the phrase; as Norman pours himself a drink, a clarinet plays an ascending figure; then the orchestra continues to develop the melody while he ponders the future of all this. A harp then plays the phrase "The night is bitter. The stars have lost their glitter," which serves as a bridge into Esther's darkened bedroom at the Oleander Arms, where she too is awake, thinking. Her restlessness is made evident by the insistent clarinet repeating the previous phrase over a rising and falling string figure. As she gets out of bed, the orchestra picks up the melody and expands it as she opens her door and goes upstairs to talk to Danny McGuire, the music diminuendoing as she knocks on his door. It is a beautifully evocative use of the song, tying the two principal characters together emotionally yet underlining their separate anguish in a completely individual manner, just by altering the chromatics and dynamics of the melody. Heindorf varied this approach throughout the film, using four songs ("Gotta Have Me Go With You," "The Man That Got Away," "Here's What I'm Here For," and "It's a New World") as principal themes, modifying their melodic structures to fit the needs of the scene.

In addition to these four songs written for the picture, he interpolated fourteen other, outside melodies throughout the film. The overture to the Shrine benefit is a rousing version of J. Fred Cootes's "Why?" from the 1929 Broadway show *Sons o' Guns.* For a jam session in the Downbeat Club that interrupts Norman and Esther's conversation, Heindorf used the Jack Yellen–Lew Pollack "Cheatin' on Me." "I brought in some jazzmen for this," recalled Heindorf, "in addition to the regular orchestra, because I wanted it to sound like improvisation. We had Buddy Cole on the piano, Nick Fatool on the drums, Babe Russin on tenor, and Hoyt Bohannon on trombone, and they made it sound improvised, even though it was written [in an arrangement by Skip Martin]." Ironic counterpoint was added by using the Johnny Green standard "Easy Come, Easy Go" as Norman points out the lights of Hollywood to Esther after her preview triumph, telling her, "It's all yours, Esther. . . . " Later, after Norman's humiliation at the Academy Awards, Esther helps him off the stage while the couples begin dancing to "Here's What I'm Here For," a bit of poignant and subtle understatement. For the final sequence, Esther's return to the Shrine Auditorium, Heindorf scored her entrance into the backstage area with a mournful guitar solo by Laurindo Almeida called "Amor Flamingo," as Esther sees the heart drawn in lipstick by Norman on the night of their first meeting. "At the end of the picture," recalls Heindorf, "after she said 'This is Mrs. Norman Maine,' she started singing 'It's a New World.' We went to preview that way, but it didn't work. It was anticlimactic, so we took Judy's vocal out and put in a choral version, which worked much better for an ending."

It took Heindorf and the Warner orchestra two weeks to record the score using the studio's new four-channel stereo sound recording system. "That was a fabulous recording," he recalls. "Years before, I'd seen the Disney picture *Fantasia* at the Carthay Circle Theatre [in Los Angeles]. I don't think that anybody has done anything better than what Stokowski did with the Philadelphia Orchestra in that. I went back to see it seven times, that's how impressed I was with it. The sound was just magnificent. When we did *A Star Is Born*, it was the first chance I had to work with stereo, and it was a completely different departure. We had a sixty-piece orchestra, and we covered the whole thing with three microphones; we had four channels, because we used what I call a 'long shot' mike, which was a microphone at the far end of the stage to pick up natural distance sound. When we listened to the first playbacks on the score, it was on magnetic tape, and the sound that came out of those big new speakers of ours—it really was something. Everybody was impressed with it. Even I was impressed with the way we sounded. It was a real thrill to hear your orchestra and your arrangements sound that good."

When the background scoring was completed, the picture was given over to the sound department for the final mixing of all the nonvisual elements: dialogue, music, and sound effects. Under normal conditions, this was one of the most time-consuming and delicate of processes. Each individual track had to be recorded in synchronization with the others. Balances had to be set so that the dialogue would not be drowned out by the music. Sound effects were immensely complicated to dub in; it was possible to have as many as six different sound-effects tracks running simultaneously in a scene: traffic sounds, wind, rain, dogs barking, footsteps, gunshots—the possibilities were limited only by the number of dubbing machines available, each of which would carry a separate track. That, of course, was with the old single-channel, monaural, optical soundtrack. With the advent of four-track magnetic stereo sound, a whole new method of putting sound on film was introduced, and with it came new techniques and methods. With stereo, if a character was talking on the left side of the screen, the sound had to come from there; if the scene cut to another angle, the sound (dialogue and effects) also had to switch positions. In the early days of stereo dubbing, sound engineers were driven to near distraction trying to work with multiple tracks, keep them all synchronized, and place the source of the sound accurately. Once this was completed, a final mix was done in which the three-channel orchestral background score was added to the previously mixed dialogue and effects tracks. It was a complex and exacting job; endless hours could be spent on one ten-minute reel.

While these final, all-important details were being meticulously attended to, Luft and Garland set forth for Europe with Jack Warner and friends on an extended three-week vacation. They were all scheduled to return to Los Angeles around Labor Day. Meanwhile, in the New York offices of Warner Bros., considerable time and discussion was being given to *A Star Is Born*. Based on the work that was being done on the film and the amount of time it would take Technicolor to make release prints, it was decided that the picture would be given its world premiere in Hollywood at the Pantages Theatre on September 29. The New York opening would take place on October 11. Due to the phenomenal interest in the film, fueled by newspaper and magazine articles, it was decided to put the picture into two Times Square theaters simultaneously, the three-thousand-seat Paramount and the smaller twelve-hundred-seat Victoria. All these initial "first run" engagements would be on a continuous-showing basis, with no intermission—and at advanced prices.

These decisions regarding the picture's handling were all being made by one man: Benjamin Kalmenson, president of Warner Bros. Distribution Corporation and a vice-president (along with Jack and Albert Warner and five others) of the parent Warner Bros. Pictures Corporation. The fifty-five-year-old Kalmenson, who had worked for ten years in the steel factories of Pittsburgh before switching over to the film business in 1927, had joined Warner Bros. in 1934 as the chief booker for the theater chain. His rise through the ranks eventually brought him to the top of the sales department, from which he subsequently moved to president of the distribution arm. Kalmenson's background and training did not imbue him with much patience for "art" or "greatness" in films. To him they were merchandise, to be sold to theaters at the highest price that could be extracted. The more stars and production values, the better the merchandise and the easier it was to sell. In his estimation, *A Star Is Born* had all those, plus the additional advantage of massive amounts of publicity due to the fascination that Garland held for the press. But he felt that the picture had one great drawback: its length. At three hours and two minutes, it was twice as long as the average film. A large first-run theater conceivably could show a hit film seven or eight times a day, filling the house for each screening—what is known in the trade as "turnover." The more people who paid to see a film, of course, the bigger the gross. Since the bulk of a picture's earnings came from its first run in large cities, it was imperative that as many patrons as possible have access to the picture. With *A Star Is Born* this would be especially important, since the final production cost had reached the astronomical figure of $5,019,770, making it the second most expensive film ever produced in Hollywood. (Selznick's 1946 production *Duel in the Sun* had cost $5,225,000.) For *A Star Is Born* just to return its negative cost to Warner Bros., it would have to take in $10 million. This was due to the cost of making prints, advertising, studio overhead, distribution costs, interest on money to finance the film, and the fact that out of every dollar taken in at the box office, seventy cents went to the distributor and thirty cents was kept by the theater. In the days before the government had made the companies give up their lucrative theater chains, this last factor was not a major problem, since all the money eventually ended up in the same corporate pot. But the 1948 "divorce decree" had turned distribution and marketing into two very different (and expensive) ball games. With *A Star Is Born* Kalmenson and his staff had a five-million-dollar piece of merchandise on their hands which would have to be sold in a manner that would bring in twice that amount. In the entire history of the American film business, only eight films had managed to gross $10 million.*

The marketing problems posed by *A Star Is Born* could be solved in several ways:

1. A road-show presentation, with reserved seats and two or three showings a day at high prices. This would give the film a prestige handling and make it special in the eyes of the moviegoing public. Later it could be exhibited in one or two first-run theaters with continuous showings at regular prices. The "playoff time" (the time a picture is in first- and second-run release) would be longer, but so would the amount of time needed for the film to recoup its cost.

---

*Gone With the Wind (1939), $33 million (including five reissues); *The Robe* (1953), $17 million; *The Greatest Show on Earth* (1952), $12 million; *From Here to Eternity* (1953), $12 million; *Samson and Delilah* (1950), $11 million; *Duel in the Sun* (1946), $11 million (including one reissue); *The Best Years of Our Lives* (1946), $11 million; *Quo Vadis* (1951), $10 million. *The Birth of a Nation* (1915) may have taken in that much, but accurate figures were not kept in the early days, so there is no way of knowing.

2. A regular, continuous-performance presentation in a large first-run house at advanced prices.
3. Showings at several theaters in every major city, also at advanced prices, so as to reach the widest possible audience in the shortest time.

All of these approaches had been used in the past to market expensive films, and all had paid off handsomely. For a while Kalmenson toyed with the idea of road-showing the film with reserved seats and an intermission, much in the nature of legitimate theater, but the slow return on the investment had pretty well scuttled that approach. Multiple openings within a city was an attractive idea, but there were not yet enough theaters equipped for Cinema-Scope and stereophonic sound, and even if there were, no chain would want to tie up its theaters for a long run with one film. So it was decided that *A Star Is Born* would be shown in one major first-run theater per city (except New York, with two) on a continuous-performance basis, with no intermission and at advanced prices, which in most cases would be two dollars top, fifty cents higher than normal. To overcome the difficulty of getting the necessary turnover, it was decided that each theater would screen the film five times daily, beginning at eight a.m.(!), with a short subject and a newsreel bringing the length of each show to three hours and thirty minutes. This was fine in theory but unfortunate in practice: with that schedule, the film would screen in the evening at six-thirty (too early) and at ten (too late). This evidently did not occur to the sales people, who felt that it was necessary to squeeze in many showings, regardless of the starting time.

Kalmenson, after attending both sneak previews of *A Star Is Born*, had insisted that the picture be shortened; but Warner, backed by Luft and Cukor, refused, reminding Kalmenson of the fact that *Gone With the Wind*, at three hours and forty minutes, had just been reissued by MGM and had been one of the summer's top-grossing films. He also pointed out that Warners' *The High and the Mighty*, which clocked in at two hours and forty-five minutes, was doing spectacular business throughout the country.

Word of the internal dissension about the cutting of the film had reached the trade press, and Warner felt obliged to issue a statement to *Variety* to the effect that the picture was going to be released at its full three-hour-and-two-minute length, assuring worried exhibitors that they were in fact getting two films for the price of one and that all they had to do was drop their second feature to show *A Star Is Born* without difficulty. With that problem apparently put to rest, Warner, Garland, and Luft went off on their European jaunt, as Kalmenson began planning the picture's release schedule while simultaneously complaining to everyone within earshot about the length of the picture.

Across town in his Madison Avenue headquarters, David O. Selznick, frustrated with Warner's lack of cooperation or response, finally started legal action, but not before sending another pleading and threatening letter to Warner, saying:

> . . . Jack, I think you are in grave jeopardy. You must think otherwise, or you would not be running these risks. My previous letters to you have elicited curious replies that seem to imply your recognition of our position, while the behavior of your lawyers continues to be nothing but aggravating . . . I am sincerely sorry that they have forced me into a position which I hope you will not regret . . . from this point on it will . . . be in the hands of my lawyers, and the lawyers for our distributors . . . as I have authorized [them] to proceed in such manner as they deem appropriate, to protect and enforce our rights. Counsel have already been engaged for this purpose here in New York and abroad.
>
> With kindest regards,
David.

The subsequent lawsuit was given front-page prominence in both daily and weekly *Variety* and the *Hollywood Reporter*, with *Variety* commenting on the fact that Selznick's suit was unusual in that "this is the first case of this kind . . . wherein Selznick is trying to restrain Warners from distributing [their remake] in any country where Selznick has rights to release his original version. . . . [Selznick] also charges that WB's threat to exhibit the new *Star* . . . in direct competition with [his] 1937 film has caused him 'irreparable damage.' Warner, in making a denial, maintains Selznick's rights aren't as broad as he maintains."

Several weeks later, after Warner and the Lufts had returned from their European trip, columnist Leonard Lyons reported on a dinner party at which both Warner and Selznick were guests:

> . . . After the ladies had gone upstairs, the men moved up nearer the host.
> I sat between David Selznick and Jack Warner. "I still can't get Jack to

listen," said Selznick. Warner wasn't listening. He was busy with his vaudeville comic patter, reaching for the only thing he covets, besides good movies—laughs. . . . And Selznick told me: "Warner cleared everything, but overlooked [the fact] that I still own the foreign rights." Warner still wasn't listening. "Print this," he said to me. "I know a man whose factory is on the blink." And I told him, "Where there's smoke, there'll be you, ha-ha."

While the attorneys prepared their briefs, preparations were going full speed ahead for the September 29 opening at the Pantages in Hollywood. Warner had instructed his studio publicity chief, Bill Hendricks, to give *A Star Is Born* the biggest, most elaborate, most glamorous opening that the city had ever seen. He wanted to return to the legendary premieres of years past, with the largest possible turnout of stars. Not only would it be great publicity, but he also wanted to eclipse Fox's opening for *The Robe*, just over one year before. To this end, Warner involved himself more than usual in the preparations for the premiere, sending personal telegrams to every major star and ex–major star in Hollywood. Those who received his invitations needed little urging; the picture and its problems, the lengthy shooting schedule, and its final astronomical cost had been the talk of the town for months. And Garland, whatever her foibles, was still an object of intense curiosity to everyone in the business. This much-touted, monumental "comeback" film of hers was awaited as nothing had been since *The Robe*, and Warner had very little trouble in getting acceptances from almost every major personality he invited—almost, but not quite. James Mason, who abhorred what he referred to as "that premiere nonsense," declined to attend, prompting Warner to wire the actor and his wife Pamela:

Just learned you have not accepted invitation to be my guest at theatre as well as party at Cocoanut Grove following the premiere. Have held tickets for you, and will personally appreciate hearing from you. Please telephone me at the studio. There's an old adage: One must put something back if they want to continue taking something out. Assure you only good can come from your attending. Affair will be covered by hundreds of radio and television stations throughout the USA and world, so why not get on the team and have a good time with us all?

Best,
Jack

Mason, however, held firm: "Many thanks for good wishes and invitations, but you have nothing to worry about. I am sure the picture will be a great success. Best wishes, James and Pamela Mason." Another disappointment was Darryl Zanuck's inability to make the festivities; Warner wanted him to see just how good an opening the studio could stage, outclassing *The Robe* festivities, and with a much better picture. But Zanuck, in his letter of apology to Warner, offered some interesting advice:

Many thanks for your personal invitation to opening. . . . Virginia [Mrs. Zanuck] is already going as the guest of Clifton Webb, and I am sure they are going to your party afterwards. I am in a very difficult position—Spyros [Skouras] is returning from Europe . . . and is bringing some financial people with him and confidentially, these are people I cannot brush off, and they will only be able to meet with me that night and then they are returning immediately. . . . I do not have to wish you good luck on your premiere as I know it is already in the bag. May I suggest that in your advertising campaign you emphasize CinemaScope, and I say this because we really do not have one important box office name in *The Egyptian* . . . and yet . . . you know . . . we are doing much bigger business than any picture since *The Robe* . . . even running ahead of *How to Marry a Millionaire*, which was the second CinemaScope release . . . and therefore I must attach enormous importance . . . to the trademark CinemaScope.

> Affectionate regards,
> Darryl

Warner had much better luck with his entreaties to Groucho Marx, although not at first, for the comedian wrote to Warner on September 16:

Dear Jack:
I rarely go to premieres, but I am deeply disappointed that I cannot go to the one for Judy Garland. Unfortunately, I give a show every Wednesday night and when I say unfortunately I am referring to the sponsor, not to me.

> Regards,
> Groucho

Warner kept after him, however, and on the 20th Marx replied:

I received your wire and contents barely noted. Seriously, folks, if you are as eager for me to go to *A Star Is Born*'s opening—I almost said Judy

Garland's—as you profess to be, I will make a deal with you: You either pick
me up with your car and chauffeur or send a car for me, and I will cancel
my Wednesday night performance. . . . In recent years I have avoided
opening nights of this kind because at the conclusion of the picture I always
find myself walking in the rain looking for my parking lot while out front
the uniformed doorman is bellowing, "Dore Schary's car." This goes on
endlessly. Either Dore Schary [head of production at MGM] has fifteen or
twenty cars or he has slipped the doorman a sizeable sum to keep howling
into the night, "Dore Schary's car! Dore Schary's car! Dore Schary's car!"

Yours until you buy a DeSoto,
Groucho

Meanwhile, as preparations for the premiere intensified, relations between Warner and Luft and Garland had been steadily worsening as the
strain of the previous year took its toll. Now that the picture was completed, Warner felt he did not have to put up with what he considered
unprofessional and unreliable behavior on the part of Garland, nor any of
her temper tantrums. While he recognized her as a major talent, she was
also, in his own words, "a major pain in the ass." Garland could still
charm him when she tried, but her tolerance was low for what she considered unreasonable and intrusive demands. Chief among them were the
plans for publicity surrounding the first four premieres of the film, which
made heavy demands on Garland. Initially she balked at the thought of
a whirlwind tour of four major cities in one week; but when she was
reminded that it was her own company that had made the film and that
she stood to gain from making herself available for the tour, she softened
her stance and agreed to attend the New York opening. Warner and
Kalmenson persisted in their demand that she also go to Chicago and
Detroit, two of the major movie markets; when Warner suggested that
she and Luft vacation with him in Europe, she finally relented and agreed
to cooperate. But this well-intentioned gesture on Warner's part back-
fired. Garland had wanted to take a quiet three weeks off with her family;
Luft, however, talked her into taking Warner's offer. In Europe she
found herself surrounded by Continental and American café society,
whose company and pursuits began to pall on her. The month had
strained her nerves to almost the breaking point, and by the end of August she was bored, irritable, and hostile. Sid Luft related to Gerold
Frank that at one point, after he left Garland in Monte Carlo to go off

to Deauville to see Aly Khan's stud farm, the actress had mixed pills and liquor in too strong a fashion, which brought on a minor nervous breakdown, and she had been confined in a psychiatric clinic for several days. Warner had returned to the United States by that time and knew nothing of this. After Garland's return to normalcy, she and Luft had gone to Paris, then London. According to Luft, Jack Warner advanced them money for the European trip out of anticipated profits from the film. (Samuel Goldwyn is reputed to have sent Warner a telegram after seeing the picture, predicting that it would gross $26 million.) At some point the couple contacted Warner, for a cable to him from the Lufts in London elicited this reply on September 5: ". . . explained emphatically to Sid at studio I personally or for company can't do more than have done . . . have been very square in all our dealings . . . company has refused to go further financially . . . all this beyond my control." Evidently, Harry Warner had stepped in and told Jack to spend no more on the film, other than what had already been budgeted for prints and advertising.

Harry Warner had finally seen his brother's $5 million gamble on the star power of Judy Garland, and he was concerned about the ability of the film and the actress to pay for themselves. His concern was shared by others in the company, including, surprisingly enough, Jack Warner himself. In a memo to head of national publicity Mort Blumenstock, the week before the picture's opening, he commented:

Analyzing and thinking about *ASIB* (as who of us isn't?) it is quite apparent that being off the screen for five years . . . Judy Garland is not a favorite . . . nor is she even known to many teenagers. . . . at a party recently at which [she] sang, there was a group of 16–17-year-olds. The kids got a kick out of her but evidently did not know her. One of the youngsters was overheard remarking "She's good . . . I don't remember seeing her before. . . . What's she been in?" . . . It might be worthwhile to think of some way of penetrating to this 12–18-year-old group . . . these youngsters influence their parents when selecting the movies they go to . . . and if there was only some way of Garland ingratiating herself with them . . . becoming "fans," it could snowball for Garland and for us.

To achieve this, it was imperative that Garland be kept happy and cooperative. Jack Warner convinced Harry to allow him to give Garland

and Luft additional monies for their own personal use during the four-city premiere jaunt—but with strict supervision, as he explained in a memo to one of the company's vice-presidents, Samuel Schneider:

> I have agreed to advance $1200 for out of pocket expenses for Judy Garland and for the people going to New York with her on the train. This is in addition to their railroad fares. I have also agreed to advance them additional money when they need it for meals away from the hotels, trips, car hire and miscellaneous expenses. . . . It is up to you fellows to hold these down. This out of pocket money should be at a minimum, but we do not want this entire operation to blow up in our faces in New York, or any of the other cities. So we will have to suffer a little.

With peace between the Warner and the Luft/Garland camps re-established, the studio now put all its energy and effort into launching the film amid a blaze of ballyhoo and excitement that was unprecedented, even by the colossal standards of Hollywood. Sixteen klieg lights made the night sky above the Pantages Theatre glow; Warner's arm-twisting resulted in a galaxy of close to two hundred and fifty major personalities alighting from their limousines to the shrieking delight of the twenty thousand fans lining the streets around the theater. The festivities were carried live coast-to-coast by NBC-TV. ABC supplied simultaneous radio coverage over two hundred stations, while kinescopes and radio tape recordings the next day started beaming the program around the world and even across the Iron Curtain into the Soviet Union.

The New York opening was even more dazzling and spectacular than the Hollywood event, with three blocks of Times Square cordoned off to all but people holding tickets to one of the two theaters. WABC-TV had four mobile television cameras stationed in front of each theater for an on-the-spot half-hour telecast highlighted by the appearance of Judy Garland at both theaters. Huge searchlights again gave the appearance of daylight to the area, while red carpeting in front of each theater covered the sidewalks from lobby to curb; when Garland made her appearances, colored stars fell from the sky. The usual superlatives and fatuous comments reached a new height of sorts when Major Albert Warner stepped to the microphone and gushed: "I really can't recall a more wonderful occasion. It's a wonderful thrill because of the wonderful Judy Garland. It's the greatest thing we have done since we brought out the first talking picture."

Sunset and Vine, looking north toward Hollywood Boulevard, 1953.

The world premiere, September 29, 1954, at the RKO Pantages Theatre, Hollywood and Vine.

A preproduction test using the WarnerScope lens and WarnerColor (the Eastman process), photographed by Winton Hoch. Both Cukor and Luft judged the results "disastrous."

Garland's first entrance in the film; costume by Jean Louis.

"Night of the Stars," outside the Shrine Auditorium. This is actually two shots combined. On the left is footage photographed for the film in CinemaScope; on the right is footage of the world premiere of *The Robe* (September 23, 1953), photographed with the inferior WarnerScope lens.

Hoyningen-Huene's artistic influence is evident in this scene backstage at the Shrine Auditorium—it is based on Degas's *Dancers Adjusting Their Slippers*.

The second version of "The Man That Got Away," shot in CinemaScope and Eastmancolor. Here the dominant color is brown and the final effect is very muddy.

The final version of "The Man That Got Away," with Garland in a new costume (by Jean Louis) and new makeup. This scene was restaged by Cukor using red and blue as the dominant colors for a striking effect.

OPPOSITE, TOP: Esther/Vicki meets publicist Matt Libby (Jack Carson) on her first day at the studio. This is a fine example of excellent CinemaScope composition and color design. Garland's costume is by Mary Ann Nyberg.
OPPOSITE, CENTER: The Oliver Niles Studio version of Vicki Lester.
OPPOSITE, BOTTOM: Norman Maine's vision of Vicki Lester.

Two scenes from the "Born in a Trunk" sequence; sets by Gene Allen, costumes by Irene Sharaff: (ABOVE) "Melancholy Baby" and (RIGHT) "Swanee."

The Academy Awards sequence, with an innovative use of the wide screen: the long shot of the glamorous audience juxtaposed with a simultaneous close-up of Vicki's acceptance speech on the television screen.

"And now here comes a big fat close-up . . . ," the most famous image from the movie (ABOVE); the 1954 poster (BELOW LEFT) and the 1983 version (BELOW RIGHT).

These two stills were composited to provide a shot for the missing drive-in sequence.

This frame of Garland and Mason from an earlier scene in the film was used to replace the deleted footage of Norman and Vicki on their way to the sneak preview of her first film. This is the way the image looks in CinemaScope before it is "unsqueezed."

This photo was taken for the 1983 reconstruction. Gloria Lewin plays the landlady and the author's arm stands in for Norman Maine. It was photographed at the original location for the Oleander Arms.

This scene was created by taking the figure of Mason from the still below and compositing it against a frame from an original location shoot.

Opening night, Radio City Music Hall, July 7, 1983.

Ronald Haver, Fay Kanin, James Mason, Clarissa Mason, and Douglas Edwards
at the Paramount Theater, Oakland, California.

James Mason and Lillian Gish
on the national tour.

James Mason, Lorna Luft, Liza Minnelli,
and Sid Luft backstage at Radio City.

"Hello, everybody, this is Mrs. Norman Maine."

The star herself managed to maintain a sense of humor about all this, for, as Gerold Frank relates, the four-months-pregnant Garland was jostled badly by the crowds around the Paramount Theatre. As the throng surged around them, Garland, Luft, and the wedge of police surrounding them were forced out of the lobby and out a side door onto Forty-third Street, where the horse of one of the mounted policemen lifted its tail and relieved itself directly in front of them, causing the richly dressed Garland to burst into laughter and exclaim, "A critic!"

Other critical reaction, however, was laudatory. In fact, the reviews from most of the major newspapers and magazines were so favorable that they could have been written by the Warner Bros. press department. *Variety*'s review of September 29 led the parade of praise:

> *A Star Is Born* is a socko candidate for anyone's must see list, scoring on all counts as fine entertainment. . . . It is among the top musicals that have come from the Hollywood stages. . . . It is a big picture for big selling . . . and big box office should be the rule rather than the exception. The tremendous outlay of time and money . . . is fully justified . . . it is to the great credit of Jack Warner that he kept his mind and pursestrings open and thus kept the project going despite . . . the insurmountable stumbling blocks. For both Miss Garland and Warner the racking months that went into the making of [the film] will soon be forgotten in the joy of an artistic and box office smash.

Life magazine agreed, saying that the picture was "a brilliantly staged, scored and photographed film, worth all the effort." *Look* proclaimed that Garland "puts on the greatest one woman show on earth." Bosley Crowther in *The New York Times* raved that "it is something to see, this *Star Is Born!* A stunning achievement." The New York *Daily News* gave it four stars, its highest rating; *Parents* magazine gave it its Award of Special Merit. And critical reaction was generally the same all across the country as the picture opened its first-run engagements in the early weeks of October. All reviewers commented favorably on the new Moss Hart screenplay, on Cukor's direction, and especially on the innovative use of CinemaScope and the imaginative and subdued production and color design. There was unanimous praise for Garland, with everyone commenting not only on her newfound maturity as a singer and performer but also on her surprising abilities as a dramatic actress. James Mason's performance was greeted with superlatives and hailed as the equal, if not the superior, of Garland's for its subtlety and bitter humor. Both performances were deemed to be of Academy Award caliber. Cukor's direction was alternately hailed and faulted, the latter primarily for allowing too much production to swamp the story. Noël Coward, a consummate theatrical professional and a friend of both Garland and Cukor, saw the film in its initial run, and his comments in his diary are lucid and pithy:

> I went to see *A Star Is Born.* What happened to the . . . once famous American timing sense? In spite of fine acting performances by Judy . . . and James . . . and a lavish, highly coloured production, it dragged interminably. Every song was attenuated to such a length that I thought I was going mad. One in particular, "Born in a Trunk," started brilliantly but by the time it was over and we had endured montage after montage and repetition after repetition, I found myself wishing that dear enchanting Judy was at the bottom of the sea. The picture ran for three hours; if it had been cut down to two, it would have been really exciting.

This was the one major criticism that was leveled at the film everywhere: it was too long, and the story was constantly being interrupted for too many lengthy musical numbers, especially in the second half. Exhibitors were complaining to Kalmenson about this; even *Variety,* the show-business barometer, while commenting on the tremendous business the picture was doing in its initial week, observed that "the tremendous length of pic is murder to the turnover." Kalmenson, armed with reviews criticizing the picture's length and with complaints from exhibitors, made a strong case to Harry Warner that if the picture were shortened, they could make even more money. In its first week, the picture was outgrossing just about every other picture in release. The second week saw a slight falling-off in attendance; at several first-run theaters, prices were dropped and schedules were revamped so that the last show started at nine instead of ten. Unfortunately, there still was no "prime time" screening at seven-thirty or eight, and once again a chorus of complaints went up about the length.

Finally, Harry Warner *ordered* Jack to shorten the film as quickly and efficiently as possible; editor Folmar Blangsted's cutting notes indicate that there had been discussion about this within the first few days after the Los Angeles opening. Blangsted's second wife, Elsa, herself a film editor, relates: "I wasn't married to him then, but he told me later that *A Star Is*

Born was a great thorn in his side. He loved Cukor, loved working with him, and apparently Cukor liked him too. But Cukor had left to go to India. It was Warner who said 'Take it out.' It's true Folmar could have said 'I'll quit before I do this,' but by that time he'd been there for such a long time, and Warner had insisted that Folmar be put on as editor—[Garland and Luft] wanted Bill Ziegler, but Warner wanted Folmar to do it. These men, and my husband was one of them, they really believed in that system. Those [moguls] were like fathers to men like Folmar—they were the boss. Folmar told me over and over that it was Jack who said 'Cut it'; Folmar started sending wires to Cukor in India: 'Please contact me, contact Warner; they're making me take out important scenes, whole sequences.' But he never got a response from Cukor, and Cukor never spoke to Folmar again; he blamed him for the cuts. He didn't dare blame Warner, because, you know, there's such a club with the big ones. In those days they patted each other's backs—now they kiss. But there is a club and they will always find a fall guy, and Folmar was Cukor's."

Just who decided what should be cut is a mystery. The only notes regarding suggested cuts in the Warner Bros. files is a handwritten memo from someone in the sales department named Barrie Richardson which says: "Here are the suggested cuts we talked about making in the picture." This is followed by a description of what was to be omitted in the new version:

> Entire scene omitted where Esther says goodbye to members of the band. Following scenes in sequence completely omitted:
>
> –Maine being led to car in front of his home and being driven to location.
>
> –Esther sitting in bungalow court and washing hair; lying by swimming pool.
>
> –Maine on boat for location filming.
>
> –Oliver Niles talking with Maine's director on phone and talk with Libby about Maine being sick.
>
> –Esther at rooming house talking on phone about singing job.
>
> –Esther singing Calypso commercial for shampoo outfit.
>
> –Esther at 'burger stand talking in phone booth with Danny and scene with customer asking what's on the menu.
>
> –Maine at Oleander Arms looking for Esther.
>
> –Maine and Lucy Marlow hearing Esther's TV commercial.
>
> –Maine finding Esther on roof of rooming house.

Thus new transcript jumps from scene at dawn in bungalow court when

Esther tells Danny she is quitting the band and jumps to studio scene of Esther being made up for screen test.

–Scene omitted of Esther and Maine driving to preview of Esther's picture.

–Entire scene omitted of recording session when Maine proposes to Esther.

–Entire "Lose That Long Face" number omitted—moves directly to dressing room scene.

–Scene omitted of Esther drying tears and singing "Lose That Long Face" again.

The announcement by Warner to Luft and Garland that the picture was going to be cut evidently ruptured their relationship irreparably. Luft bitterly blames both Warner *and* Cukor for the cuts: "The only person who can cut a picture is the director. George Cukor made those cuts. George denies it, but . . . he had to cut it to get his money. Think about it—Jack Warner, a cigar-smoking idiot, sitting up there in that studio saying 'Cut the goddamn movie' because the Paramount theater chain says we're losing a fortune! The only person who could cut is Cukor, or myself, or maybe Moss Hart could cut it, but Jack Warner couldn't cut it. Moss thought it was too long; I never did. We wanted an intermission—with that, it never would have been too long. They said, 'With an intermission we're gonna lose more money,' and they were absolutely wrong. I wouldn't cut it; I walked away. Judy and I, we wouldn't touch it. I tell you it was George who cut it. He said, 'Remove "Lose That Long Face" '—it was done on the telephone and in his presence—one meeting in the projection room with Blangsted and the cuts were made. . . . [Judy and I] were heartbroken." Garland's daughter Liza Minnelli, who was eight years old at the time, recalls her mother coming home after hearing the news that cuts were being made, throwing herself on the bed, and sobbing, "They just don't care . . . they just don't care."

No matter what Luft thinks, it would have been impossible for Cukor to cut the film, as he had been out of the country since early September. It is true, however, that he thought that "Born in a Trunk," the proposal sequence on the sound stage, and "Lose That Long Face" could all be removed without materially damaging the story. But what angered and hurt Cukor was, as he later related, "the way they just hacked into it. It was very painful. . . . Some terribly funny and touching scenes [were taken out] that were crucial. If they thought it was too long there were other ways of shortening it besides chopping and hacking out vital bits. Had we been allowed, Moss Hart and I could have sweated out twenty minutes which would have been imperceptible to the audience. That's something which I can't understand. Producers spend millions of dollars to do pictures and then suddenly, right out of the blue, they say, 'Let's chop this out, then that. . . .' It's very painful, all this. . . . It's one of the great sorrows of my career, the way the picture was cut by the studio. Judy Garland and I felt like the English queen who had 'Calais' engraved on her heart. Bloody Mary, wasn't it? Neither of us could ever bear to see the final version."

Just exactly why the picture was cut as it was is very simple when you consider that both Harry and Jack Warner wanted the picture shortened as quickly and as economically as possible. This meant no meticulous recutting, no rerecording, no making of new prints. Instead, the picture was to be trimmed by lifting out whole reels, or portions thereof. For studio editorial purposes, the length of a 35mm reel is considered to be one thousand feet, lasting ten minutes, give or take a few minutes, depending on the amount of footage. For exhibition, two of these reels are combined to form a two-thousand-foot projection reel. Each of these projection reels is made up of an A section and a B section. To make the cuts in *A Star Is Born* as indicated by the Richardson memo, Blangsted was obliged to shorten both reels 3A and 3B and combined them to form a new reel known as 3AB. Cuts were also made in reels 4A, 5A, 6B, 9A, and 9B. This was done in utmost secrecy, as Jack Warner was still not entirely convinced that the picture would work with the cuts. Blangsted worked from a finished print, completing all deletions and changes within a week, and after this new version was screened for Warner, he wrote to Kalmenson, "We have eliminated 27 minutes . . . [and I] am certain we have lost none of the values . . . in fact we have gained a lot by sharpening the story line and eliminating any 'sore fanny' restlessness. We are sneaking this 'shorter version' at the Pantages tomorrow night [Sunday]."

This new version was shown, unannounced, at the six o'clock evening screening. Columnist Joe Schoenfeld of *Variety*, who had been alerted, showed up to see what was happening with the film and recounted later in *Variety:*

Warners' tested its cut version of *A Star Is Born* at the Pantages the other night. Jack Warner, Steve Trilling [his assistant] and other execs were in the lobby talking it over afterwards. Out of the auditorium came an angry youth of around 19. Seeing J.W., who looks like an exec, the young man came over and asked, "Are you the manager?" J.W. answered, "Yes." The youth then demanded his money back. "This picture has been cut," he charged, "and I didn't get my money's worth." "What makes you think the picture's been cut?" asked Warner. "Because I've seen it before" answered the kid and again demanded his money. Warner, knowing that the uncut version was going on again for the next and last showing, then asked the kid to describe exactly what scenes had been omitted. The kid reeled them off as though he had lived most of his life in a cutting room. After he had described the trimming in detail, Warner looked him straight in the eye and said, "You must have been dreaming! But I'll tell you what I'll do. You go back in there and see the next showing, and when it's over, if you tell me again that the picture has been cut, I'll give you your money back." 3½ hours later, the house manager, on instructions from Warner, was waiting for the 19-year-old as he came out of the theatre. His eyes looked as though they had been looking at film for 10 hours. The manager told the kid he was the assistant manager, and asked whether he still thought the film had been cut. The kid never answered. Just shook his head, dazed and completely perplexed.

The trimming that had so outraged this young man was damaging to the film, as it eliminated scenes that added considerably to the understanding of the motivations and development of the two central characters. The deletion of this expository material diminishes the growing emotional involvement of Norman and Esther and mutes the final tragedy of the story. The two songs removed from the second half had been designed to complement and enhance the dramatic structure of the story; cutting them not only lessened the impact of certain scenes but also seriously damaged Moss Hart's carefully structured continuity, which, in the original, maintained a careful balance between the musical and the dramatic. Warner, however, was evidently at the point where he was sick of the whole project and just wanted to put it behind him.

After seeing how the picture went over with an audience (who, after all, did not know what was missing unless they'd seen it before), Warner was considerably heartened and gave orders that the short version should be supplied for all future engagements; the picture would continue to play in the full-length version where it had already opened. The fact that the film had been shortened was made public by Warners in a news release dated October 27, with the announcement that the new version would be for subsequent runs only, and primarily for second-run and neighborhood houses, which remained resistant to films over two hours in length. But according to one irate patron in a letter to the editor of *Variety:*

> The Victoria, here in New York, is now showing the abbreviated version . . . without . . . however . . . a price cut . . . still at a fancy $2.00 top. . . . This action is highly objectionable . . . nor can it be excused on artistic grounds. I would defy any of the critics who complained of the . . . length to suggest that any improvement has been made in the film's quality by the trimming. On the contrary, the film suffers noticeably by the fadeouts where it is obvious a musical number has been dropped, to say nothing of dialogue which is now meaningless because it refers to earlier scenes which have been indiscriminately scissored. It seems to this writer that the New York showcase for such a long-awaited attraction has acted most unwisely in the matter and with contemptuous disregard of the public interest.

As the news of the editing done on the picture spread, the studio was suddenly flooded with dozens of letters from moviegoers protesting the action. An angry patron from the Bronx took Warner to task, saying:

> I saw *A Star Is Born* twice . . . [it is] a finely wrought, lovingly created moving piece of entertainment. . . . The length was inconsequential to the enjoyment of the film. Now I read that there is a different *A Star Is Born* being shown, a picture which has lost forty [sic] minutes of priceless footage. . . . Frankly, Mr. Warner, a long time has passed since a really good picture has come from the Warner lot, and when one finally did come along it was only to be slashed to conform to the mold. A very sad thing has occurred [over] which I, as an ordinary moviegoer, have no control, and I wish to know what prompted you and your associates to do this terrible thing. . . .

And it was not just fans who were irate. A letter from a theater manager in Maine complains: "What they have done to this film is inexcusable. The studio should certainly back down to the extent of making both versions available to [exhibitors] and let us select which version we will show. We played the picture last week and received many letters and calls from customers stating that they would not pay advance prices to see a picture with more than thirty minutes cut out of it. Consequently we lost money on the picture." Controversy spread as far as the pages of *The New York Times,* where critic Bosley Crowther, who had high praise for the original version, declared himself to be "in a grave dilemma" in considering *A Star Is Born* for his ten best list of 1954. He deplored the trimming of the film and called for reviewers to "show disfavor for such post-release tampering."

The picture did extremely good business everywhere for its first month of release; then, about the middle of November, as other, newer films were released for the holiday season, attendance at *A Star Is Born* began to fall off sharply. Everyone in the sales and distribution departments of Warners had expected the picture to maintain its first run for at least two months before business slackened, so there was immediate surprise and concern, for the film had not yet recouped the bulk of its negative cost, let alone shown signs of moving into the profit area. By late December, it was obvious that the film was not going to be the financial bonanza that Warner and his people thought it would. Irv Kupcinet, in his column in the Chicago *Sun-Times,* remarked that "Hollywood has been quick to label Judy Garland's [film] a box office flop. 'Taint quite so. Some 300,000 persons have laid it on the line to see the movie at the Chicago Theatre, which means that the picture will show a tidy but not huge profit locally. The same is true all around the country. What *is* true is that *Star,* after one of the biggest buildups in Hollywood history, hasn't been the tremendous hit expected."

The picture was generally released in the shorter version in mid-January 1955. The existing full-length prints were shortened at the various Warner Bros. film offices around the country, as per detailed instructions from the studio's editorial department in Burbank. The cut material was shipped back to the studio, and the long version, for all practical purposes, ceased to exist. Even the studio print was cut to conform to this new length. Over the next months this version of *A Star Is Born* did fair business; as it wended its way down the theatrical release ladder, the sales department added another $2 million to the picture's gross, bringing its total to just over $4.3 million for the first six months of its release.

In February, however, the announcement of the nominations for the 1954 Academy Awards gave *A Star Is Born* a temporary new lease on box-office life. Both Garland and Mason were nominated for their performances, and the film also was cited for art direction, song ("The Man That Got Away"), scoring, and costume design. The picture stood to gain a great deal of income depending on how many awards it received and in what categories. If Garland and Mason both won, that could add another $2 million or more to the gross. Garland alone would probably be worth a little over a million. Awards in the subsidiary categories could bring in an additional quarter- to half-million dollars. So the nominations and the awards were a valuable marketing tool. Indications were all in favor of Garland winning. The competition was strong (Dorothy Dandridge for *Carmen Jones,* Audrey Hepburn for *Sabrina,* Grace Kelly for *The Country Girl,* and Jane Wyman for *Magnificent Obsession*), but she was the sentimental favorite. When *Look* gave her its award for best female performance of the year, it seemed a harbinger of things to come.

Cukor, however, was nowhere in sight on the Academy's list of nominees. In fact, all of Cukor's extensive efforts on this film were obscured by the flood of publicity on Garland: his direction was praised, but not extensively; most remarks concerned the performances he had gotten from the two leads. At the time of the premiere, he was off in India scouting locations, and there had been almost no acknowledgment of him at all. Gene Allen, who was with him at the time, recalls, "He got a wire from his aunt—I think her name was Maude—and she said, 'George, don't work hard. Don't kill yourself for these people. Do you [know] that nobody except Lucille Ball mentioned your name at the premiere?' He laughed— he thought that was wonderful."

A Star Is Born had played the bulk of its bookings by the time the nominations were announced, so it needed all the help it could get. Musicals were seldom deemed worthy of awards except in music, design, costumes, photography, and other technical areas. Performances, direction, and script were seldom given serious consideration, though *An American in Paris* had won in 1951.

The awards were to be given on March 30, just about the time Garland was due to have her baby; Lauren Bacall would accept for her if she won. Garland gave birth to her son, Joey, on March 29; and the next night, the evening of the Academy Awards, she later recalled very vividly in an interview with Joe Hyams for *Photoplay* magazine: "Just picture this. There I was, weak and exhausted . . . I was lying in bed and three men came into my room in the hospital with three huge television sets . . . and I said, 'What's this for?' and they said, 'When you win the Academy Award, you've got to be able to talk back and forth to Bob Hope,' who was emceeing. And I said, 'You can't just bring a whole crew and lights and all that stuff in here; there are other women in here having babies' and they said, 'Don't worry about that,' and they pulled up the venetian blind and they had built a four-story-high tower outside the

hospital for the cameras to point into my room. And there were a lot of
people running around on that tower; what with all that excitement and
everything they got me all worked up, and I was positive I was going to
win so I had the nurse put a new bed jacket on me and there I was flat
on my back trying to look cute. Then they found out they had some
trouble with the sound, so they strung wires all over the room and put a
microphone under my nightgown and taped it to my chest. My nurse had
been assigned to open the venetian blinds on cue, so that the cameras could
get me making my acceptance speech; they scared the poor woman to death
when they told her, 'If you open that window while the show is on we'll
kill you!' By this time it's getting near the point . . . I was flat on my back
in bed trying to look cute, I was ready to give a performance, then Bob
Hope [opened the envelope] and said Grace Kelly had won and I said
'WHAATT??' I'll never forget it to my dying day. The technicians in my
room all said 'Kelly! Aah,' then they started lugging all that stuff out again,
you should have seen the looks on their faces! I really thought I would have
hysterics!"

This was retold much after the fact (on one of her 1964 CBS television
shows), and with the self-deprecating humor that was so much a part of
Garland's defense mechanism; but to someone as insecure and sensitive to
public reaction as she was the pain of not winning must have been intense.
Lauren Bacall, who joined Luft and Garland at the hospital almost immediately after the announcement, relates: "The big night came and we were all
praying—and Judy lost. She carried it off beautifully, saying her son Joey was
more important than any Oscar could be, but she was deeply disappointed—
and hurt. It's pretty hard to put your heart and soul into something and then
get your face slapped. . . . Emotionally it was terrible for her. It confirmed her
belief that the industry was against her. She was very upset about it; it was the
peak of her career, and she knew it was then or never. Instinctively, all her
friends knew the same. Judy wasn't like any other performer. There was so
much emotion involved in her career—in her life—it was always all or
nothing. And though she put on a hell of a front, she was bitter about it—and
for that matter, all closest to her were."

Surprise upsets are one of the fascinations of the Academy Awards, and
this one is still legendary. Everybody in Hollywood seems to have been
convinced that Judy Garland would win—or at least everyone professes
surprise that she didn't when you bring up the subject, even now. So, if
everybody *expected* her to win, why didn't she? Probably because not
everybody *wanted* her to win. The Hollywood filmmaking community is a

very tightly knit society. There are rivalries, resentments, reprisals, and a great deal of hostility toward overachievers, larger-than-life genuine artists, who are volatile and demanding; they are lightning rods for the "who the hell does she think she is?" attitude. In Garland's case, the Hollywood press had been satiated with stories about her; her activities on *A Star Is Born* were largely public knowledge. And then there was the intratrade gossip: grips, hairdressers, and costumers all knew the stories of Garland's behavior during the making of the film, and these folks are the true citizenry of the town and the industry. Their attitudes differ from those of the creative level above them—executives, directors, writers, agents—in that they seldom harbor grudges, but they have little patience or sympathy for what is considered to be temperamental "star" behavior. Too many of them had seen examples of that kind of nonsense to be anything but resentful of it. Even though Garland was always liked by the crews she worked with, they were uneasy about her ability to lose her temper and throw tantrums. There is a photo in the *Life* layout on the film that shows a furious Garland clutching a cigarette and evidently raging at someone, and there is a hostility and a ferocity in her person that is most revealing. So there was this perception of Garland on the part of the rank-and-file workers in Hollywood. Then there was the film itself, which many thought overblown, too long, and too much a showcase for Garland; it conjured up images of a monumental ego and a demand for attention that could be offputting. As far as much of the industry was concerned, Garland and *A Star Is Born* were overdone, overrated, and exhausting.

The hostility toward both performer and film is evidenced by the fact that out of the six categories in which it was nominated, *A Star Is Born* did not win a single award.* There was also the perception of the picture as an expensive flop; Academy voters in those days seldom gave awards to pictures that had failed financially. Moreover, Warners had not aggressively promoted the picture during the voting period and had even shown the short version of it for the nomination and voting screenings. These screenings were important, since this is where many of the Academy members finally get to see the films that have been made in the past year.

"Judy Garland [gave] a brilliant performance," stated George Cukor, "marred only by the way in which the picture was cut by the studio. . . . I'm convinced that it cost Judy [the] Academy Award." The cutting had elimi-

---

*In addition to Kelly, the other winners were: actor—Marlon Brando for *On the Waterfront*; costume design—*Gate of Hell*; art direction—*20,000 Leagues Under the Sea*; scoring of a musical picture— *Seven Brides for Seven Brothers*; and song—"Three Coins in the Fountain."

nated much of the vulnerability, warmth, and humor of her character; what was left was a slightly overbearing performance, both vocally and dramatically. Grace Kelly was young, patrician, unassuming, and well liked. Her performance in *The Country Girl* had startled most people, as the popular perception of her was of a well-bred ingenue; here she was effective primarily because she was cast against type, allowed herself to be "deglamorized," and gave a restrained yet intense performance. Both MGM, where she was under contract, and Paramount, where she had made *The Country Girl,* mounted large advertising campaigns in the trade journals on her behalf. So all of these factors must be considered when trying to analyze why Garland lost an award that everybody thought she would win. And then, of course, there is the inescapable fact that Academy Awards are given on the basis of a simple majority; Garland could have lost by a single vote.

The loss of any Academy recognition more or less sealed the commercial fate of *A Star Is Born.* It played off the balance of its theatrical engagements in the short version, going on record in *Variety*'s list of top U.S. grossers for 1955 as having taken in $6 million. The figure was supplied to *Variety* by Warners, which evidently was doing a little creative bookkeeping: according to the studio records, the picture had grossed only $4,355,968 domestically by November 1955; it had taken in another $1,556,000 overseas. (*A Star Is Born* had opened in London on May 29, 1955, in the short, 154-minute version. As it played in Europe, the local Warners distributor kept cutting until it ended up running 100 minutes, in which version it played from 1956 through 1970 and then was taken out of release and put on television.)

Warner did not want to admit just how big a failure his gamble had been. If the picture grossed $4.3 million, that meant it returned roughly $3.5 million to the studio—a loss of approximately $2 million on just the negative production cost. At the inflated $6 million gross, *A Star Is Born* placed fourteenth on *Variety*'s list, following *White Christmas* (Paramount, $12 million), *Gone With the Wind* (MGM reissue, $9 million), *The Caine Mutiny* (Columbia, $8.7 million), *Mister Roberts* (Warner Bros., $8.5 million), *Battle Cry* (Warner Bros., $8 million), *20,000 Leagues Under the Sea* (Disney, $8 million), *Not as a Stranger* (United Artists, $7.1 million), *The Glenn Miller Story* (Universal, $7 million), *The Country Girl* (Paramount, $6.9 million), *Lady and the Tramp* (Disney, $6.5 million), *Strategic Air Command* (Paramount, $6.5 million), *To Hell and Back* (Universal, $6 million), *The Sea Chase* (Warner Bros., $6 million), and

The High and the Mighty (Warner Bros., $6 million). At the actual $4.3 million gross, *A Star Is Born* came in at twentieth place, after *Seven Brides for Seven Brothers* (MGM, $5.6 million), *Rear Window* (Paramount, $5.3 million), *Magnificent Obsession* (Universal, $5.2 million), *Three Coins in the Fountain* (20th Century–Fox, $5 million), and *Desirée* (20th Century–Fox, $4.5 million). After the year's tally was in, Ben Kalmenson wrote to Jack Warner: "It became apparent a few months ago that, while Judy Garland is young enough to be the daughter of Mary Pickford . . . she is in a way like her in that she is the little girl who grew up and is a favorite of adults. There is no question but that we overrelied on our star on this one."

Warners and Transcona had called off their three-picture deal after *A Star Is Born* proved so troublesome and unsuccessful.* Warner had unkind words for both Garland and (especially) Luft in his autobiography, *My First Hundred Years in Hollywood.* Luft, never a man to dodge a fight, related: "I sued him. Jack was nuts—he got carried away. . . . [In his book] he accused me of all this nonsense: 'Aw, the son of a bitch,' he'd say, 'he stole all the furniture.' That's the kind of guy he was—he'd make a joke out of everything. There was no loyalty with Jack. All this crap he put in his book—he made up all this stuff for self-aggrandizement." The lawsuit was settled out of court and over the years, many people have insisted that one of the reasons *A Star Is Born* was mutilated was because Warner wanted to "get back" at Garland and Luft for causing him so much personal and financial trouble with the film. This is nonsense. Warner, as we have seen, was ordered to cut the film by his brother Harry; he put up a good fight to maintain the integrity of Cukor's work but finally had to back down when faced with the intractability of his brother and of Ben Kalmenson. The only thing Jack Warner can be faulted on was not keeping a full-length version of the film for archival purposes. Even the studio print, the last existing "long version," was cut to conform to the 154-minute edition, as was the master negative; and the footage cut from this print and from all the prints playing around the country was sent back to the studio and put through a silver reclamation process.

Warner's acquiescence in this, and the finality of it, were certainly known to Cukor. Gene Allen recalls: "He would never discuss it, but his lips would go white if you brought it up. I remember once the USC cinema

---

*Nominally at least, Transcona had made *two* films. The other one, *The Bounty Hunter,* was a Randolph Scott western produced by Warner staff producer Sam Bischoff; the Transcona label was for studio bookkeeping and tax-shelter purposes.

department asked him to come down and talk about the film, and he said he would if they would show the original version. So they told him they did have the long version and he was very excited. So we went down and sat there, and when the first cut came on, he grabbed me and we got up and left and we walked around till it ended and then we went back in and he apologized and said he just couldn't stand to see it that way."

As Elsa Blangsted pointed out, "the big ones don't blame each other." Cukor never spoke to Blangsted again, but he remained on cordial, even friendly, terms with Warner. He later referred to Warner as "tough . . . but a showman. Quite a remarkable showman, I might add. He's very intelligent . . . he is a perfect gentleman . . . generous . . . and courageous." This was said in 1964, ten years after *A Star Is Born* and just after Cukor had finally won an Academy Award for his direction of Jack Warner's personal production of *My Fair Lady*. In an extreme bit of circular irony, Cukor won his award with work based on Moss Hart's stage direction of the play.

The failure of *A Star Is Born* marked the end of Judy Garland's career as a major film star. Thereafter, she confined herself primarily to concerts, including one legendary appearance at Carnegie Hall in 1961. That same year she did a short dramatic bit in Stanley Kramer's *Judgment at Nuremberg*, following this with a critically acclaimed straight dramatic lead in another Kramer-produced film, *A Child Is Waiting*. Her film career came to an end after she starred in a 1963 British production called, ironically, *I Could Go on Singing*. Luft continued to advise her on her career, including a series of weekly hour-long television shows on CBS in 1963–64; they were finally divorced in May 1965.

A Star Is Born is one of Sid Luft's proudest accomplishments, and he recalled a poignant memory of it to Gerold Frank. It was the night of the first national telecast of the movie; Garland and Luft had been separated for some time. Luft was watching the film in his hotel room in New York; at midnight,

there was a telephone call from the lobby. "This is Miss Garland's chauffeur," came a man's voice. "Miss Garland is here in her car, and she would like to see you." . . . When he went downstairs and walked outside, there was Judy, dressed to perfection, sitting in the rear seat of a limousine, a fur blanket over her knees, beside her was a bucket with a bottle of champagne. . . . "Hi, darling," she said, as though they'd seen each other a few hours ago. "How are you?" He said, "Just fine." She said, "You watched the picture?" He nodded, not trusting himself to speak. "Wasn't it great?" she asked. And then: "You produced a great picture, Sid." He said, "Judy, it was your picture and you were great in it and it's great to see you again." She said, and her voice broke, "Let's celebrate." They did—at El Morocco. That night . . . on the drive back, he noticed she was wearing neither her wedding ring nor the engagement ring he had bought her. . . . "Where are they, darling?" he asked. She snuggled up to him. "Somewhere between here and Scarsdale," she said. . . . "I got sore at you one night and threw them out of the car."

Jack Warner, too, remained proud of *A Star Is Born* over the years. Despite the headaches, the heartaches, and the final fiscal disappointment, all who knew him or worked with him recall him listing it as one of the best pictures ever to carry the Warner shield. He stayed head of production at the studio until 1966 and outlived his feared older brother Harry, who died in 1958, and brother Albert, who followed ten years later. Jack, finally tiring of the role of mogul and seeing the rules of the game of moviemaking change in ways that he could not adapt to, sold his shares in the company to Seven Arts Productions for $32 million; at seventy-five, he officially retired. He made two unfortunate forays into independent moviemaking: *Dirty Little Billy* and the film of the hit Broadway musical *1776*, both released in 1972 to profound public indifference. Warner died in 1978, at the age of eighty-six. Literally the last tycoon, he presided over the making of more good movies for a longer period of time than anyone else in Hollywood, and those films are his legacy.

Moss Hart died of a heart attack in 1961, a year after the opening of the Arthurian musical *Camelot,* which he directed. Jack Warner later personally produced film versions of both this and Hart's 1956 *My Fair Lady.* In 1963, the studio released an unsuccessful adaptation of Hart's posthumously published autobiography, *Act One.*

As for David O. Selznick's lawsuit against Warners, it was settled in late 1955 when Selznick turned over his foreign distribution rights to the original production of *A Star Is Born;* for an additional payment of $25,000, he was given the remake rights to *A Farewell to Arms.* He produced the film under his Selznick Studio banner in Italy in 1956–57 at a cost of $5 million. Starring Jennifer Jones and Rock Hudson, it was filmed in CinemaScope and Eastmancolor and released by 20th Century–Fox in 1957; it was a failure, both critically and financially, and Selznick never made another movie. He died in 1965 of a heart attack at the age of sixty-three.

James Mason went on to a string of artistic successes that ended only with his death in 1984 at age seventy-five. He, too, had subsequent experi-

ences with *A Star Is Born:* "It continues to be shown all over the world
both in theatres and on television screens," he wrote in his 1981 autobiography. "If there is no pressing appointment to stop me, I will always watch
it when it shows up on my nearest television set. When I was taking a walk
with [my daughter] Portland on the side of our local mountain in Switzerland, we stopped in at a cafe for a cup of tea when the voice of Judy singing
made us turn towards a corner of the room where a small black-and-white
set was lodged. When she stopped singing another voice took over her share
of the dialogue. Both she and I had French-speaking voices attached to us
and Portland and I sat through it spellbound to the end. I have seen it again
a couple of times since . . . and the last time we saw the French version
I noted that it ran for not more than an hour and forty minutes. The
uprooted sections were mostly musical. . . . In most of our lives this film
meant a great deal. The Hollywood Establishment saw little virtue in it.
. . . It was by no means a commercial success at the time. But now it has
been revived so often that I think we may call it a retarded success. When
the film first came out, the people of Hollywood knew Judy as a person who
had 'trouble' written all over her. But now . . . people all over the world
. . . rate her among the two or three great popular singers of our century,
an irreplaceable treasure."

Judy Garland was found dead in a London hotel room on June 21, 1969,
apparently of an "accidental overdose of sleeping pills." Her body was
brought back to New York, where it lay in state at Campbell's Funeral
Parlor as thousands of fans gathered outside to pay their last respects. James
Mason delivered the eulogy, which ended: "The little girl whom I knew
. . . when she was good, she was not only very, very good, she was the most
sympathetic, the funniest, the sharpest, and the most stimulating woman
I ever knew."

At the time of her death, Warner Bros., which now owned *A Star Is Born*
outright, announced that the picture, in its full-length version, would open a
limited engagement at the 8th Street Playhouse in New York. The theater
was jammed for the first showing, but it soon became apparent that this was
the short version, and the studio was forced to admit that it had no idea
where, or even what, a "long version" was. Thereafter, *A Star Is Born* was
relegated to the film cemetery of late-night television and seedy "grind"
houses. An expensive footnote in movie history, it was evidently a picture
that the Hollywood film industry had no further use for nor interest in.

Or so it seemed until the night of July 19, 1983.

PART
TWO

A
STAR
IS
BORN
AGAIN

On July 19, 1983, twenty-nine years after its first Hollywood premiere, *A Star Is Born* was given another searchlighted and celebrity-studded unveiling. This one took place at the new Beverly Hills headquarters of the Academy of Motion Picture Arts and Sciences: there were some limousines, a red carpet, photographers, and television news cameras—no premiere would ever be complete without them—but this event was much less hysterical and spectacular than the original opening. Once again George Cukor was not in attendance; nor, for obvious reasons, were Jack Warner and Judy Garland. But her daughters, Liza Minnelli and Lorna Luft, were there, as was her son, Joey Luft; so was Sid Luft. James Mason made it to this premiere—along with Gene Allen, Sam Leavitt, Lucy Marlow, Earl Bellamy, Russ Llewellyn, and eleven hundred of Hollywood's elite, old and new, including Gregory Peck and Lillian Gish. All of them crowded into the Academy's Samuel Goldwyn Theatre to take part in a unique filmland event: the hometown premiere of a "reconstruction" of the original version of the film, funded in part by the Academy Foundation and by Warner Bros., the same studio that had produced, then diminished, the masterpiece a quarter of a century before.

The intervening years, however, had wrought many changes, not only in Hollywood the town but also in the film industry. The old moguls of legend were all gone; the studios over which they had ruled so colorfully and successfully for so many years were now largely small plums in large corporate pies. Some had simply ceased to exist; nothing was left of RKO except its backlog of 744 films and an art deco address plate at 780 Gower Street. The company had been bought by the TV production firm Desilu, which was later absorbed by Paramount Pictures, which in turn had been acquired by Gulf and Western Industries. Columbia Pictures was a subsidiary of Coca-Cola and had given up its production facility on

Gower Street in Hollywood to move out to Burbank, where it shared space at the Burbank Studios with Warner Bros., which had evolved first into Warner Bros.–Seven Arts, then into Warner Communications, a unit of Kinney Services, operator of parking lots and mortuaries. United Artists was now merely an appendage of the once mighty MGM; both were reduced to being just chips in the high-stakes money games of their owner, Kirk Kerkorian, who preferred building hotels and gambling casinos to making movies. Real-estate mania had begun in Hollywood in the late 1950s when 20th Century–Fox sold its studio at Western and Sunset to a developer who demolished it and built a shopping center. Fox's Beverly Hills studio still stood, but the extensive back-lot acreage had been sold off in the early 1960s and the facility was now backdropped by the spectacular skyscrapers of Century City. The Pico Boulevard frontage of the studio had been converted into an amazingly detailed replica of 1890s New York City, complete with miniature elevated railway—an elaborate reminder of the disastrous 1970 film version of the Broadway hit *Hello, Dolly!* In 1962, Darryl Zanuck had ousted Spyros Skouras and taken over the presidency; he, in turn, was deposed in 1971 after the failures of *Hello, Dolly!*, *Dr. Doolittle*, *Star!*, and *Tora! Tora! Tora!* had squandered the $82 million profit of the 1965 blockbuster *The Sound of Music.* Universal Pictures was now owned by MCA, the former talent agency. When in the early 1950s the government forced the production companies to sell off their theaters, it freed the studios from the burden of churning out picture after picture to keep those theaters supplied with product. Consequently, there was no need to keep expensive stars and other creative talent under contract. As performers and directors formed their own companies, their managers and agents became the dominating force in the business. Adept at making deals, they were not quite so skilled at making pictures; costs rose as quality fell. The cost of an average film was $1.5 million in 1960; by 1983 it had risen to $11.8 million, largely because of the wage demands of the unions. And fewer pictures were being made. In 1957, 533 features were released by the major distribution companies; by 1983, the figure had dropped to 280. In 1960, 40 million moviegoers paid an average of seventy-five cents weekly to get into a first-run theater; by 1983, audiences had dwindled to 22 million a week, but admission prices had quadrupled to an average of three dollars.

With fewer and more expensive films, the game of moviemaking was played for higher stakes; but when a film caught the public fancy, the winnings could be tremendous. In 1977, *Star Wars* grossed an astounding $193 million; in 1982, *E.T.* topped even that by taking in $209 million. But for each spectacular success, there were equally sensational failures, the most celebrated of which, 1980's *Heaven's Gate*, cost United Artists $44 million and grossed $1.5. This resulted in the parent firm, TransAmerica, selling the company to MGM, which had its own series of unbelievable disasters, such as the 1982 Luciano Pavarotti vehicle *Yes, Giorgio*, which cost $18 million and took in less than $1 million.

As the old studio owners retired or died, their places were filled by a succession of agents, lawyers, and accountants, few of whom had the training, the knack, or—most importantly—the love for making movies. Audiences were now smaller and much more selective in their choices of entertainment; few of the new production executives, with their degrees in business or finance, had any sense of what these audiences wanted and instead relied on marketing surveys and previous successes in place of imagination or instinct in making their production decisions.

Television had broken the hold the movies had on family entertainment habits. The mass audience had largely defected to the smaller and less expensive pleasures of commercial television, and it was the production of filmed television programs that now accounted for the bulk of the output of the Hollywood film industry.

While television was responsible for the decline in theatrical attendance, paradoxically, it also created a new market and a new interest and respect for movies, especially films from the so-called "golden age" of the 1930s and 1940s. An anonymous writer for *Time* magazine in April 1954 has been proved amazingly prophetic with the statement that "Hollywood could stop work tomorrow and still keep the wolf out of the patio with its past potential." He was writing about theatrical reissues of older films, but his prediction has come true in ways he could not have foreseen. For with the release of the studio backlogs to television in the mid-1950s, a whole new generation was given a crash course in the art and pleasures of Hollywood's past accomplishments. Millions of children grew up on a steady diet of some of the finest films ever made (and some of the worst!). This penetration of the subconscious by the constant telecasting of old films created a new breed of film enthusiasts. These new fans, born in the 1940s and 1950s, were literally reared on, and fell in love with, the film medium and its achievements, fragmented and disjointed as these seemed to be when seen between endless commercials on a tiny black-and-white screen. But the films, with their storytelling power, their superb craftsmanship, and their talented, charming, and glamorous performers, transcended these limitations and gave young viewers a new cultural awareness of and curiosity about the history and techniques of film that their parents seldom, if ever, possessed.

In the decade between 1957 and 1967, a whole new industry sprang up around this love of older films. The study of moving pictures became an accepted and popular discipline in universities. From these educational centers emerged graduate students with elaborate theories on the impact and meaning of film and filmmaking. An entire subculture in the academic and publishing worlds appeared. As these youngsters matured, matriculated, graduated, and decided on careers, thousands of them migrated to Hollywood in the 1960s and 1970s, drawn by the lure of what they had seen on TV and been taught in their film classes.

The reality of what they found there was a jolting disillusionment. By the mid-1970s, the city of Hollywood itself, far from being the glamorous capital of make-believe, was a shabby, dirty eyesore of decaying buildings, seedy discount stores, and greasy fast-food restaurants. Populated largely by lowlifes of every class, the litter-strewn streets were teeming with muggers, druggers, and pimps and prostitutes of both sexes, drawn by the same magnet that had attracted their more fortunate and educated peers: the lure of the movies, of fame and wealth and the fabled hedonistic lifestyle that was so much a part of Hollywood myth. Faced with the influx of the sordid and squalid, the "respectable" white middle-class population had fled to the suburbs in the early 1960s, as had most of the film production companies. The only tangible reminders of Hollywood's past glories were the stars on the Walk of Fame, a series of commemorative insignias laid down on the sidewalks of Hollywood Boulevard by the Chamber of Commerce in the 1960s, which paid homage to the famous and the forgotten names in the entertainment world. Grauman's Chinese still stood, but it now bore the name of its new owner, who had carefully obliterated that of its founder. The New View Theatre on Hollywood Boulevard, which had featured revivals and newer films of merit, had been converted to a "pussycat" theater, specializing in pornography; the silent movie theater on Fairfax Avenue was closed and boarded up; the venerable Hollywood Hotel was long gone, replaced in 1956 by one of the worst examples of that decade's utilitarian architecture. The same fate had befallen the Garden of Allah, the NBC studios at Sunset and Vine, the Trocadero, the

Mocambo—all demolished to make room for banks, high-rise apartment buildings, and other examples of contemporary urban necessities. Charlie Chaplin's old studio at LaBrea and Sunset still stood, but now it housed A&M Records. The Pantages Theatre, where *A Star Is Born* had its original premiere, was now a "legitimate" theater; it at least had been spared the fate of so many other famed movie palaces, which had fallen under the wrecker's ball, victims of dwindling audiences and real-estate speculators. In some cases, the cavernous interiors of these old theaters had been subdivided into two or three smaller theaters, with tiny screens, poor sound, and rowdy patrons. The famed HOLLYWOOD sign, long a symbol of the glamour that once was, had fallen into disrepair; pockmarked, covered with graffiti, crumbling, and structurally unsound, it was symbolic of the decay that engulfed Hollywood and the Sunset Strip, now a tawdry thoroughfare of strip joints, massage parlors, and sex shows.

From the hills of Griffith Park one could see the results of voters' 1957 decision to rescind the old thirteen-story building height limit. From east of the Santa Monica city limits, the Wilshire Boulevard corridor was lined with eruptions of steel and glass, while the downtown L.A. area was now highly visible because of the monolithic monsters that had all but obliterated City Hall from view, announcing to the world that Los Angeles was finally a major U.S. financial and architectural center. The same was true of Westwood, which by the early 1980s was so jammed with buildings and people that the police had to close the streets to vehicular traffic on the weekend evenings. Beverly Hills had not escaped the blight of bigness, either. Once a charming, if overpriced, section of shops, hotels, restaurants, and theaters, by 1983 it was considered the Fifth Avenue of the West. Major department stores, banks, and hotels proliferated, while almost every theater within the city had been razed to make room for more banks, more stores, and more parking lots.

The elimination of nearly all the major movie theaters in Beverly Hills was an indirect result of yet another technological revolution: the introduction to the United States by Sony of the home video recorder in 1975. A year later, an entrepreneur named André Blay broke through the barrier of studio fear and hostility and licensed the home video rights to fifty films from 20th Century–Fox. By the end of 1982, there were as many video sales-and-rental stores in the United States as there were film theaters, and movies on video cassette were bringing in millions of dollars in profit to the film companies. This unexpected income was much greater than the studios had ever been able to collect from booking their films to the second-run and neighborhood theaters over the years. As the number of VCR-equipped homes rose, there was a corresponding decline in the patronage of these theaters, with the inevitable result: the closing and demolishing of another former mainstay of the American film industry. Once again, television, through the video revolution, had killed off an aspect of the film business, only to give birth to another even more profitable and widespread form of film distribution.

To gain this new source of revenue, however, the studios and distributors had to relinquish the cherished and closely held regulation of their films. Until the advent of the VCR, the ownership of every single copy of a movie never left the control of the copyright owner. Not even the creative personnel involved in the making of the film could obtain a copy without complicated and arduous legal negotiations and agreements. But the profit to be made from this new market was potentially so great that the seventy-five-year-old tradition of allowing the patron to pay to *look* at a movie rather than take it home, as with nearly all other merchandise, finally gave way, as so many traditions do, to the onslaught of money.

An earlier and indirect synergy to the 1975 introduction of the Sony Betamax was Congress's formation of the American Film Institute in 1967. Its mandate, among others stated, was to "serve as national center for progress in film art . . . supporting other organizations and agencies involved in related activities." The formation of the Institute could conceivably be traced back to the explosion of interest in the history of film set off by the fusion of old movies and television. With so much film history on view, it quickly became apparent, to those who cared, how much was missing. It was estimated that by the time of the Institute's founding, over half the feature films produced in this country since the invention of the motion picture camera in 1888 had been lost through neglect, disinterest, and purposeful destruction, as the film industry, seeing seemingly useless and valueless films taking up expensive storage space, burned, melted, and otherwise destroyed a great portion of early film history. It was not until 1935, when the Museum of Modern Art in New York began searching out and preserving films, that any concerted effort was made to treat motion pictures an an independent art form. MOMA's pioneering efforts in this area, led by one of its founders and trustees, John Hay Whitney, and its first film curator, Iris Barry, sparked similar efforts by other far-sighted cultural institutions. Following MOMA's lead, the George Eastman House in Rochester, New York, and the Library of Congress and the National Archives in Washington, D.C., began collecting and preserving film. These efforts, however, were all hampered by lack of money, lack of coordination, and the refusal of the production companies to assist in this monumental task, with either funds, materials, or permissions to save much of what had brought their companies to prominence and power.

The main preservation problem lies in the fact that until 1950 all professional film stock manufactured in the United States, both negative and print, was on a nitrocellulose base, which was unstable and highly flammable. It could and did crumble into dust or turn into a gooey mess if not stored and cared for properly. The introduction of acetate safety film as the professional standard in the late 1940s meant that every negative and/or print made on nitrate stock would now have to be transferred onto safety film—a monumental task that should have been undertaken by the private firms that owned the films. In some cases this was done, as MGM did in the 1940s, but until television came along with its promise of untold riches based on the marketing of these films, there was no thought or concern given to the preservation of older films by the major companies. And even when television did spur them to action, it was only to save films made after the introduction of sound: the thirty-five years of film history previous to *The Jazz Singer* were considered expendable and inutile. So the AFI, with public funds provided by the newly formed National Endowment for the Arts, began a concerted effort to find, preserve, and exhibit as many of these films as possible and to assist the other, older institutions which were committed to the same goals but hampered by the lack of money, manpower, and the cooperation of the film industry.

One institution that should have been involved in this effort was the Academy of Motion Picture Arts and Sciences. Since its founding in 1927, it had undertaken various preservation projects, but these were largely activities that were the particular enthusiasm of specific individuals on the Academy's board of governors. Sadly, there was no ongoing commitment or effort by the Academy to locate and preserve films deemed of historical importance. Even Academy Award nominees and winners were seldom deposited in the Academy archive, the consensus evidently being that if an older film was needed, for whatever purpose, it could be borrowed from the studio that owned it.

Not until the late 1970s did the Academy embark on an ambitious preservation program. It had been a long time coming, and the catalyst that set it in motion was the election of Fay Kanin to the presidency. Fay has been a part of the Hollywood community since the mid-1930s, when she first went to work for RKO as a writer. She loves movies and the people who make them, and is quick to defend against what she feels are unjustified attacks on Hollywood and the film industry. One of her pet hates is the name "Tinseltown," denoting, as it does, an attitude of smug condescension toward the place, the people, and the work they do.

Her affection for the movies and for what they represent to us all—our past, our sense of ourselves, and our aspirations—is deep-rooted and passionate; and because of this she was able to convince the board of governors that film preservation was an activity to which the Academy should commit itself. As its president, Fay was also a member of the National Committee for Film Preservation, along with Frank Hodsoll of the NEA, Jean Firstenberg of the AFI, Mary Lea Bandy of MOMA, film historian Jeanine Basinger of Wesleyan University, and representatives of several other important media arts institutions. This committee decided to make the 1980s "the decade of film preservation," to "alert the film community and the public to the need for preserving our great film heritage."

Fay expressed her feeling about film: "All art forms are buffeted by time, but ours has proved unexpectedly ephemeral. Museums can show us sculpture from fifteen hundred years ago and beautifully preserved books and paintings from before the fifteenth century. But most of the movies made before 1920 have already been lost to us. . . . The roster of once admired, now lost pictures—including the Oscar-winning *The Patriot* [1928]—makes uneasy reading. . . . The nation's film archives have done a heroic job . . . but they need help and they need it soon." Fay made these remarks at the repremiere of *A Star Is Born* in 1983, and they reflect the feelings of all of us who were part of that evening.

How that evening came about is a story in itself, one that began at the Academy two years earlier. In November 1981, I had been asked by Douglas Edwards, coordinator of special programs for the Academy, to moderate a tribute to Ira Gershwin. Doug and I had known each other socially and professionally for about ten years. Along with thousands of others in the sixties and seventies, we had come to Hollywood because we wanted to have something to do with the movies. Dazzled by their history, we were both a little disillusioned by their present state.

But we loved what films had accomplished in the past; we were—and are—optimistic about their future; and both of us delighted in putting the best examples of past work before often unknowing but ultimately appreciative audiences. In the case of the Ira Gershwin tribute, this meant looking at every film for which he had written lyrics and excerpting those to illustrate every facet of his skill and the enormous range and artistry of his work. In particular, we wanted to show as much as possible of his lesser-known pieces while highlighting some of the more familiar songs. This took us from some of his earliest creations, for the shows *Lady, Be Good!* and *Funny Face,* through songs for the Fred Astaire films *Shall We Dance?* and *Damsel in Distress,* to the mini-opera "The Nina, the Pinta, the Santa Maria," which Gershwin had co-written with Kurt Weill for the film *Where Do We Go from Here?;* the evening ending with Judy Garland singing "The Man That Got Away."

Before that, however, Doug and I had decided to include a rarity: a piece that Gershwin had written for *A Star Is Born* that had not been heard publicly for twenty-nine years, as it had never been recorded, even though Garland performed it in the film. It was the commercial for "Trinidad Coconut Oil Shampoo," and a scratchy, muffled recording of it had been turned up by Michael Feinstein, who then was working for Ira Gershwin and assisting us in the preparation of the tribute; I introduced it, commenting that it was one of the pieces cut from the film after its initial release. The audience listened to it respectfully, but the abysmal quality of the sound and the lack of visuals caused it to have very little impact.

"The Man That Got Away," however, was another story. The screen at the Academy's Samuel Goldwyn Theatre is one of the largest in the city, and the audio system has been designed to extract and reproduce sound with superb fidelity and power, no matter the age of the track. For this excerpt, we were using the only existing four-channel magnetic stereo print in existence. When the curtain opened and the full width of that early CinemaScope image filled the huge expanse of screen, and Garland's voice, backed by the dynamic three-dimensional orchestra, poured out of the multiple speakers, the effect on the audience was electric. At the conclusion of the song, the ovation was tremendous—it was almost as if no one there had heard the piece before. And in a sense they hadn't, for most people knew it only from old phonograph records, tiny television speakers, or the muffled, faded prints that were sometimes shown in revival houses, where the sound systems usually left much unheard.

The impact of the image and sound on the audience that evening was exactly the same as it had been on me one hot Sunday afternoon in early

1955, when I first saw the film in my local theater, the Bal, in San Leandro, California. San Leandro was very white, very working-class, very dull—a forty-minute bus ride from San Francisco, and light years away from the glamour and excitement of Hollywood and the movies. Except, of course, at the neighborhood theaters, of which the Bal was one of the newest. Built right after the war to serve the new housing developments that had sprung up to provide homes for returning servicemen and their new families, the Bal was a medium-sized, one-thousand-seat, "stadium"-type theater, meaning it had no balcony but, instead, a raised terrace area of seats in the rear that served as the loge and the smoking section; it was also very useful for necking. In the center of the ceiling was a large, ornate chandelier hung with what was supposed to be crystal but was really just heavy plastic. On this particular Sunday *A Star Is Born* was double-billed with the ironically titled *How to Be Very, Very Popular,* which neither of them were, for even on this scorching day there were fewer than fifty people in the air-conditioned auditorium. The Bal was equipped with a big new CinemaScope screen and a decent stereophonic sound system, and I can remember vividly being open-mouthed in awe at the sound of Garland singing "The Man That Got Away." Later, at the conclusion of "Born in a Trunk," when she belted out the final phrase, " . . . in Pocatello, Idaho!," the sound was so intense and thundering that even after the song had died away, the plastic fragments in the chandelier were still swaying and tinkling, causing dust to sift down from it onto the audience.

I was sixteen when I first saw *A Star Is Born,* and it was one of my primal moviegoing experiences, the kind of epiphanic film that burrowed itself into my subconscious and reverberated there. Movies were always important to me. I had grown from an indiscriminate kid enjoying Saturday matinees with my friends into a teenager fascinated with movies as a phenomenon, curious about their origins and history, their impact on people, how they were made, and the excitement of how they were advertised and sold to the waiting public. My friend Gary Essert was the only person I knew of my own age who shared this early fascination. We maintained a bulletin board in the school library on which we mounted elaborate displays of new films. To gather material for this we would take bus trips across the Bay to San Francisco, haunting the various film exchange offices, occasionally conning our way into film inspection rooms, where we would pick up miscellaneous frames, sometimes pilfering a still or snatching a trailer. We considered ourselves fairly sophisticated: we read weekly *Variety*, and for further insight I subscribed to *Showman's Trade Review*, an exhibitors' magazine that offered news of films in production, technical articles, weekly grosses, theater exploitation ideas, ads, news of premieres, and reviews of films, and generally gave what, to my teenage mind, was a comprehensive inside view of the movie business.

Every Monday morning at school, we talked about the movies we'd seen that weekend at the Bal, the Del Mar, the Granada, or the Lorenzo. Several of my classmates had also seen *A Star Is Born* that weekend; none of them, it seemed, had quite the same experience with the film as I did. One girl admitted to having "cracked up" when Garland began singing to Mason in the wedding-night sequence, while another fellow was impressed with the symbolism of the bathrobe being washed out to sea in the scene of Norman's suicide. Most of them felt that the picture was too long. Our teacher Mr. Levine felt that there was too much emphasis on Garland, and I tended to agree; I had been more intrigued by Norman Maine than by Esther Blodgett/Vicki Lester; there seemed to be something missing about Norman, some aspect of his character that was not explained.

I attributed this to the fact that I had seen the picture in its shortened form. I knew there was a longer version; reading the trades had kept me abreast of the controversy over its length, and a fan magazine called *Screen Stories* had published a story version of the script that contained many scenes that were not in the film I saw—and the soundtrack album contained two songs that weren't in the picture. But even if I hadn't known about this, the picture itself was full of maddening inconsistencies, and oblique references that indicated to even the most obtuse viewer that something was missing. A line delivered by Maine's manservant, "He'll sure be surprised when he finds himself on location in the morning," was meaningless, as Maine never went on location. Maine's remark to Esther "Think about a man in a car eating a nutburger" was incomprehensible; the disappearance of Lola Lavery after her initial scenes also seemed strange, as did Esther's abrupt rise to stardom.

Almost immediately after my first viewing of the film, I tried to track down the full-length version. My reasons are best summed up by a speech written by Moss Hart for Norman Maine: "There are certain pleasures you get—little jabs of pleasure—when a swordfish takes the hook . . . or watching a great dancer—you don't have to know anything about ballet. That little bell rings inside—that little jolt of pleasure. That's what happened to me just now." He was describing to Esther the thrill of recognizing greatness; and so it was with me and *A Star Is Born*. I wanted more of those "little jabs of pleasure," the nuances of characterization, the hundreds of directorial details with which Cukor had so delicately imbued the film. I wanted more of the art direction, so carefully and tastefully understated, the subtle richness of the photography, which filled the screen with compositions such as I'd never seen in a film before. I wanted to see and hear the two cut musical numbers. I wanted more of the delicacy and charm of James Mason and the warmth and vulnerability of Judy Garland; more of Hart's and Cukor's observations of the Hollywood social scene, the studio atmosphere, the ambience of Los Angeles and its environs; more of the elegance and wry sense of humor that permeated the film—all of which, taken together, made *A Star Is Born* a visual, aural, and emotional feast.

I contacted the Warner Bros. office in San Francisco, asking where the full-length version could be seen. They had one print, but it wasn't booked for any theaters in the near future. I kept calling, kept going to theaters playing the film in the Bay Area in the hope that it would turn up. But it never did, and finally the man at the Warners office told me the print had been sent back to the studio. So I wrote to the studio asking that they put the full-length version back into the theaters. My letter was never answered, and after a while the hope of ever seeing all of Cukor's masterpiece faded.

. . . Until years later. After living in New York during the 1960s, I moved to Los Angeles and went to work at the American Film Institute in Beverly Hills as a projectionist. Around this time, in early 1970, author/critic Gavin Lambert was preparing a book on the films of George Cukor, and he and Cukor were looking at all of the director's work. I was running the films for them. I was completely in awe of Cukor—he was as witty, unsentimental, and forthright as his films, and I hesitated to approach him. But finally, several days before we were scheduled to screen *A Star Is Born*, I introduced myself, told him how much I enjoyed his films, and what a good time I was having running them all for him. He received all this graciously, though he seemed somewhat taken aback by my unquestioning enthusiasm ("You liked them *all?* Well, that's certainly more than *I* can say"). I told him of my admiration for *A Star Is Born* and then asked if we could show his print, as I'd always wanted to see the film complete. "I don't have a copy," he said. "I don't have any of my films. All I have are scripts and stills." I was shocked. In my naivete, I had assumed that all directors had copies of their work, an assumption that was proved unfounded in most cases. So I implored the AFI's film librarian to try to get the 181-minute version from the studio. Back came the word: all they had was a stereo print that ran 154 minutes. The day of the screening, Lambert showed up alone. "Where's Mr. Cukor?" I asked. "He's not coming." How strange, I thought, not to want to see one of your best films.

Two years later, I had left the AFI to join film historian David Shepard in putting together a permanent film program for the Los Angeles County Museum of Art, and we both agreed that George Cukor should be the subject of our first retrospective. By this time, I had met Cukor several times and worked with him on a professional basis in putting together a three-and-a-half-hour compilation called "The Movies" for the fiftieth anniversary of the Motion Picture and Television Fund. (An interesting sidelight: the producer of this marathon undertaking was none other than my old friend Gary Essert, with whom I had maintained that library bulletin board so long before.) Sharp, practical, and feisty, Cukor brooked no nonsense from anyone, nor had he patience with pretentiousness and airs. He could be, and was, brutally direct with his dissatisfactions, and downright earthy in his succinct observations about people and situations. I delighted in the stories he told of his famous (and not-so-famous) friends, in his wit, his taste, his rare outbursts of temper, and his unfailing good humor; even under the most trying of circumstances he was almost always gracious and considerate, if sometimes a bit testy.

Wanting to please him, I came up with an idea for our screening of *A Star Is Born* at the County Museum as part of our Cukor retrospective. Since so many people knew that cuts had been made in the film but no one seemed exactly certain of what was missing, I would put together a brochure, using stills and script extracts to show exactly what had been deleted. Over the years I had managed to find stills of all the missing sequences; the studio supplied a copy of the script, and the end result was given out at the screening of the film and quickly became a collector's item.

I was very proud of this brochure, but when I gave Cukor the first copy off the press, he looked at it cursorily, murmuring almost to himself, "They don't deserve a good picture," and then, beyond a brief "It's very nice," never said another word about what I had hoped would give him some kind of pleasure. Evidently and unfortunately, it only served to remind him of one of the major disappointments of his career.

One thing the brochure did do was to generate a renewed interest at Warner Bros. in finding the missing footage. Rudi Fehr, who was then vice-president in charge of postproduction at the studio, called to tell me that he had his people go through their records and their storage vaults and that they had turned up nothing. Evidently the cut sections had been kept for several months and then destroyed, in what was then the accepted practice at every major studio. Fortunately, this had all changed with the advent of the television movie market, and now everything that might possibly be of use for alternate versions of a film was saved. But *A Star Is Born* had been too early a case.

In the interim, another version of *A Star Is Born* had been produced, this one starring Barbra Streisand. While dramatically incoherent, it had been a great box-office success, due primarily to Streisand's star power. If contemporary moviegoers could enjoy this lackluster remake, I thought they would really appreciate the Garland-Cukor version—if only it could be restored to its full CinemaScopic and stereophonic glory. If this could be done, I was convinced, it would once again prove to be an overwhelming theatrical experience for everyone who loved good movies and good movie-making.

Then one day, from out of nowhere, a call came in to my office from an apprentice film editor at Warner Bros. named Dave Strohmeier, who had been at the screening of *A Star Is Born* at the County Museum. The brochure with the missing sequences had kindled his interest in the film, so he began a little research of his own. It had evidently paid off, for he excitedly told me that in the sound department storage vaults, he had come across the complete three-hour soundtrack to the picture: dialogue, music, and sound effects, mixed and ready to be put to picture. He had not, however, been able to turn up any footage, try though he might.

The discovery of the complete soundtrack gave me the idea of screening the film at the museum using this soundtrack, illustrating what was going on by showing stills of the missing sections—a sort of aural version of the brochure. This would necessitate all kinds of expense for special sound reproducers to play the magnetic soundtracks, copying stills, and running everything in synchronization; and unfortunately, our budget at the museum wasn't up to it.

In preparing the Ira Gershwin evening with Doug Edwards, I brought the idea up to him—but again it was rejected as too expensive and cumbersome. In the course of our conversations, however, I told him of my conviction that somewhere out at the studio the missing footage was just sitting in some vault or mismarked can, waiting for someone to dig it out.

Over the years, first at the AFI and then at the museum, I had been out to the Warner Bros. facility in Burbank many times to pick up and deliver film, and I had seen the way films were shipped back and forth, in and out of the studio, and how many different people handled the prints. Due to the many changes of studio administration and ownership, the films were constantly being shifted from vault to vault, and there were times when nobody knew exactly where a print or negative could be found. In the case of *A Star Is Born,* I was convinced that the missing sequences were somewhere out there in one of these numerous storage facilities. But I knew it would require a careful vault-by-vault, can-by-can inspection before they could be found, and the job would have to be done by someone who knew what to look for. This could not be managed without the permission and cooperation of the highest levels of Warner Bros., and there just wasn't enough time to organize this before the Gershwin evening. But Doug thought that we should pursue this later, through the Academy.

Immediately after the tribute to Gershwin (which, unfortunately, he was too ill to attend), Doug, Fay and Michael Kanin, and I went out to celebrate. Fay brought up the subject of the missing sequences in *A Star Is Born* and remarked how wonderful it would be if a full-length print of the picture could be found. She and Michael had seen the film in its original form and had been shocked to hear that it later had been so heavily cut. Both of them had a long and close relationship with George Cukor. Michael had produced one of Cukor's best films, *A Double Life,* which had won an Academy Award for Ronald Colman and had marked the film debut of not only Shelley Winters but Fay Kanin, who had a small part in it; thirty-two years later, George cast Fay in a role in his last film, *Rich and Famous.* Doug and I immediately explained our hope that the missing footage might indeed be found, if a complete and thorough search of all the film storage facilities of Warner Bros. was made on both coasts, and especially at the studio. Our enthusiastic conviction evidently piqued Fay's interest, for she decided to call Robert Daly, the chairman of the board of Warner Bros., explaining what we wanted to do and why, and asking whether Warners would put its corporate efforts behind this project. We all wanted to restore the film; but Fay, as a member of the National Committee for Film Preservation, was aware of how a project such as this could vividly illustrate the necessity not only of film preservation but also of film restoration. Kevin Brownlow's recent reconstruction of Abel

Gance's *Napoleon* had demonstrated both the ability of this kind of project to be culturally valuable and the extent to which it could capture the public's imagination in a way that no amount of proselytizing could.

Literally millions of feet of irreplaceable film are moldering in vaults around the country because there is not enough money to copy them. Some early color films no longer have negatives, just prints, which must be copied accurately and expensively. Time and a shortage of money are the twin perils here: both have to be made highly visible so that funds can be raised to do what's needed with all possible speed and efficiency. *A Star Is Born* seemed a likely candidate for this: it was famous, it featured some of the best work of some of the finest talents of the time, and it was an outstanding example of the artistic and technical standards of the art and industry that are generically known as Hollywood. It would also point out the fact that film preservation is not simply a matter of copying silent film, as many people seem to think; it is also dealing with the infinitely more complex problems of preserving and reconstituting both color and sound films. *A Star Is Born* was less than thirty years old, but already questions had been raised about the stability of its color negative; existing prints were on the old Eastmancolor release stock, which has an unfortunate tendency to fade. So if the film could be reconstructed as closely as possible to its original form, it would be a clear illustration of the problems and rewards of the craft of film preservation.

Fay explained all this in her letter to Bob Daly, and back came permission to go through the company's film storage facilities to see what could be found. We decided not to say anything to Cukor just yet so as not to get his hopes up.

Earl A. ("Rusty") Powell III, the director of the Los Angeles County Museum of Art, encouraged me to take as much time as needed to conduct this search properly. The next week I was to be in New York City on museum business, and I began the hunt at the very beginnings of the American motion picture—the old Vitagraph film storage facilities out in Brooklyn, owned by Warners since the late 1920s. Built fortresslike sometime in the teens, the films here are meticulously organized and antiseptically maintained. I found nothing useful, though, and the same was true at the laboratories in midtown Manhattan that had manufactured prints: the only material they had was the cut final negative, both 16mm and 35mm.

Back in Los Angeles, my first stop was the Technicolor labs in Universal

City, where I was aided by Bob Schulte, who went through *A Star Is Born*'s printing history with me. Technicolor had made the first set of prints for the full-length road-show version back in 1954. According to their September 1954 records, they printed 150 four-track stereo prints on Eastmancolor stock for the first runs. Then no more work was done until mid-October, when an order came through to cut the master negative. This was done on October 10. For the revised *A Star Is Born,* reels 3A and 3B were shortened and combined to form a new reel known as 3AB. Cuts were also made in reels 4A, 5A, 6B, 9A, and 9B. The excised material—the "trims and deletions," as the order phrased it—were put in cans, numbered 430 through 440, and shipped back to the studio. Thereafter, the print orders called for another 150 optical prints of the short version made by the dye-transfer process, for second-run usage. From this shortened master negative were made all the subsequent printing materials for 16mm and foreign 35mm use. So much for a full-length version being printed overseas.

The next step was trying to find out what had happened to the 150 full-length, four-track prints. According to the studio files at USC and the Warner Bros. distribution records now at Princeton University, orders went out from the editorial department to all film exchanges across the country, instructing them how to cut the prints and to send the excised material back to the studio. At this point, we thought it was worth a try to contact people who had worked in the film exchanges, to see if possibly some zealous editor/inspector had cut it and kept it. The Academy placed ads in daily and weekly *Variety* and the *Hollywood Reporter;* the response, while gratifying in numbers, turned up nothing of interest.

And then, of course, there were the film collectors. If you love movies and you live in Hollywood, eventually you will have some contact with that strange, obsessive group of film fanatics whose passions are the possession of movies—the rarer and more eclectic, the better. Some do it for love; some do it for money; some do it for pride of ownership; and some do it for no reason that they can articulate. In fact, most film collectors will not talk of their hobby, their mania. They are secretive, and with good reason: they could be, and have been, prosecuted for possession of stolen property, since the only way they could gain most films was to buy stolen merchandise or steal the films themselves. For years, film collectors, whom the industry despised as a group of eccentrics, did what the studios and other corporations failed to do: saved, preserved, and otherwise cared for the priceless relics of our so-called cultural heritage. When big money moved into the area of old film in the way of television sales, then the studios and other copyright owners set loose the minions of Jack Valenti and the Motion Picture Association of America, who contacted the FBI, which began a series of confiscations and prosecutions that terrified and intimidated illegal collectors. So it was no wonder that the Academy's ads in the trade papers were greeted with a wall of silence from the film-collecting community. It *is* a community, albeit a tiny and tightly knit, paranoid one, and its members are careful to let few outsiders be aware of their secrets. However, word does get out. In the case of *A Star Is Born,* there were rumors: that a collector in the Chicago area had the footage; that Peter Sellers had a complete 16mm print. Regarding the latter rumor, Liza Minnelli is reputed to have joked that the only reason she dated Sellers was in the hope that he would show her the movie. Her hope was unfulfilled.

Her sister, Lorna Luft, told of an encounter with one of these movie mysterians, who evidently wrote her a note regarding *A Star Is Born,* telling her to call a certain number at a certain hour. The conversation, according to Ms. Luft, was cryptic: "I've got what you want." "You have? Can I see it?" "Call tomorrow—same time."

The next night: "I really would like to see what you have." "All right, come to a phone booth at the corner of Pico and Sepulveda at ten p.m. tomorrow night, and wait for further instructions." She went to the phone booth, armed with champagne, caviar, and money, just in case it might be needed. The phone rang—instructions were given as to how to find a certain house. Her excitement rose; the house was found; the door was opened; and a furtive gentleman of indeterminate age whisked her into a chair. The lights went down, and onto the screen came a black-and-white print of *Good News.*

My own experience with tracking down leads of this sort on *A Star Is Born* dates back to 1970 when I was a projectionist at the AFI. A film historian who frequented the Greystone Mansion headquarters of the Institute took me aside one day and said he knew the mysterious collector in the Chicago area who had the material I was looking for. He hadn't seen it personally, but the collector was a respectable type who seldom claimed to have something unless he did. All he wanted in exchange for the footage was a 35mm Technicolor print of *The Adventures of Robin Hood,* the 1938 adventure classic starring Errol Flynn. Even though Warner Bros. had produced the film, it no longer owned it, having sold all its pre-1948 movies to United Artists in the mid-1950s. However, I put in a call to Rudi Fehr, then the vice-president in charge of postproduction at Warners. Rudi never could understand all the fuss about the missing footage of *A Star Is Born;* he thought it was a better film in the shorter version. But he was fond of Cukor, and he agreed to try to obtain a print of *Robin Hood* from United Artists. But the collector upped the ante: now he wanted *The Private Lives of Elizabeth and Essex,* also in Technicolor. I told Rudi, who said he would see what he could do. The message was then relayed to the collector, and that was the last anyone heard. I inquired several times about the status of the deal, and all my contact would ever say was that he was waiting to hear from the collector, whom he described as "weird." Weird indeed!

The ad in the trades did prompt a provocative telephone call. A local revival-house owner, a *Star Is Born* fanatic, called to tell me that he knew of a collector who had the footage. When I expressed my doubt, based on previous experience, he assured me that he had seen it: it was the "Lose That Long Face" number! The exhibitor was not the type to invent stories like this, so I was intrigued. But Mr. Exhibitor could not and would not tell me who the elusive gentleman was, having been sworn to secrecy. I asked him to try to convince his friend that he would be doing a great service if he would make the footage available to us to copy. Mr. Exhibitor said he would try. My hopes went up a bit—not much, but a bit. Several days later, Mr. Exhibitor called back to tell me that Mr. Elusive Collector had had a fit when told that I knew of the footage; he denied everything and threw the exhibitor out of his house. My slight hope was dashed, and I began concentrating on real possibilities.

Everything seemed to point to the studio. If the material wasn't there, then it was pretty certain not to exist. The Burbank Studios are concentrated next to the usually nonexistent Los Angeles River, across from Forest Lawn and sandwiched in between Universal to the west and Disney to the east. As a filmmaking facility, it teems with activity; as a Hollywood haunted house, its streets and stages are rife with the ghosts of people and films: Warner, Wallis, Flynn, Davis, Bogart, Cagney, Robinson, Steiner, Korngold, Tiomkin. Everywhere you turn there is some reminder of the studio's history: walking up a flight of stairs, you pass a wall filled with dusty blueprints for sets and your eye is caught by the titles *Casablanca* or *A Midsummer Night's Dream.* Dozens of other familiar sights leap out at you, including the automobile called the General Lee from the television series "The Dukes of Hazzard," parked incongruously in the famous New York street.

You enter the studio from, appropriately enough, Hollywood Way, which leads to the editorial departments and film library, all under the calm but firm control of Fred Talmage, successor to Rudi Fehr as vice-president in charge of postproduction. This area is the nerve center for everything that happens to a picture after it comes off the stages. Here are the true veterans of the movie business: Fred Talmage started with Warners in 1955; Ralph Martin, Fred's assistant, has been there almost as long; Frank Murphy, one of the oldest editors in terms of service, has been putting films together since 1959; Don Adler has been film vault supervisor since 1960. But the longevity champ of the entire studio is probably Lillian Harr Wilson, the sweet-tempered and efficient head of the film library. She's been with the studio for thirty-eight years, and in fact did the dialogue transcript for *A Star Is Born*—a script in dialogue form only. Warners was one of the rare studios that did not make detailed "cutting continuities," a shot-by-shot description of each scene in a film, broken down into angles, movement, and footage measurements—something that helps an editor replace exactly any damaged footage or to time a given sequence precisely down to the frame just by reading the footage numbers. These are invaluable aids, and I was somewhat taken aback to find that Warners didn't make them. "Jack L. never wanted us to spend the time or the money to do those," explained Lillian ruefully. "The labs made footage-count scripts, and he thought those were enough."

Fred, who had his hands full with all the television and theatrical production work that was going on at the studio, seemed a little bemused by the whole project; when I told him that I was looking forward to spending my summer vacation prowling through the studio vaults, he just smiled, shook his head, and said, "Well, Ron, whatever turns you on."

Our first stop at the studio was the sound department's storage area under what was known as the old Technicolor building, to make certain that Dave Strohmeier had been correct about the complete track being there. A huge subterranean basement, it stretches under the studio for nearly an acre; here, lit by bare bulbs and in some areas thick with the fine dust of the years, are thousands of cans of soundtrack film and magnetic tape. Fred and I went through the narrow aisles and finally located cans of film marked "*A Star Is Born*, Long Version YD-YF Mag Track," which, translated, meant that this was a monaural dialogue, music, and sound effects track on magnetic film. (The original stereophonic master tracks had all been erased in the mid-1960s. This was done on orders from Jack

Warner himself, who reasoned that old films with stereo tracks were never in demand in television or for theatrical reissue. All those expensive reels of magnetic tape were erased and reused. The sonic splendors of those early Warners stereo tracks were obliterated, and only the single-channel mixes were saved.) There were twenty-three separate cans, and the only way to find out whether this was what we were looking for was to play back one of the reels to see if it had the missing material on it. Reel 3A was pulled. If all was well, it should have Esther saying goodbye to the band—and by God, it did! Things were off to an auspicious start. Finding the soundtrack was half the battle; now all we had to do was find the picture to match it. To try to do this, Fred turned me over to Don Adler, who had been working in the production film department for close to thirty years, cataloguing every single piece of photographic film from camera to release print, from sound stage to laboratory. He was a large, quiet man, who whisked around the studio in an electrically motorized cart, appearing and disappearing with equal parts of speed and silence. I asked him what would have happened to the cans shipped back to the studio from Technicolor with the cut negative in them. "In those days, we'd keep it for six months, then junk it." What about the cut sections from the various exchanges around the country? "Same thing. If it was sent back to us, we'd hold on to it for a while, then junk it." Was it possible that some of it might not have been junked? "Possible, but not likely."

Our first step was to go to the negative storage vault to make sure that the Eastmancolor printing negative was trimmed as the records indicated. If it had been, reels 3A and 3B should have been in one can marked 3AB. And so it was. This was the only 35mm printing material on the picture; and since it was trimmed, it seemed that the material had indeed been junked. According to Don's inventory, however, there were some miscellaneous cans of *A Star Is Born* material in one of his storage areas. Back to the old Technicolor building and into another locked and dank area of the basement. More rows and rows of rusty cans of film, stacked darkly on metal shelves, by decade: *April in Paris; Stop, You're Killing Me; Storm Warning; Young at Heart* . . . and, finally, *A Star Is Born.* I looked at those rusty cans in the light of Don's flashlight and realized that I had been thinking of the film in terms of images on a screen and sounds, all of which made it live for me; but to most of the people here in the studio, this must be what the film was: rusty cans with frayed adhesive labels, dead and buried.

There were about twenty cans for *A Star Is Born,* none of which bore the appropriate Technicolor numbers to indicate that they might be what we were looking for. Mostly, they were trailer negatives, foreign-language titles, and background negatives. But there were also nine cans marked "YCM Printing Masters," which meant that each primary color record had been converted into a black-and-white positive image, which could there-upon be recopied on color film to form a duplicate color negative. In those days it was standard practice to make these separation masters, so that as many duplicate color negatives as needed could be struck for printing purposes. This was a promising lead. Unfortunately, the entire picture had not been done; evidently, work was halted when it became obvious that the picture was going to be cut further. None of the reel numbers on the cans matched up with the reels that had been trimmed. Still, here was my chance to prove or disprove my theory about the possibility of mismarked cans.

Don and I carried the nine cans into a small office that had a set of rewinds, and I opened the containers one by one. The film was still in the black waxed bags in which it had originally been wrapped: apparently, these cans hadn't been opened in close to thirty years. I wound through the film, squinting at the 35mm images, looking for something that was familiar to me from the stills of the missing sequences. Can 7A had the first love scene between Norman and Esther, immediately after her preview triumph. It took place on the terrace of an exclusive Hollywood nightclub, and in the cut version it was supposed to dissolve into a scene in Oliver Niles's office, when they announce to him that they're going to be married. But it didn't. Instead, I found I was staring at the scene on the recording stage with Esther singing "Here's What I'm Here For," followed by the proposal and live microphone pickup.

I must have let out some sort of loud yelp, because Don came running back into the office to see if anything had happened to me. I was literally jumping up and down with excitement: the entire scene was there on all three reels of black-and-white images (one for each primary color), includ-ing the fade and dissolve at the beginning and end. All that had to be done was to copy it, print it, match it up with the track, and drop it back in where it had been originally. If this one sequence was there, could the others be far off?

After Don had helped me carry in the twenty other cans of film, he left me alone, reeling through negative can after negative can, hoping that lightning would strike twice. Alas, it didn't. For the next four days

I examined every single rack and every single label on every single can of film in that basement storage area, looking for anything that might conceivably contain something to do with *A Star Is Born*. But there was nothing else.

"Where next?" I asked Don.

"Try the stock footage library. I think they have a lot of leftover material from the film."

Every studio has one of these libraries. After a picture is put together, an editor goes through all the unused film and picks out material that might be useful at some future time in another film: crowd scenes, exterior shots, buses, cars, houses, nonspecific bits that can be integrated into another film to save money.

The Warners stock footage library was under the iron rule of Evelyn Lane, a large, imposing woman who stands for no nonsense from anyone. Her long days are spent in a cramped bungalow office, stacked with miscellaneous cans of film, file cabinets, rewinds, and editing tables; she answers telephones, fields requests, demands, and complaints, and deals with interlopers like myself while trying to get on with the business at hand: locating footage needed for theatrical and television productions and keeping track of the thousands of cans and millions of feet of film that flow in and out of her tiny office.

"*A Star Is Born?* Down there in the bottom drawer," she pointed, while cradling a telephone on her shoulder and typing up a requisition at the same time. She hung up and swung around in her chair to explain that all of the Warners features are listed by title, with individual index cards for each piece of stock footage from that particular film. She pulled out the bottom drawer, and there, neatly typed on five-by-seven file cards, were descriptions of all the unused negative footage from the film with a sample frame on each card. It was all broken down into categories—Theaters, Premieres, Apartment Houses, Los Angeles Exteriors, Automobile Traffic, Drive-ins, Life Rafts, Studio Production, Interior Sound Stages—with one-line descriptions of what is on the film.

I pulled out the card marked "Bus" and read: "Day. Bus with lettering GLENN WILLIAMS ORCHESTRA on side pulls away from motel." I began to get excited again—this was Esther's goodbye to the band. I pulled out the card marked "Drive-in": "Dusk. Robert's Drive-in Restaurant on Sunset Blvd. Watch for Judy Garland"; then "Hotel": "Day. Old three-story house turned into Hotel Lancaster. Watch out for James Mason as he runs up and enters hotel." Card after card listed bits and pieces of missing sequences. There were close to two hundred entries on *A Star Is Born,* some of which had been printed up for various uses.

Evelyn took me over to the vault where this printed material was stored, and I began going through the cans, finding dozens of takes and angles on these scenes, mostly long and medium shots, carefully edited so that the principals were not visible. This was particularly frustrating in the scenes around the fictional Hotel Lancaster, which was the location of Norman and Esther's reunion on the roof. There would be an establishing shot, and just as Judy Garland or James Mason would appear, the film would end. Hoping there might be more of this on the negative material itself, I asked Evelyn to take me over to the storage vault: long, narrow bunkers filled with rank upon rank of film cans—150 of them from *A Star Is Born.* Each can had several tightly wound rolls of negative material with a paper label describing the contents.

The first cans I opened corresponded with the inventory cards; there was Norman Maine on location, bobbing up and down in a life raft; there was his limousine pulling away from his home in the early morning hours, as he sleeps off his hangover in the backseat; there was Judy Garland inadvertently left in as a carhop at the drive-in, serving a customer and reeling off a list of hamburgers to a man in a convertible. The contents of can number 90, however, were not all listed on Evelyn's inventory. The paper label read very plainly, "Judy Garland sings 'Lose That Long Face.'" Examining other cans, I discovered that Folmar Blangsted, the original editor, had saved every single alternate take for all the musical numbers in the film, including the puppet commercial! I didn't want to get my hopes up, but there seemed a good chance that all of the missing dramatic footage might be there, too, in alternate takes. For the next week, I went through the 150 cans, examining every roll; but in spite of the musical numbers being there, and the miscellaneous shots from the exterior sequences, the all-important close-ups and medium shots of the two leads playing out the missing dramatic scenes were nowhere to be found. It was doubly frustrating because so much *was* there.

For the next month I scoured every vault in the place, trying Evelyn's patience with my repeated requests of "Are you sure there's no place else to look?" She gave me a set of keys to the double-decker storage vaults behind the old Technicolor building, under which I had found the sound stage proposal sequence. There were forty-eight of these vaults, narrow concrete rooms with row after row of film cans carefully held in metal slots.

Most were neatly ordered, but some were in disarray, and in this disarray I discovered some rarities. Here were a negative and print for the 1932 version of *The Animal Kingdom,* which Warners had purchased from RKO in the mid-1940s for remake purposes. *The Animal Kingdom* was considered a "lost" film, since no copies were known to exist; so this was a major find. So was a pristine 35mm print of RKO's 1934 *Of Human Bondage* starring Bette Davis and Leslie Howard, later remade by Warners. In the same vault were the original black-and-white camera separation negatives for the 1937 Technicolor *A Star Is Born;* this, too, was an important discovery. If I had not been so anxious to find the missing sequences from the remake, I would have been extremely excited.

I kept on searching. I was even allowed in the sanctum sanctorum, Jack Warner's own personal vault, which was chock full of all sorts of miscellaneous footage, including costume and photographic tests for *A Star Is Born,* but no missing footage. How absolutely crazy, I thought to myself, that he would hold on to that but not to the deletions! Having exhausted every possibility in these stock vaults, my last hopes were the storage areas for the library prints themselves, the copies that are kept for use by the studio. Some of these are stored in individual 1,000-foot cans; some are kept in "shipper" cans, which are 2,000-feet reels in metal containers, ready to be sent to studio projection rooms, schools, museums, or other studios for single viewings. Several of these vaults were no longer used for storing film but had been given over to housing departmental records of one sort or another: stacks upon stacks of cardboard boxes, which at this point, to my fevered mind, might well contain film.

Over a period of days, I worked my way through all these storage vaults, finding nothing, until finally only one more vault remained. By this time I was pretty much resigned that there was nothing more to be discovered, and I was just going through the motions. Vault 120 looked no different than all the others before it, except that in the very back were two tall cardboard boxes of the type that film cans are shipped in. I climbed over crates, working my way toward the back, looking at the labels on everything, opening what wasn't labeled, still finding nothing, until I reached the air duct grating in the very rear. There were the two cardboard boxes, about three feet high, sealed, with no labels other than the Technicolor emblem. I opened the first one and looked at the cans: *The Bounty Hunter,* a Randolph Scott western from 1954. I had a bit of trouble with the next box; it was sealed tightly with masking tape, and my efforts to peel it off weren't entirely successful. From the look of it, it had never been opened. But I finally managed to peel off the tape and break open the sealed top: there was a silver can inside with the distinctive Technicolor blue label, and on the label were the words "*A Star Is Born* R12A." A yellow shipping receipt bore the date October 14, 1954. I opened the top can, and inside were the distinctive black waxed bags in which film was shipped, still sealed—they had never been opened. I began pulling those cans out furiously, looking for the two reels, 3A and 3B, which would tell me if this was a complete, uncut, original print. By the time I got down to the bottom of the box, I was shaking so much that I dropped my flashlight and couldn't read the numbers on the top; there was 4B, then 4A, and the next can was it—I looked and read "Reel 3AB." It was the cut version!

I sat there for a couple of minutes, completely depleted and dejected. It was so close. I went back through everything once again. No mistake, it was cut. I tried to take some comfort in the fact that here was a pristine original Technicolor dye-transfer print; but the disappointment was so strong that it was almost physical; I felt as if someone had hit me in the stomach. After that, I had to admit that the missing sequences were irretrievably lost.

Still, the search had unearthed a great deal of material. Out of the missing half-hour, approximately twenty minutes of usable footage had been found. There were the complete 181-minute monaural soundtrack; 154 minutes of stereo soundtrack on the studio print; and the mint-condition Technicolor short version. So, even though everyone involved felt the disappointment of not finding all the material, there was still the possibility of putting much of the picture back together. I wanted to take the bits and pieces of film that had been found in the stock footage vaults and, using the soundtrack and the editor's script as a guide, put the shots back where they belonged. The sections without the necessary visuals could be filled in using stills of the missing scenes. These had all been shot on the set simultaneously with the principal photography, and the still photographer generally matched the angles and the action of the CinemaScope camera. Panning, zooming, and otherwise moving across these photos in a variation of TV news technique, would, I felt, give a fluidity and a sense of drama to these otherwise static shots. It seemed feasible, at least in theory.

But before proposing this, I wanted to get some idea of what was involved technically and financially, so I called Robert Swarthe, special effects genius and animator par excellence. Bob, busy with Francis Coppola's *The Outsiders,* listened to my idea and nodded yes, it could be done, but it would be expensive. When I asked him *how* expensive, he explained that it would depend on how many camera moves we made over the stills and how elaborate these moves would be. Obviously, we would need someone experienced in working with an animation camera and in laying out camera moves. Bob wanted to take on the project, but because of his work on *The Outsiders* he reluctantly had to give up on the idea. He recommended several people who he thought could do what was needed.

The first one I called was Lize Bechtold, mainly because I knew she was a prize-winning animator, a filmmaker of sensitivity and imagination; it turned out that she was also a young woman of energetic charm and humor. When I spoke to her, she was flabbergasted. *A Star Is Born* was one of her favorite films, but she had no idea that large sections of it were missing. She agreed at once to take on the project if we could get approval and money, and she immediately worked out a budget based on her examination of the stills and hearing tape recordings of the missing scenes. She estimated that her work alone might cost upwards of ten thousand dollars. Then, the costs of printing up the negative material in the Warners vaults had to be figured in; raw stock and printing of approximately six thousand feet of color film would add another seven or eight thousand dollars, not to mention the cost of rerecording the stereo track (replacing missing frames, repairing tears and splices, and generally bringing it up to present-day standards)—all of which added up to an approximate total of $25,000.

But at least the project seemed feasible, so Doug Edwards and I presented the idea to Fay. She was a bit uncertain about the concept and the costs and decided to get Gene Allen's opinion. Gene had a long-standing close relationship with George Cukor, and if Gene didn't like the idea, then we wouldn't go any further with it. After listening to what we wanted to do and how we proposed to do it, he was all for it and, even more encouraging, offered to work with us in the still photography to make certain that the tints and colors we used were coordinated with the existing color and design scheme of the film. Fay and Gene now felt that George should know what was going on. He might be very opposed to the idea—it was, after all, yet another compromise on a film that had already been compromised enough. So Gene explained what was happening and asked George what he thought of the whole idea. "Very intriguing, by all means—go ahead with it" was the reply.

Having worked out a budget and received the approval of George and

Gene, Fay now felt prepared to go to Robert Daly of Warners and ask for the company's financial support not only in restoring the film but also in setting up a series of fund-raising screenings in selected cities across the country. At a meeting in his office, Daly was interested but cautious. He thought the project worthwhile but did not want to commit the company to it until everyone was certain that the concept would really work. He proposed that we do a test reel and asked how much we'd need. I did some quick calculations and pulled a figure of $5,000 out of my hat. "You've got it," he said. "How long do you think it will take?" One or two months, I told him, and he said to let him know when we were ready and he'd look at what we'd done and give us an answer. It was a quick, productive meeting.

Several weeks earlier, I had been talking about all this with a young editor named Craig Holt. He thought it "sounded like fun" and volunteered his services if we ever got to the point where we needed them. Now he, Lize, Gene, Doug, and I met in the Academy's editing room to figure out the best place to start. We decided to begin right at the beginning, with Esther's farewell to the band, and proceed through the scenes of Norman being driven off to location, Esther waiting for his call, and all of the other missing bits, right up to Esther doing the voice-over for the commercial. Evelyn Lane pulled the negative segments we needed, which caused me some worry, because there recently had been questions in some quarters about the supposed instability of Eastmancolor negative. It looked fine when I was winding through it, but the material *was* thirty years old. However, all my doubts proved relatively unfounded. When the material came back from the laboratory, aside from a slight yellow tint to some scenes, it was visually superb.

Craig and I then began the arduous task of looking at these various takes and trying to match them up with what was happening on the soundtrack. It was very much like putting together a jigsaw puzzle. We put in blank film where we had no picture, then Lize and I sat down and timed this blank footage and worked out the camera moves across the stills, again as dictated by what was happening on the soundtrack. It was a matter of painstaking trial and error. We could not really be certain of how the original shots had been put together: there were so many takes and angles to choose from, and nobody at the studio or at USC, where the early Warners files were deposited, had been able to turn up Folmar Blangsted's cutting script. (Unfortunately, Blangsted had died several months before the project got under way.) So Craig was working in the dark, and it's a testament to his instincts that when Evelyn Lane finally did find the cutting script, Craig's choices were almost all identical to the original edit.

One of our biggest headaches was the proper photography of the stills. *A Star Is Born* was the third film in Hollywood to go into production in CinemaScope, and that was the proportion we wanted to use for the stills. To make certain that the photographic quality matched that of the original, the Warners camera department located the anamorphic attachment with which the picture had originally been photographed. But it turned out that when Lize went to her cameraman to start photography, she found it impossible to get the kind of moves we wanted with this lens, as it was not possible to follow focus; after every movement the cameraman would have to refocus, a time-consuming and expensive process. None of the other computerized camera stands were set up for CinemaScope photography, and we were stumped. To our rescue came Bob Swarthe. He suggested copying the stills themselves through the CinemaScope attachment, which would give us a "squeezed" image which we could then photograph on the animation stand with a standard lens. When the film was projected through a normal CinemaScope lens, we should get a wide, full-screen picture.

After this had been tested and had proved effective, our major problem was in gathering the necessary stills to flesh out the sequences. Previously, there had been some discussion about this: Why go to all the trouble of manufacturing footage for these sequences—why not just restore the musical numbers that had been found and leave out the sections that would need stills? But my intent all along had been to find and restore the missing *dramatic* sections. Their deletion had caused Cukor the most pain and had fragmented the early part of the story to such an extent that a clear understanding of the characters of Norman and Esther was impossible. I didn't really care about the missing musical numbers that much, though it was wonderful that they had been found, and they were, of course, the most interesting aspect of the picture to Garland fans. But for myself and for George, and for all the people who loved *A Star Is Born* as more than a Garland vehicle, the real joy in reassembling the film would be the inclusion of all this early expository material. As our project got under way, I pointed out that it would be impossible to say that we had reconstructed the film without doing something about this deleted footage. If we put back just the songs, it would still leave gaping holes in the beginning. Audiences would feel cheated—and George still would not sit through the film.

Fay, in her best logical manner, argued forcefully and persuasively that we could make a virtue out of necessity by using this section to demonstrate in a very dramatic fashion just what film preservation was all about. I must say that if it weren't for Fay Kanin, *A Star Is Born* would never have been restored. Everyone who loves the movie—and loves movies—is in her debt.

Now that everyone agreed on the approach, and with the support of the entire Academy, we set about trying to solve our difficulty about the stills themselves. Warners had been run very economically by Jack Warner. The still photographer assigned to the film, Pat Clark, had been under strict orders not to overshoot, which meant that he shot only one still of each camera setup. (As I mentioned earlier, these stills would be used for publicity purposes.) Normally, this would probably be sufficient, as most directors break these scenes up into a multitude of shots. Cukor, however, liked long takes and would stage his action to move in and around this single take. So the still photographer would do one or two shots of an entire three-to-four-minute take, usually at the beginning of the scene or at a crucial dramatic moment. But after going through my own stills from the film and the files at Warner Bros., USC, the Academy, and the Museum of Modern Art and ransacking all the stills stores in the New York and Los Angeles areas, we had almost enough photos to do the job.

Our first section of photographs and live-action footage set to the soundtrack was the sequence of Esther saying goodbye to the band. We had a number of stills that could be used for this sequence: stills of the bus, shots of Noonan and Garland in the scene, and production shots showing the scene being photographed. The scene continued after the bus pulled away with Esther going back into her room to wait for Norman's call; she decides to wash her hair and then lies by the pool drying her hair and waiting for the call that never comes, while across the city, a hung-over Norman is being poured into his car and driven off to a seaside location. This was a long sequence, and half of it was nothing but music as Esther waits and waits: almost three and a half minutes, all scored to a lush rendition of "The Man That Got Away." We tried everything we could think of to make those stills interesting for three and a half minutes, but we just didn't have enough variety. Finally, in desperation, we decided to trim the track, eliminating two minutes of music. Ironically, this was done by Elsa Blangsted, the widow of the original editor on the film and a superb music editor. Her cut was barely discernible on the track, and now we were finally able to assemble the sequence, using our combination of stills and live action to make clear to the audience what was happening.

Unfortunately, there were some scenes for which evidently no stills had ever been shot. One of these was a transitional scene that showed Esther having a long-distance conversation with Danny McGuire in a phone booth. He has stayed in touch with her after she has left the band, and he calls to tell her that Glenn Williams is willing to take her back. She refuses, saying that while Maine may have been insincere in his job offer, he convinced her that she could do it and she's going to stick to that. It's an important scene because it sets up Esther's belief in herself, her determination. It also has a kicker at the end—for, according to the script, it isn't until the very end of the sequence that the audience discovers that she is a waitress, something she vowed earlier that she'd never do again. We had the sequence of Garland as a carhop, inadvertently left in the stock footage of the drive-in; the soundtrack we had didn't quite synchronize with this alternate take, but it was close enough, and Garland's reading of the final line—"Everything in the place, all burgered!"—matched the picture perfectly.

The problem was what to do about the sections showing Danny McGuire placing the call from the lobby of his hotel. There were no stills of this. There were, however, stills of the set of the hotel lobby, seven publicity shots of actor Tom Noonan seated on a divan with different expressions on his face, a still of the drive-in, and one of Garland in a phone booth in her carhop uniform. So we took the photos of Noonan (which were two-by-three images on a proof sheet), cut his figure out, took the phone-booth shot of Garland, cut her out of the booth, put Noonan's figure in the booth, and placed this mock-up against the still of the hotel lobby. Then Lize did a quick series of dissolves, showing Noonan's change of expression as he hears Esther explain that she's decided to stay in Hollywood. On the cut to Esther on the soundtrack, we opened on a close-up of her face talking, and as Lize slowly pulled the camera back, we revealed to the audience that Esther is a carhop. Then we cut to the live action of her waiting on customers.

Lize was working with a very creative animation cameraman named Ken Rudolph, and there was almost nothing we could devise that he couldn't figure out a way to accomplish. Of course, we had to give him the material to work with; and on one crucial sequence, there was absolutely nothing. Norman has returned from location and is making frantic efforts to locate

Esther. He even goes to the Oleander Arms Motel (which name he could not remember) and harangues the landlady, who has no idea where Esther has moved. This was important because it showed Norman's concern for Esther, his chagrin and frustration over his inability to locate her, and made clear to the audience that he was not just on the make. It also served as a bridge into the next scene, where he is lying on his sofa talking with Lola Lavery when he hears Esther's voice-over for the Trinidad Coconut Oil Shampoo commercial. All we had here was one stock footage shot of Norman driving away from the curb at the Oleander Arms after berating the landlady for naming her place something stupid like "Oleander Arms." There were no shots of the landlady, no stills of the Oleander Arms, no shot of the signboard that prompts his furious remark. We tried to find Kathryn Card, the actress who played the landlady, in the hope that she might have a still of the scene, but she had died several years before, with no known survivors.

We were stymied. My one last hope was George Cukor. He had, I knew, a complete set of stills from the film, and he had indicated through Gene that we could use them if necessary. I hadn't wanted to bother him unless we were unable to find or create what we needed; moreover, he was not feeling well. But I put in a call to him anyway, and he told me to come up to his home immediately and go through his files and take what we needed.

George lived in a walled villa in the hills several blocks above Sunset Boulevard near Beverly Hills. You entered through an electronically controlled door and were immediately transported into another world: the grounds of a Mediterranean-style home, surrounded by trees, lush vegetation, and splashing fountains. Down a flight of stone steps was an Olympic-sized pool, on the other side of which were terraced formal gardens. A slightly longer flight of stairs led up to the door of the main house, where George would usually be waiting to greet whomever he was expecting. Today, however, one of his servants opened the door and ushered me through the suede-lined living room hung with Mirós and Braques to a door on the far side of the hallway.

A knock on the door and a "Yes?" from inside and I was in a tiny, sunny bedroom overlooking the garden and the pool. George was sitting in a chair facing me; he had on a white shirt, a pair of suit trousers, and carpet slippers. I had not seen him in some time and was appalled at how thin and frail he looked. His voice and manner, however, were the same as ever, strong and purposeful. I explained what we were doing again and why we needed his stills, but he impatiently cut me off: "Yes, yes, I understand perfectly what you're doing. Let's go up to the attic and you can see what I have."

As we made our way slowly through the house, he kept up a steady stream of conversation, much as he always would, but it seemed to me that he was studiously avoiding talking about *A Star Is Born* and what we were doing to it. The air was permeated with the smells of something tasty cooking—he was expecting guests for dinner—and as we neared the kitchen he saw that the door was open and took the chef to task: the door should be closed so that the smells of food didn't fill the rest of the house.

He led the way slowly out the back door and up a short flight of stairs to the attic, a large, bright, carpeted room filled with shelves, lined with cabinets and tables, all neatly and efficiently ordered. He apologized for having to leave me, but he had to get ready for his dinner guests.

As he slowly made his way out, I began searching through the volumes of stills—a set for every film he'd ever worked on, beginning with *All Quiet on the Western Front* in 1930. There were almost two hundred stills from *A Star Is Born*, scenes and production shots, including one of Cukor standing talking to Lucy Marlow that I recognized immediately as being one of the images on the original advertising campaign for the film. It was used in all the magazines and posters for the film: a tiny silhouetted image of a man standing and gesturing to a girl in front of him, evidently imparting some words of wisdom. The impression it gave in the poster and the ads was of Esther being tutored by Norman. I marveled at the use of this shot, a stout George being redrawn into a trim movie-star figure and standing in for James Mason in the advertising campaign. With all the stills that he had in his collection, however, there was not one of the landlady. There were some miscellaneous shots of Mason in sport clothes, taken as candids in the downtown location, which might come in handy. I gathered up what I needed, locked the attic, took the stills downstairs, signed a receipt, and went to say goodbye to George. He was sitting in the chair in his bedroom while his manservant helped him dress for dinner. After asking me if I had found anything useful and being assured I had, he apologized for not seeing me to the door.

Then, just as I was leaving, he spoke up. "I think it's remarkable what you're doing. I keep getting reports on how it's progressing. I appreciate all the effort and the work and I'm very grateful to you. Keep at it and good luck."

Buoyed by these words of encouragement, I went back to the Academy determined to find a solution to the problem of the landlady sequence. The stills I had found of Mason in George's files at least gave us something to work with, since there were several full-figure poses of Mason standing in various attitudes which could be used over the track as he expressed his irritation and outrage at the name "Oleander Arms." But we still needed some visual representation of the sign on the motel.

The only time the motel is seen previously is at night, when Esther is driven home by Norman after their first meeting. As they pull up to the building, they stop in front of the sign. I remembered that in my searching through the stock footage vaults, I had found a roll of film marked "Oleander Arms—Night" which had been used for background process plates. I went back to the vault and pulled out the negative, hoping that there might be a "flash frame"—an overexposed frame that occurs sometimes at the very end of a reel when the electronic shutter disengages. My hunch paid off, for just before the end there were three frames with the sign "Oleander Arms" as bright as daylight. We took those frames, blew them up into eight-by-ten stills, composited the figure of James Mason onto them in such a way that he seemed to be looking at the sign, and Lize worked out the timing so that the line "Oleander Arms! Well, no wonder I couldn't remember it!" seemed to be prompted by his looking at the sign. Then we could cut to his driving away and put the rest of the line over that.

That was fine for the end, but we still needed the beginning of the scene—the dialogue with the landlady. The location for the Oleander Arms was an apartment complex that in 1982 was still standing at the corner of Fountain and Crescent Heights in Hollywood, a mile or so away from the Academy. I passed it almost every day—it was easily recognizable because of the distinct railings that were all over the building. Looking at the scene where Norman drives away from the building, I noticed that he wears a tweed jacket much like one I owned. In mulling over what we could do to save the beginning of the scene, it suddenly occurred to me that we were manufacturing stills from bits and pieces of other stills—why not just photograph what we needed? The building had changed barely at all in the intervening years. And no one knew what the actress playing the landlady looked like; we could find someone, make her up to look the part, give her the lines to say, put her in front of a recognizable part of the building, and photograph a set of stills that would serve our purposes. As for getting Mason into the scene, it wasn't necessary to show his face, just his back or his arm gesturing to the landlady. My jacket matched his pretty closely— I could stand in for Norman Maine! Doug thought I was a little crazy, but after I explained my plan in detail and sketched out how it would work, he fell in with the idea. An actress friend of his, Gloria Lewin, agreed to do the job, and the photography was done by Bob Kensinger.

It worked beautifully, except for one minor flaw: Doug had not had a chance to listen to the track of the landlady's voice, which—cultured, querulous, older—just did not match up to Gloria's appearance. But the sequence did convey all the points that needed to be made. And I must confess to a certain satisfaction in knowing that I'm in the movie—even if it is just my arm, and only for a fleeting moment at that!

All of the photographs we were working with, whether originals, reconstructions, or newly photographed, had to be retouched to eliminate spots, dirt, scratches, and unwanted details before they could be given to Ken Rudolph for photography on the animation camera. Fortunately, Lize had brought with her into the project Kevin Kutchaver, whose ability to doctor and enhance these photos was truly unique. Many of these were tiny images on proof sheets. Kevin had to go through six separate steps for each normal photo: rephotographing, special processing, enlarging, retouching, rephotographing again, and then once again through the "squeeze" lens. Composite photos, where we were adding images, were even more complex and time-consuming.

Not all the photo uses were so complicated. Just before the "Born in a Trunk" sequence, there was a scene deleted showing Maine driving Esther to the sneak preview of her first film: she is nervous; he is trying to reassure her; she makes him stop the car and is sick to her stomach all over an oil derrick. This is a sequence that many people remembered in the original version, partly from the beauty of the California sunset that backdropped it and partly because it showed a tender side of Norman. It would have been easy to leave it out, as it did nothing to advance the plot, but it was one of those unique Cukor uses of location to set a mood and to enhance the development of characters and relationships. I had found the alternate takes for the driving and oil derrick scenes, all long and medium shots. What was needed were close shots of Mason and Garland in the car for

the dialogue sections; again, no stills had been photographed for this. But
in the first part of the film Norman drives Esther home at night in his
convertible: there was enough variety of facial expressions in this earlier
sequence so that if we picked out some frames, blew them up, and intercut
them with the driving scenes and oil derrick shots, we could maintain the
continuity, the charm, and the pictorial effectiveness of the segment. However, to maintain audience interest throughout the stills, we were forced
once again to edit the soundtrack, eliminating much of the steady stream
of conversation with which Norman tries to calm Esther.

This was something we had to do several times throughout the stills
sequences; and it accounts for the difference in running time between the
original release version of 181 minutes and our reconstruction, which runs
176 minutes. In one instance we had to leave out a portion of a crucial
scene. When Norman finally tracks Esther down in a seedy rooming house,
they have an awkward reunion on the roof of the building, where she is
drying her hair. In the Hart-Cukor original, the two are set upon by the
landlady and the neighbors, all demanding autographs and photographs
and generally being extremely boorish. When Norman gets angry, they
turn on him in a nasty fashion, and it takes all of Esther's tact to quiet
everyone down and smooth things over. Unfortunately, we only had two
stills of this sequence, and no matter what we did and how we edited the
track and juggled the stills, we could not make it work. When we showed
the scene to Fay and Gene, they didn't like it, feeling it stopped the flow
of the reunion scene. I wasn't happy with it either, but I felt it should stay
in, choppy and awkward though it was. Fay's and Gene's logic prevailed
and I realized that the scene did work against the sequence; so we lost that
one bit.

This first eleven-minute photo-and-film section took almost five weeks
to complete. We had looked at bits and pieces of the material on the
editing table as we worked, but we had never shown it to anyone in
continuity and on a big screen. On the day of our first full-scale screening
for Fay, Gene, and other Academy executives, we were all extremely nervous. Craig had spliced the footage into the appropriate places on our reels
of re-edited film and gave the picture and separate soundtrack to the
projectionist. The lights went down, the picture faded in, and the camera
traveled across a still of the Glenn Williams Orchestra bus, coming to rest
on Judy Garland as, on the track, the voices of the men in the band said
their farewells. The sound and the image matched up beautifully; when we

cut to an actual shot of the bus pulling away in full color, the effect was striking. The rest of the technique worked equally well. I was greatly relieved, and everyone else seemed generally pleased.

We set to work in earnest, trying to complete the segment in time to show Bob Daly before he went off to Europe. We estimated that it would be done in two more weeks, so Fay made an appointment with Daly to come to the Academy on Tuesday, January 25, to see the results.

Gene called George Cukor to tell him that we were almost ready to show what we had, and George agreed to come down and take a look with Daly. We decided that to make the best possible presentation, we would run the picture up to the point where the cuts had been made, then switch over to our reconstructed material. This would not only demonstrate how the technique worked in terms of story continuity but also show off the film itself, along with the superb stereo track. (I defy anyone to sit through the first two reels of *A Star Is Born* without immediately getting caught up in the excitement, the glamour, and the sheer artistry of the film.)

On the Monday before our screening, Craig and I were feeling anxious about Cukor's and Daly's reaction to what we had, especially George's, because if he didn't like it, that would end the project immediately. I was still thinking about all this later that night when the telephone rang and someone's voice told me that George had died. I can't remember who called; I only remember not being able to say anything, a reaction of stunned silence. A whole era of sophistication, elegance, good manners, and civilized behavior seemed suddenly to have vanished with George. Fay and Gene, who were both extremely close to him, were devastated, and for a time we considered postponing the screening. But we decided to go ahead.

It was a very depressed group that met at the Samuel Goldwyn Theatre that Tuesday morning. Fay made a brief speech in which she pointed out that although we all felt a great sense of loss, we were gathered there with a remarkable feeling that we had a great opportunity to make a kind of lasting tribute to George and his artistry.

We went through the screening; the picture looked beautiful, the sound was impressive, and the virtuosity of what George had done seemed to rouse everybody from their depression. Three days later Fay called me to say Bob Daly had agreed to back the project and that we should go ahead full speed.

In order to keep our costs down, Jim Roberts, executive director of the Academy, suggested going to Eastman Kodak and enlisting its aid. Eastman had been receiving a great deal of unfavorable publicity about the stability of its product. The longevity of the old color negative had been attested to in the excellent quality we were getting from the stock footage. We wanted to put our restored sequences on the new Eastman Kodak print film #5382, with its vastly improved dye stability—up to thirty years with no loss of color. Eastman agreed to donate the amount of film we needed to complete the project properly. That act of generosity freed a large chunk of our budget, which was then used to restore the stereo track.

This rerecording was being done at the studio and was a time-consuming and complex task, especially for Craig. The one existing four-track stereo print was the short version. Over the thirty years of its life, it had weathered numerous screenings; it was torn and spliced, it had frames missing, and its metal oxide soundtracks had undergone considerable wear, with a consequent diminution of the high frequencies. Before it could be rerecorded to obtain a new stereo master, Craig had to go through it foot by foot, measuring it against the original negative. Where frames were missing, he inserted the appropriate lengths of blank film; there was a twenty-five-foot rip down the center of one section which he had to carefully tape over so as not to lose the four magnetic tracks. After Craig had accomplished this painstaking task, Bob Buescher, the engineer at the Burbank Studios, took over the print to transfer the sound to a new magnetic four-track master. To do this, the sound department had to manufacture special sound heads, since there were no longer any sound units at the studio that could reproduce the thirty-year-old track. After this was done, the four-track original print was carefully run past three heads in synchronization with the single-track sound masters of the long version. Wherever Craig had spliced in blank film, the recorder picked up the sound from this long version and thus filled in the "holes" in the stereo master. At the same time, a special processor "rechanneled" these monaural fillers to give them a pseudo-stereo sound, matching as closely as possible the stereo sound of the original.

While this was being done at the studio, back at the Academy, D. J. ("Zig") Ziegler of the Academy's Film Department was working on the reconstruction of the "Lose That Long Face" musical number. She began looking at the numerous silent takes for this sequence that had been found in the stock footage vaults. There were close to twenty-five separate takes on this one number, which had been filmed over a period of several weeks. The technique for filming was to break the song down into bars; these sections would be played back on the sound stage and the choreographer/director would film each section in a separate shot. Some of these shots were done as often as ten times, depending on their complexity and whether any mistakes were made. Watching this silent material was fascinating, as you could see the physical strain in Garland as the takes wore on and on. Missteps, miscues, wrong camera moves, and colliding dancers all caused scenes to be retaken. Zig's job was to match each sequence with the appropriate musical accompaniment. She had to do this largely by eye, matching Garland's lip movements with her voice on the track. Matching the track to the dance section was relatively simple, as the sound effects on the track dictated what was happening on screen: for example, Garland splashing in a puddle, tap dancing, being joined by two children for another section. (For a while we toyed with the idea of using a bit of the takes done with Garland's dance double, but the difference in technique and style was too apparent.) Inevitably, what Zig had to work with was inferior to what had been used in the film originally, and when we looked at the completed number, while pleased that we had been able to reconstruct it, we all felt that it was not as good as it should have been.

At this point, I was contacted again by the local theater exhibitor who knew the collector who supposedly had the original footage of "Lose That Long Face." Once again, he assured me that it *did* exist—that he personally had seen it—and after an extensive bit of cajoling, persuading, and other entreaties he reluctantly told me the man's name, adding that he was an editorial assistant at the very same Burbank Studios where Craig and I were working. Suddenly, I realized that if this fellow did indeed have "Lose That Long Face," then he must have the missing dramatic sections as well, probably having obtained them all at the same time right there at the studio. (I still had not given up my conviction that the *original* negative material had not been destroyed—that it had been saved, and that somehow it all had fallen into this fellow's hands.)

Craig and I devised a strategy. Knowing that the man was a fanatic about Garland and *A Star Is Born,* we would invite him over to the editing room to see what we were up to. Craig and I felt that this bit of privileged viewing might dazzle Mr. Elusive Collector. The plan was to enlist his aid and his knowledge of *other collectors* who might have the material: that way, we wouldn't be confronting him directly, but instead would appeal to his love of film and of this particular movie to help us locate what we needed.

The appointed time arrived, and in the door came a medium-sized man in his mid-fifties, wearing Levi's and a plaid shirt, balding, with a mustache and a quiet manner. He was appreciative of our offer to see what we were doing and appropriately enthusiastic about the results. After showing him the material, I launched into my spiel about how much we wanted to find the original material; could he, as a collector with wide knowledge of the field and acquaintanceship with other collectors, give us any help? No expense would be too great and no questions would be asked.

He sat there on the stool, arms folded, looking at the Moviola, having stared at it all during my impassioned plea. He said nothing for a moment, then looked up at me and smiled ruefully and shook his head. "I sure would like to help you, but I don't know anybody who has this stuff. I've heard for years that some collectors claim to have it, but I've never seen it and I don't know anyone who has, except when the movie first came out. I really can't help you. I wish I could." He looked at me the entire time—straight in the eye—and I felt that he was telling the truth.

After he left, I put in a call to my source and told him the outcome of the conversation. He was infuriated, swearing that he'd seen the material. Alas, all we could do now was hope that eventually, after all the publicity broke, the material would somehow find its way to us.

Meanwhile, we still had to finish putting the picture together. The soundtrack, having been rerecorded, was now being re-equalized to restore to the stereo sound the luster and sonority that had been lost in the transfer. This was being done on one of the rerecording stages by dubbing editor Wayne Artman and his staff. At the beginning of their work, they more or less, I think, considered it just another dubbing job—more of a curiosity piece than anything else, with no particular creative work needed, as the track was already mixed and ready for putting to the picture. In my zeal to make sure that the spectacular sonics of the original not be lost (I still recalled vividly those tinkling chandeliers at the Bal), I began bird-dogging Wayne and his crew, second-guessing them, criticizing and otherwise making a nuisance of myself to the point where he almost ordered me off the stage. The work they were doing was delicate and time-consuming but, to them, not particularly exciting until one afternoon when they were working on the section showing Esther on her first day at the studio. Evidently neither Wayne nor his assistant, Tom Beckart, had seen the film before; and when the scene of Garland getting weak-kneed on the high studio bridge flashed on the screen, they sat up in surprise, for the catwalk she was crossing was right outside their dubbing stage. In fact, the door she walked through after crossing the bridge was the door immediately to the right of their dubbing console. After that, *A Star Is Born* was as much their movie as it was Cukor's, or mine, or Craig's, and they fussed and fretted over every detail of the sound, striving to make it as close to the original as modern technology allowed, so that it would show off the full breadth and depth of the old four-track magnetic process, with its almost palpable bass impact.

We had been working on all these final details for the better part of a month; while we labored at the studio, the Academy was orchestrating a publicity campaign for the announcement of the reconstruction while simultaneously organizing a series of fund-raising presentations of the film in six major cities around the country. In Los Angeles, the film would be presented at the Academy's Samuel Goldwyn Theatre; but it was the plans for New York that floored me—the picture would premiere at the Radio City Music Hall! Doug had been in the theater for one of the first performances of Kevin Brownlow's restoration of *Napoleon.* To hear him tell it, it was a truly monumental and memorable film evening, and he wanted to have that experience again, only this time with *A Star Is Born.* Fay and I had been seen *Napoleon* at its Los Angeles opening at the Shrine Auditorium and, along with thousands of others, were dazzled not only by the film but by its presentation. Memorable nights at the movies, with excitement, glamour, genuine enthusiasm, and, most important of all, a terrific movie, are few and far between these days. So when the Academy turned its collective professionalism loose on the proper publicity and presentation of *A Star Is Born,* I watched in admiration.

A series of interviews were arranged for *The New York Times,* the Los Angeles *Times, Daily Variety,* and *The Hollywood Reporter* to announce the discovery of the material and the reconstruction of the film. That happened in April. In May, the first announcements went out that the film would have its premiere in New York on July 7, 1983, to be followed over the next few weeks by single evenings in Washington, D.C.; Chicago; Dallas; and Oakland, California; and by three evenings in Los Angeles. To me, the Oakland evening was particularly meaningful, as the picture was to play at that 1930s art deco masterpiece the Paramount, a theater wherein I had spent much of my early life and where I had started my "career" in film as a doorman in the mid-1950s. (Oakland was chosen instead of San Francisco because no available theater in that city was as large or as glamorous as the Paramount.) In each city, the presentation would be in association with an appropriate film institution. Thus, the film department of the Museum of Modern Art would co-sponsor the Radio City Music Hall presentation; the American Film Institute would co-host in Washington, D.C.; the Chicago Film Festival in Chicago; the USA Film Festival in Dallas; and the Pacific Film Archive would co-sponsor the Oakland Paramount event. In Los Angeles, of course, for all three evenings, the Academy would present the picture in association with Warner Bros. All the proceeds from each event would go toward film-preservation projects of the cooperating institutions.

Why open the picture in New York, not Los Angeles, the home of legendary premieres? Because of the unfortunate truth that, barring an earthquake, a fire, a plane crash, or an assassination, the Eastern press pays practically no attention to anything that happens in Los Angeles. The plan was for a splashy New York opening that would make headlines across the country and be picked up by all the major print and electronic media.

Warner Bros. commissioned a new poster for the film by noted graphic artist Richard Amsel. His four-color design reproduced the original classic image of Garland, hands framing her face, with a wistful look on her face—in the film it's a caricature movement in the "Someone at Last" number, where she announces, "Now, here comes a big, fat close-up." All the humor and irony removed, it now became the dominant advertising image for the film, concentrating on Garland to the exclusion of any other idea of the film: no music, no spectacle, no drama—nothing but the face of Garland with searchlights coming out of the background behind her head.

After the first news stories broke and the dates were announced for the picture's screenings, we started the final phase of work to ready the film for its official unveiling. The soundtrack had been rerecorded and now had to be meticulously trimmed to match the cuts we had made in our working copy. The stills sections needed a final touching-up. They were given a slight color tint under Gene Allen's supervision to more closely integrate the material into the body of what already existed. Fades, dissolves, and other optical devices to link all this disparate material together had to be carefully devised, and some of the stills sequences needed to be reshot because of technical difficulties. Lize and her husband, Alan, were leaving for China and a Ping-Pong tournament, but she had arranged for Eric Durst, another animation expert, to come in and help us finish up the details.

Publicity continued to build, and we began doing interviews with selected members of the press. Jim Brown and a camera crew from the

"Today" show did a piece on how we were working with the stills; Leonard Maltin put together a segment for "Entertainment Tonight"; and Stephen Harvey from the Museum of Modern Art came out to do a Sunday piece for *The New York Times*. And as the New York opening drew closer, the Academy made arrangements for Liza Minnelli and Lorna Luft to attend, along with James Mason (who had just lost a Best Supporting Actor award for his role in *The Verdict*). The presence of Lillian Gish would add a grace note to the event—not that it needed one; but Miss Gish, the only surviving great actress from the birth of the movies, was enthusiastic about anything to do with film preservation. With her, the evening became more than just the repremiere of an outstanding film from the 1950s; it now had a continuity with the past, with the very beginnings of film history. With these personages as part of the event, the evening became more ambitious. A premium price ticket of fifty dollars entitled the bearer to attend a prescreening party in the lounge of the Music Hall; as soon as this was announced, there was a stampede for tickets that gave the lie to the legend that New Yorkers are blasé and indifferent to celebrity gawking.

As an added fillip for the evening, Craig and I put together a compilation of newsreel footage of the original 1954 premiere at the Pantages in Hollywood. I'd found the material in the stock footage vaults—ninety minutes of coverage in black-and-white and color, showing just about every major star in Hollywood getting out of limousines, stopping to say a few words, then going into the theater. We cut it down to approximately fifteen minutes, keeping the high spots and the recognizable greats: James Dean was in the crowd, unknown and unrecognized; Clark Gable briefly flashed by. This was newsreel footage shot by the studio. The live television coverage was much more detailed, but there was no way we could make the existing kinescopes of the event match up to our 35mm footage, so we lost shots of several major stars of the time. The compilation ended with the tumultuous reception given Garland as she made her way into the theater.

In these same stock footage vaults, I had also found the first Cinema-Scope version of "The Man That Got Away," which later had been re-thought and reshot by Cukor. I thought it might be interesting to screen this earlier version before the film, showing the way the creative process worked; but it was decided that this would detract from the actual performance in the film. Also, Cukor hadn't liked it, and the sequence failed to show Garland to her best advantage. (When the restored *A Star Is Born*

was given a theatrical reissue, the Warner Classics Division added this
sequence to the beginning of the picture, and it indeed worked against the
song in the film itself.)

At this point, we agreed that the picture should be presented with an
intermission. According to studio records and the recollections of everyone
involved, it had been designed to have one; the only reason it didn't was
exhibitor resistance. *A Star Is Born* builds to a first-act finale with "Born
in a Trunk," which ends on such a rousing note that a break is mandatory—
the audience needs to "blow off steam," so to speak. Moreover, it is here
that the story shifts gears. The first half, detailing the struggle, the excitement, and the glamour of the star-building process, has reached its climax.
The second part now moves into the darker, more tragic aspects of the love
story. Without a break, the shift is too jarring. And the length of the film
itself demands a breather, for, as George Cukor himself commented,
"neither the human mind nor the human ass can stand three hours of
concentration."

We were now less than two weeks away from the scheduled New York
opening and began working out the details of the presentation itself. We
would be showing the dye-transfer Technicolor print that I'd found un-
opened in the studio vault. This, of course, was the short version, but the
quality of the image was so extraordinary that we decided against making
a new print, as it could not match the beauty of this original. It had, in
the words of one critic, "Technicolor that you could eat with a spoon." Our
reconstructed sections could easily be spliced into this print, and the picture
would be run in synchronization with the new four-track stereo master—
what the engineers call "double system." Picture and track on separate reels
meant that the possibility of mistakes in the presentation would be in-
creased; it meant, too, that expensive equipment would have to be installed
in all the theaters showing the film. It also meant extra expenses for
transportation, rehearsals, stagehands, extra projectionists, and myriad
other problems and stumbling blocks.

Doug and his assistant, Ric Robertson, were scheduled to leave for New
York on June 30 to arrange all the details for the press conferences, the
party, and the premiere itself. But so far no one had seen the completed
film in a theater with our new stereo track, and Doug in particular was
anxious to see what we'd finally done, as it was the most vital component

of his organization of the tour. So on the morning of June 30, Doug and I, Fay, Gene Allen, Craig, Lize, and an invited group of about one hundred Academy staff and friends gathered in the Goldwyn Theatre, where the project had begun almost two years ago. A short introduction that was appended to the beginning of the film read: "The Academy of Motion Picture Arts and Sciences dedicates this film to the cause of preserving the world's motion picture heritage. We particularly thank Warner Bros. for their help in locating missing material and for its generous support during the reconstruction of this motion picture."

Three hours and one intermission later Doug was a self-proclaimed "emotional mess." To see the film almost restored to the way George had always envisioned it, to see it looking and sounding so splendid, and to know that he had had an important part in "repolishing the gem" made that morning's screening a highlight of his entire *A Star Is Born* experience.

To be truthful, I don't recall anything about that screening except Doug's reaction. The audience was small, and they were all involved in the project in one way or another, so whatever their reaction, it must have been favorable. In fact, I don't have any recollection of the next few days until I arrived in New York the day before the Music Hall opening. There was a press reception at the Quo Vadis restaurant, and I remember finally meeting Sid and Lorna Luft and Kitty Carlisle Hart, but even that is vague. What does stand out in my memory is seeing the picture in its first runthrough at the Radio City Music Hall. There in that empty, echoing palace, watching it come to life on one of the biggest screens in the world, hearing it as I've never heard it before or since, it became entirely *my* movie—everything and everyone else faded away, and I just gave in to the selfishness of the moment—proud, happy, and pleased to know that later that night six thousand people would have an equally memorable experience that I'd helped create!

The evening's festivities were scheduled to start at six-thirty with a cocktail reception in the downstairs lounge of the theater. I took my time walking down Sixth Avenue from my hotel; arriving at the Music Hall, I stood for a while across the street near the Time-Life Building, watching the crowds throng around the theater and looking at the marquee: "The Academy Foundation Presents *A Star Is Born.*" Approaching the stage-door entrance on Fifty-first Street, I passed a mass of photographers, fans, limousines, and other accoutrements of big-time premieres; but once inside I was stunned by the number of people who were jammed into the grand lobby. I couldn't recall ever seeing so many people in one theater.

And there suddenly was James Mason, gracious, unflappable, every bit as charming and as handsome as he was in the film. He and Liza Minnelli and Lorna Luft were kind and generous in their warmth and praise as we all posed for the photographers.

Then it was time for the show. The theater was filled to its art deco rafters. We all took our seats. The lights dimmed, and on the screen came the newsreel footage of the original premiere. I doubt whether anything could have stirred the crowd up more than seeing that parade of glamorous figures. It was nostalgic, funny, foolish, and ultimately touching as you realized how many of these well-loved personalities had made an impact on all of us there. At the end of the newsreel, Fay walked on stage to an ovation and proceeded to put the entire evening in context by saying, "It was an exciting event then, and twenty-nine years later it's still an exciting event." Then she introduced Gene Allen and me; the applause for us was gratifying, but it was nothing compared to that for "someone who embodies everything about the movies—the legendary Lillian Gish." She received a standing ovation, as did Lorna Luft and Liza Minnelli. It was a touching moment when Lorna introduced her father, Sid Luft, sitting in the audience, and said, "All my life I've wanted to see this movie the way my mother and father made it, because it's the only film they made together." Liza recalled seeing the original version when she was very young; she remembered the "nutburger" scene and her mother's hurt at learning that "Lose That Long Face" had been cut from the film. Finally, Fay introduced James Mason, who almost shyly walked on stage to an ovation that rivaled that for Lillian Gish. He seemed a bit taken aback at the clamor and the cheering but warmed to the occasion, and, gentleman that he was, paid tribute to "three names seldom mentioned in connection with stories about this [film]: Charles Bickford, Jack Carson, and Tom Noonan." He then thanked "another bunch of human beings, who come under the heading of film buffs, especially the film buffs of New York. These are the people who go up to the theater manager and complain loudly and bitterly if a film is cut or badly shown—and especially this film. These people," he said, "I think contributed greatly to this evening."

After Mason finished, Fay concluded her remarks by saying: "The rebirth of A Star Is Born is a testament to the enduring artistry of our colleague and friend George Cukor. For twenty-nine years, this uncompromising artist refused to look at the cut version of his masterpiece. On the night before he was to see this reconstructed version, he died. Tonight's screening has a very special meaning for all of us, for tonight would have been George's eighty-fourth birthday." Suddenly, I felt cheated. I wanted George to walk out onto that stage and get the kind of screaming, whistling, hat-throwing standing ovation that would have let him know how much everyone there loved his work, and especially this particular aspect of it. For, as Fay said, "what's so wonderful about movies like this is they fill the theater with magic."

And that's exactly what happened that night, for as soon as the lights went down and the image and the sound of *A Star Is Born* filled the stage and the theater, the audience was electrified. I was so excited that I had to leave my seat and paced back and forth in the back of the theater with Craig, who was as nervous as I was. I had no doubt that the audience would love the movie. There was ample proof of that—applause began almost immediately at the credits and reached a sustained crescendo at the conclusion of "The Man That Got Away." What was worrying me was whether or not they would accept the stills sequences. As the first reconstructed sequence flashed on the screen, I stood in the back watching as the audience quieted down in—what? Rapt attention? Appreciation? Puzzlement? It was the quietest audience I'd ever encountered . . . until Garland had sung the "Trinidad Coconut Oil Shampoo" commercial. Then, laughter and applause. More laughter at the "nutburger" scene; and as the stills sequence ended on the rooftop of the rooming house, there was applause loud and sustained. I suddenly had chills up my spine "and some thrills I can't define," to quote Ira Gershwin.

The rest of the first half of the film played beautifully, and at the end of "Born in a Trunk" there was pandemonium. It was exciting, gratifying, vindicating, and during intermission the crowds and the enthusiasm were extraordinary. Standing in the back of the theater, I saw Doug and other Academy and Music Hall staff hard pressed to keep the fans from deluging Lorna, Liza, Lillian, and James. Looking around, I caught glimpses of Andy Warhol, Helen Hayes, Candice Bergen, Patricia Neal, Betty Comden, and Adolph Green.

Once the second half started, I walked all over the theater, in and out of the mezzanines, the loges, and the balconies, watching the audience watching the movie. It was the most exciting night of my adult life, and it's impossible to explain why in any rational, unemotional manner. David

Denby in *New York* magazine summed it up as well as anyone could when he called the premiere

> the most stirring event of the summer movie season. . . . What made the evening extraordinary, apart from the movie itself, which in any version is devastating, was the all-round film savvy and fervor of the audience. Walking around the sold-out hall, one felt gratified by the presence of a true film community. These were not people merely latching onto a glamour occasion; they were people still capable of being moved by the emotional qualities of a favorite movie . . . six thousand adults concentrating on a thirty-year-old film that meant something to them emotionally.

And when the two restored musical numbers came on in the second half, these six thousand adults responded like opera lovers at a Callas concert. Those who knew the film well began applauding as soon as these unknown scenes faded in. When Garland walked out onto the sound stage in her ragamuffin costume to do "Lose That Long Face," the audience went crazy. It was several seconds into the number before they stopped applauding; when she began tap-dancing and when the number ended, the applause again was frenetic. It quieted down for the dramatic dressing-room scene, then began again with the tag reprise of "Lose That Long Face." (After this number, which evidently was all some individuals wanted to see, we lost several dozen people, which surprised and irritated me.)

My pacing back and forth in the back of the theater had been watched for some time by a young usherette, who was alternately fascinated by the movie and by my behavior. Finally, she walked up to me and asked me if I had something to do with the film. When I told her I did, she smiled at me and said, very genuinely, "Well, don't be nervous. It's a terrific movie and it should be a big hit!"

The film moved toward its climax, and I remember one image very vividly. The back area of the Music Hall, the "standing room" section, has a chest-high partition running the length of the theater, separating the seats in the auditorium from this rear area. For the last twenty minutes of the film, about twelve of New York's Finest, police who had been assigned to the event, were lined up solidly, leaning against this partition, elbows and arms resting on the divider, all in exactly the same position, one foot crossed over the other, billy clubs and pistols hanging at their waists, staring raptly at the screen, unmoving, completely involved in the proceedings. I wished at that moment that I had a camera—it was absolute proof of the picture's power to engross even the most hardened audiences.

As Judy Garland walked toward the microphone at the film's climax, the theater became so quiet that you could hear the collective breathing of the audience. As she spoke her curtain line—"Hello, everybody. This is Mrs. Norman Maine . . ."—the audience in the film began applauding but was drowned out by the sound of the audience in the Radio City Music Hall, who started clapping, then cheering—and continued for the next two minutes that it took for the film to end and the curtain to come down. And even then they didn't stop. I tried to get down the aisle to reach Doug and Fay, but the crowd was too dense and too clamorous. I saw a flying wedge of policemen and ushers surrounding the celebrity party, moving them swiftly through a side door and into the backstage area. Doug told me later that both Liza and Lorna had to be taken into a dressing room, where they cried and held on to each other for the better part of twenty minutes: the emotions generated by the film and by seeing their mother in her favorite movie, and the intensity of the audience involvement, were more than they could handle.

Afterwards, we all went back to our respective lodgings. Doug, who was staying in the Village, later related to me that he walked home and, too excited to go to sleep, went up to the roof of the building in which he was staying and watched the moon go down. Just before dawn, he looked toward the city skyline, and at that moment a shooting star arced across the beginnings of the morning sky—a symbolic ending to a memorable event.

My own favorite story about this evening involves two friends of mine who had been to the Music Hall and seen the film, then took the subway home. Their car was near-empty except for one other passenger, one of New York's less fortunates, who evidently lived in the subway, or at least did most of his drinking there. He was bleary-eyed and truculent; seeing my two friends, he weaved his way unsteadily toward them. Holding onto the pole, he stared at them, then noticed the program for *A Star Is Born*. He looked at it quizzically, then sat down abruptly next to them and in a very slurred voice asked: "Tell me—is it really her best work like everybody says?"

Epilogue

The New York premiere of the film was a triumph for the Academy Foundation and for the cause of film preservation. Following the Radio City Music Hall opening, we took the picture to Washington, D.C., where we had the only mishap of the entire tour. As the "Lose That Long Face" segment began, the picture and the sound went out of synchronization; instead of stopping, the engineer handling the track tried to speed it up to catch up to the picture. Meanwhile, the audience was having fits— the one number everyone wanted to see was being ruined. The engineer paid no attention to anyone. It finally took Gene Allen's rushing up to the projection booth and *ordering* him to stop before we could quiet the crowd and start the number over.

James Mason and Lillian Gish traveled with the film to Oakland; in Dallas, Mason was joined by another celebrity guest, Ginger Rogers, who had started her show-business career as a chorus girl at the Majestic Theater, where we were showing the film (and which had been the scene of its original Dallas premiere in 1954). In these cities and in Chicago, the film was greeted with enthusiasm and appreciation, almost as if it were a new movie—which in a sense it was, since most of the people in the audiences for these presentations had never seen it in its full glory. These audiences were made up of an eclectic group of moviegoers; the picture's appeal cut across all barriers of age, race, and class. In Los Angeles, the three-day-long engagement at the Academy's Samuel Goldwyn Theatre was such a success that several more performances had to be scheduled to meet the public demand.

The second night of the picture's presentation at the Academy, I was approached by a young black man who informed me that his wife was one of the children who had danced with Garland in "Lose That Long Face." He took me over and introduced me to her, and I tried to get to Gene Allen, who was the emcee that evening, to let him know so that he could introduce her. But he had already started speaking; then the film started, and it was too late. After the screening, I looked for them, but they were gone, and I could not remember their name. If they read this, I hope they will know how much I regret not being able to introduce the young lady, who was listed in the credits as Patricia Rosamond.

Another, more bizarre incident came about because of the screenings at the Academy. On the third or fourth night of the screenings, I was standing in the lobby talking to some people. In another corner of the lobby, a young man was loudly proclaiming to a crowd of listeners, who evidently knew him, that we were misrepresenting our reconstruction as "complete." He was outraged because we had not included the scene on the rooftop with the landlady, the neighbors, and the children. I knew this fellow as one of the more obnoxious Garland fans. On this particular night, after the film had started, he became involved in a shouting match with another patron, who objected to his constant talking to a companion during the screening. At the intermission, I noticed that the companion was none other than the local exhibitor who had insisted that the film editor at the Burbank Studios had the original "Lose That Long Face" footage. The two came up to talk to me, and once again the exhibitor bewailed the fact that we had been unable to convince the film editor to give us the negative. I agreed that it was unfortunate but remarked that even if he did have the negative, there was no way of getting it from him short of turning him in to the police as a possessor of stolen merchandise—something I did not want to do. As we talked, I noticed the loud friend turn abruptly and go over to a pay phone. It was such a purposeful and sharp movement that it caught my eye and stuck in the back of my mind briefly. I then thought no more of it.

Several days later I received a call in my office from Gerald Loeb, who identified himself as a senior investigator from the district attorney's office. He asked if he could come and show me something that I might be able to help him identify—some film that they had recently seized. An hour later, he was in my office at the museum with a can of 35mm film. I opened it, looked at it through the film viewer, and found I was staring at the negative to "Lose That Long Face"! I was flabbergasted—where had this come from? It was evidently the original, Cukor-approved version of the number. Loeb explained that the film security office of the Motion Picture Association of America had received an anonymous tip that a man in the San Fernando Valley had an enormous collection of stolen and other illegally gotten films. Loeb and several other officers had driven out to a place called the E.Z. Storage Company in Burbank and found this collector loading dozens of film cans into a rental truck. They had confiscated the material, and the one can they brought to me because it had "Garland— Star Is Born" written on the outside. When I asked who the collector was, Loeb told me his name. It was the film editor from the Burbank Studios, whom I had believed when he said he knew nothing of this very film!

Suddenly I became enormously excited. Maybe he had the rest of the footage! Loeb took me and Dan Woodruff, the Academy's film archivist, down to the Bekins film storage facility, where all of the seized film had been stored. There were literally hundreds of cans and boxes of film, some that had been missing from Warner Bros. for years. Two of them were the only existing 35mm nitrate prints of the last two-color Technicolor features Warners had made in 1932–33: *Dr. X* and *Mystery of the Wax Museum.* There were also 35mm nitrate Technicolor prints of *The Adventures of Robin Hood* and *The Private Lives of Elizabeth and Essex,* and nearly twelve hundred additional cans of 35mm and 16mm films that this fellow had either bought or stolen over the years. Dan and I spent the next several days going through this mass of miscellaneous material, hoping to turn up the other missing negative sections of *A Star Is Born,* but we found nothing. The collector, on the advice of his attorney, would tell us nothing: he was facing criminal charges, he'd lost his job, and he'd lost the one thing that evidently gave meaning and purpose to his life—his film collection, which he'd carefully (and perhaps illegally) built up over a number of years.

We took the negative of "Lose That Long Face" to the Technicolor labs immediately; they printed it up for us, and the next night it was cut into our print of *A Star Is Born,* where it turned out to be infinitely superior to our reconstruction of the number.

The success of the road-show screenings of *A Star Is Born* across the country was no surprise to anyone at the Academy. The executives at Warner Bros., however, were caught completely off guard. Almost immediately after the Music Hall screenings and the additional screenings at the Academy, Warners announced that the film in its new form would be given a first-run reissue all across the country. New prints were made with a Dolby stereo soundtrack. The picture opened in New York, then played a series of modestly successful engagements all over the country and in Europe, where it had generated a great deal of attention at the Venice, Deauville, San Sebastian, and London film festivals. Europe had never seen anything but the short version, and in many countries the picture had been trimmed to less than two hours, with most of the musical numbers deleted.

A year after the Music Hall premiere, Warner Home Video asked me to supervise the preparation of the picture for release to the home video market. The current tradition in home video is to reduce all CinemaScope films to fit the three-by-four proportions of television sets, which means that the image must be "panned and scanned"—a process that involves a technician's rephotographing the film using a three-by-four frame, eliminating almost half the image. I made a strong appeal to Warner Home Video not to do this with A Star Is Born, arguing that it would violate the film's artistic integrity once again. I implored them to "letterbox" the image—put the full CinemaScope frame on the video release—which necessitates having a black area above and below the image to give it the correct proportion on a television set. But they were adamant in their refusal: the public would never stand for it. So, ironically, I found myself sitting at a video console, electronically trimming the image to fit the new technology.

Still, even with this compromise, the picture does look beautiful in its video incarnation, and the stereo track is astounding when heard on a good home system. Some folks with chandeliers may even manage to recapture my own experience at the Bal Theatre thirty years ago.

There are two concluding incongruities in this chronicle of ironies. As the Decade of Preservation draws to a close and hundreds of films have been saved, they may never be seen, except on video, and perhaps not even there. One of the reasons is the complicated legal status of these films: the institutions that have taken on the responsibility for preservation have no legal claim on the results of their work, other than to store it. For one of these preserved films to be shown publicly, either by the preserving institution or by anyone else, permission must be granted by the copyright owner, or the firm or individual that deposited it with the institution that preserved it. In many cases, the copyright is no longer valid, which means ostensibly that the film is in the public domain. The film may be, but if it is based on a novel or a play, or if it has songs in it, then there are underlying literary and musical rights that must be cleared. This web of permissions, coupled with the reluctance of most archives to allow their films to circulate except to other archives, means that much of the preservation work that has been done in the last decade will not be seen by more than a few hundred people, except perhaps on video—which is the other incongruity.

Since 1903, movies have been designed, directed, and produced to be exhibited on large screens. In part this was due to economics: the more people that could see a film at one sitting, the more money could be taken in. But an anonymous congregation sitting in the dark being engulfed by larger-than-life images shares a collective emotional and visceral experience. This is one of the intangibles that give the movies their particular power, their magic. This power and magic is diluted considerably when the circumstances of the viewing are not ideal. The video revolution has been a boon in many areas for the film business and for devotees of older films, but it has largely eliminated the opportunity to experience these films as they were meant to be experienced—and this is a psychological and cultural loss. Over and over again during the theatrical tour of *A Star Is Born*, people would come up and say that the experience of seeing the film in a theater on a huge screen made it an entirely different movie from the one they had known on television. The revival theater movement, which flourished briefly in the 1960s and 1970s, has largely died off, because of video and because of the reluctance of exhibitors to pay high rental and transportation prices for spliced, scratched, and faded prints. (Distributors feel that it is economically unwise to spend $5,000 to $10,000 to make a print that might not return the cost in rental fees.)

So the situation is, ironically, little better than it was in the 1940s and 1950s. Until a method is devised for projecting video tapes or discs onto theater screens with image quality equal to that of film, film will be the dominant method of projection, as it has been for nearly a hundred years. As long as commercial theater owners refuse to believe that properly presented older films could be a viable commercial undertaking, it must be the responsibility of the nation's museums and universities to keep older films alive, to give them the status they deserve as an art form, and to exhibit them in the manner, style, and technological form in which they were designed to be viewed. This last is particularly important, for the anamorphic and 70mm stereophonic sound formats are crucial to the visual and aural effectiveness of many films made after 1953. Unless proper respect and attention are given to the technology with which these films were produced, the craftsmanship suffers and the art form is diminished. To do this, to make state-of-the-art prints from all eras of film history available, will take commitment and funds from the motion picture industry, which so far has refused to consider its "product" as anything more than that. It is time that this attitude changed. A concerted, cooperative effort must be made by the studios, the distributors, and their service organization, the Motion Picture Association of America; working with accredited institutions, they should develop a national program and policy for preservation *and* exhibition. The expense of preserving, maintaining, and exhibiting this most perishable of all arts is a responsibility that must be shared equally by the industry that has produced it and by the institutions that identify and define it. Technology and the proper theaters are both important in the presentation and appreciation of motion pictures. Without these, it is impossible to do justice to the preservation efforts of the past and of the future. The movies, and the audiences they were made for, need and deserve this respect.

Appendix

CREDITS

Director:
George Cukor

Producer:
Sidney Luft

Associate Producer:
Vern Alves

Screenplay:
Moss Hart

Based on the screenplay by
*Dorothy Parker, Alan Campbell,
and Robert Carson*

From a story by
William A. Wellman and Robert Carson

Art Director:
Malcolm Bert

Set Decorator:
George James Hopkins

Production Design:
Gene Allen

Cinematographer:
Sam Leavitt

Photographed in
*CinemaScope and Eastmancolor
(1954–55 prints by Technicolor)*

Special Visual and Color Consultant:
George Hoyningen-Huene

Editor:
Folmar Blangsted

Costumes:
Jean Louis and Mary Ann Nyberg

Costumes for
"Born in a Trunk":
Irene Sharaff

Assistant Directors:
*Earl Bellamy, Edward Graham,
and Russell Llewellyn*

Dance Director:
Richard Barstow

Songs:
"Born in a Trunk"
Leonard Gershe
"Gotta Have Me Go With You,"
"The Man That Got Away,"
"Here's What I'm Here For,"
"Someone at Last,"
"It's a New World,"
"Lose That Long Face"
*Harold Arlen (music) and
Ira Gershwin (lyrics)*

Musical Director:
Ray Heindorf

Orchestral Arrangements:
Skip Martin

Vocal Arrangements:
Jack Cathcart

Additional Choreography:
Eugene Loring

A Warner Bros. release of a
Transcona Enterprises Production

Premiered at the RKO Pantages Theatre,
Hollywood, California, Thursday evening,
September 29, 1954

Original running time: 181 minutes

CAST

(In order of appearance)

AT THE SHRINE AUDITORIUM

Autograph Seekers:
*Jerry DeCoe, Wayne Taylor, Melvin Pogue,
Janet Stewart, Sylvia Arslan, Colette
McMahon*

Announcer:
George Fischer

Ass't. Announcer:
Jim Hyland

Lola Lavery:
Lucy Marlow

Oliver Niles:
Charles Bickford

Matt Libby:
Jack Carson

Woman Announcer:
Joan Shawlee

Stage Manager:
Sam Colt

Musician:
Jay Johnson

Glenn Williams:
James Brown

Norman Maine:
James Mason

Danny McGuire:
Tommy Noonan

Esther Blodgett/Vicki Lester:
Judy Garland

Reporters:
*Tom Kingston, George Kitchell,
Robert Dumas, Duff Whitney*

Graves:
Irving Bacon

Doorman:
Louis Mason

AT THE COCOANUT GROVE

Bruno:
Frank Puglia

Agent:
Michael Hathaway

Starlet:
Havis Davenport

Pasadena Girl:
Elmera Smith

Chef:
Jack Pepper

Driver:
Dub Taylor

Director:
Louis Jean Heydt

Cameraman:
Don Richards

Eddie:
Bob Jellison

Director (TV):
Don Shelton

Boom Man:
Robert Stevenson

Man in Car:
Chick Chandler

Landlady:
Kathryn Card

Woman:
Geraldine Wall

Rooming House Women:
Nancy Kulp, Mary Young

1st Makeup Man:
Alan DeWitt

2nd Makeup Man:
Rudy Anders

3rd Makeup Man:
Joe Dougherty

Photographer:
Ross Carmichael

Miss Markham:
Lotus Robb

Miss Fusselow:
Blythe Daly

Director:
Leonard Penn

Cameraman:
Eddie Dew

Ass't. Director:
Charles Conrad

Ass't. Director:
George Becwar

1st Cashier:
Charles Halton

2nd Cashier:
Joseph Mell

Charley:
Olin Howlin

"BORN IN A TRUNK" SEQUENCE

Producer:
Dick Simmons

1st Agent:
Joe Greene

2nd Agent:
Joe Hamilton

3rd Agent:
Phil Arnold

Father:
Jack Baker

Mother:
Ila McAvoy

Esther (age 6):
Nadene Ashdown

Esther (age 3):
Heidi Meadows

1st Night Club Man:
Jack Kenney

2nd Night Club Man:
Dick Ryan

Sound Men:
Ted Thorpe, David Armstrong, Bob Hoy, Larry Rio

1st Vagrant:
Al Thompson

2nd Vagrant:
Oscar Blank

Justice of the Peace:
Emerson Treacy

Malibu Party Guests:
Ruth Bradee, Shirley Whitney, Jean Engstrom, Almeda Fowler, Mae Marsh, Arlene Karr, Paul Levitt, Rodney Bell,

Richard Bauman, Marshall Bradford

Butler:
Eric Wilton

Libby's Secretary:
Hazel Shermet

Male Secretary:
John Monaghan

1st Signboard Man:
Louis Tomei

2nd Signboard Man:
Carey Loftin

Express Man:
Strother Martin

Artie Carver:
Grady Sutton

Emcee:
Rex Evans

Susan Ettinger:
Amanda Blake

Wallace:
Richard Webb

Nigel Peters:
Steve Wyman

Price Waterhouse Man:
Tom Cound

Makeup Man:
Mort Mills

Hairdresser:
Kay Ridhl

Director:
Tristram Coffin

"Cuddles":
Henry Kulky

Secretary:
Riza Royce

Manager:
Charles Watts

Sam:
Sam Colt

Bartender:
Paul Bryar

Young Man:
Tom Blakiston

Race Track Patrons:
Pat O'Malley, Gertrude Astor

Marian:
Valerie Vernon

Bert:
Pat Sexton

Pinkerton Detective:
Jack Ellis

Judge:
Frank Ferguson

Bailiff:
Timothy Farrell

Gregory:
Percy Helton

Rails:
Michael Hall

Clerk:
Arthur Space

Rodriguez:
Nacho Galindo

Reporters at the Courtroom:
Benny Burt, Ralph Volkie, Robert Strong

Women at Funeral:
*Josephine Whittell, Sheila Bromley,
Elizabeth Flournoy, Ruth Warren,
Cele Kirk, Eileene Stevens, Helen Eby
Rock, Hilda Plowright, Ezelle Poule*

Men at Funeral:
*Harte Wayne, Louis Mason,
Frank Kreig, Paul Brinegar*

Reporters at Shrine Auditorium:
*Dale Van Sickel, Don Richards,
Robert Dumas, Jean Woodley*

Photographers at Shrine Auditorium:
*Pat Miller, Al Hill, Frank Marlowe,
Charles Morton, Gordon Finn*

Emcee:
Wilton Graff

THE RECONSTRUCTION

Film reconstruction produced for the
Academy of Motion Picture Arts and
Sciences and Warner Bros. by
Ronald Haver

Production Consultants:
Gene Allen, Fay Kanin

Production Associates:
Douglas Edwards, Bruce Davis

Still photograph sequences designed
and directed by
Lize Bechtold Blyth

Still photograph sequence assistance by
Eric Durst

Editor:
Craig Holt

Assistant Editor:
D.J. Ziegler

Computer Camera:
Ken Rudolph

Photographic Effects:
Pacific Title

Bibliography

Alicoate, Jack, ed. *The Film Daily Year Book of Motion Pictures.* New York: The Film Daily, 1950–1958.

Behlmer, Rudy. *Inside Warner Bros.* New York: Viking Penguin, 1985.

Bordman, Gerald. *The American Musical Theatre.* New York: Oxford University Press, 1978.

Coward, Noël. *The Noël Coward Diaries.* Edited by Graham Payn and Sheridan Morley. Boston: Little, Brown, 1982.

Finch, Christopher. *Rainbow.* New York: Grosset & Dunlap, 1975.

Flynn, Errol. *My Wicked, Wicked Ways.* New York: G. P. Putnam's Sons, 1959.

Fordin, Hugh. *The World of Entertainment.* Garden City, N.Y.: Doubleday, 1975.

Frank, Gerold. *Judy.* New York: Harper & Row, 1975.

Gershwin, Ira. *Lyrics on Several Occasions.* New York: Alfred A. Knopf, 1959.

Harmetz, Aljean. *The Making of "The Wizard of Oz."* New York: Alfred A. Knopf, 1977.

Hart, Moss. *Act One: An Autobiography.* New York: Random House, 1959.

Hopper, Hedda, with James Brough. *The Whole Truth and Nothing But.* Garden City, N.Y.: Doubleday, 1963.

Jablonski, Edward. *Happy with the Blues.* Garden City, N.Y.: Doubleday, 1961.

Lambert, Gavin. *On Cukor.* New York: G. P. Putnam's Sons, 1972.

Lerner, Alan Jay. *The Street Where I Live.* New York: W. W. Norton, 1978.

Leyda, Jay. *Voices of Film Experience.* New York: Macmillan, 1977.

Mason, James. *Before I Forget.* London: Hamish Hamilton, 1981.

Minnelli, Vincente. *I Remember It Well.* New York: Doubleday, 1974.

Quigley, Martin, ed. *The Motion Picture Almanac.* New York: Quigley Publications, 1950–1958.

Sarris, Andrew, ed. *Interviews With Film Directors.* New York: Atheneum, 1975.

Schickel, Richard. *The Men Who Made the Movies.* Indianapolis: Bobbs-Merrill, 1967.

Wallis, Hal, with Charles Higham. *Starmaker.* New York: Macmillan, 1980.

Warner, Jack, with Dean Jennings. *My First Hundred Years in Hollywood.* New York: Random House, 1965.

Index

A NOTE ON THE TYPE

The text of this book was set by CRT in Avanta, a film version of Electra, a Linotype face designed by W. A. Dwiggins (1880–1956). This face cannot be classified as either modern or old style. It is not based on any historical model; nor does it echo any particular period or style. It avoids the extreme contrasts between thick and thin elements that mark most modern faces and attempts to give a feeling of fluidity, power, and speed.

Composed by The Haddon Craftsmen, Inc., Scranton, Pennsylvania

Color separations by Colotone, Inc., North Branford, Connecticut

Printed and bound by Fairfield Graphics, Fairfield, Pennsylvania

Designed by Iris Weinstein